Avoidant Restrictive F Disorder in Childhood Adolescence

MW00783624

Avoidant Restrictive Food Intake Disorder, more commonly known as ARFID, is a relatively newly introduced diagnostic category. Research in the field, although growing, remains limited, with clinical knowledge and expertise varying across clinicians. There may be uncertainty how to correctly identify and diagnose the disorder as well as how best to direct treatment.

This clinical guide sets out to be a trailblazer in the field, providing up-to-date information and comprehensive clinical guidance on ARFID in childhood and adolescence. Chapters in the book are divided into five sections, the first focussing on the importance of attending to the perspectives of those directly affected by ARFID. Three subsequent sections cover diagnosis and presentation, including chapters on aetiology, epidemiology, assessment, and outcome measures; clinical assessment, including psychological, family, nutritional, medical, and sensory components; and management, discussing nutritional, medical, psychological, and wider system approaches. The final section discusses prognosis and outcomes, and considers future research directions.

This clinically focussed book, with contributions from a multi-disciplinary authorship, is intended to function as an accessible, practical guide, and reference resource. It includes summaries of available evidence, with related recommendations for clinical practice. The advice and suggestions included will assist clinicians in targeting their attention appropriately, to ensure that children, adolescents, and their families receive the best possible care.

Rachel Bryant-Waugh is a highly experienced clinician and researcher whose career has been dedicated to the treatment and study of feeding and eating disorders in children and adolescents. She is an internationally leading figure in the fast developing field of ARFID.

Claire Higgins is a highly experienced clinician working in the field of feeding and eating disorders. She has a background of working in child and adolescent mental health and as a tutor on a national training programme for clinical psychologists. She is dedicated to the development of treatment for children presenting with ARFID.

"Disorders such as ARFID which sit at the interface of physical and mental health represent a challenge to patients and clinicians. The child who does not eat and seems unable to eat can be a testing and risky clinical problem. This accessible book is unique in making the challenge of diagnosis and treatment of ARFID surmountable. Experts from a range of disciplines describe and explain the disorder. Its outstanding strength is practical detail on psychological management – ensuring that clinicians get children and families on the road to recovery."

– Professor Isobel Heyman, Consultant Clinical Psychologist, National, Great Ormond Street Hospital for Children, London

"This book is an excellent, comprehensive contribution to the field of eating disorders. *Avoidant Restrictive Food Intake Disorder in Childhood and Adolescence* addresses a challenging topic and I recommend this book, written by experts in the field, to multidisciplinary teams working in the area of eating disorders. Professionals and families will find answers to a broad range of topics: diagnosis and presentation; assessment; management; course, outcome, and future research directions. This book brings together available evidence very nicely."

– Professor Kate Tchanturia, King's College London, Psychological Medicine/Consultant Clinical Psychologist, National Eating Disorder Service, South London, and Maudsley NHS Foundation Trust

Avoidant Restrictive Food Intake Disorder in Childhood and Adolescence

A Clinical Guide

Edited by Rachel Bryant-Waugh and Claire Higgins

Routledge
Taylor & Francis Group

LONDON AND NEW YORK

First published 2020
by Routledge
2 Park Square, Milton Park, Abingdon, Oxon OX14 4RN

and by Routledge
52 Vanderbilt Avenue, New York, NY 10017

Routledge is an imprint of the Taylor & Francis Group, an informa business

© 2020 selection and editorial matter, Rachel Bryant-Waugh and Claire Higgins; individual chapters, the contributors

The right of Rachel Bryant-Waugh and Claire Higgins to be identified as the authors of the editorial material, and of the authors for their individual chapters, has been asserted in accordance with sections 77 and 78 of the Copyright, Designs and Patents Act 1988.

All rights reserved. No part of this book may be reprinted or reproduced or utilised in any form or by any electronic, mechanical, or other means, now known or hereafter invented, including photocopying and recording, or in any information storage or retrieval system, without permission in writing from the publishers.

Trademark notice: Product or corporate names may be trademarks or registered trademarks, and are used only for identification and explanation without intent to infringe.

British Library Cataloguing-in-Publication Data
A catalogue record for this book is available from the British Library

Library of Congress Cataloging-in-Publication Data
A catalog record has been requested for this book

ISBN: 978-0-367-22438-7 (hbk)
ISBN: 978-0-367-22441-7 (pbk)
ISBN: 978-0-429-27486-2 (ebk)

Typeset in Times New Roman
by Swales & Willis, Exeter, Devon, UK

Visit the eResources: www.routledge.com/9780367224417

Contents

Illustrations

Tables

Figures

Contributors

Louise Bradbury BSc, MSc, PsychD, Clinical Psychologist, Feeding and Eating Disorders Service, Great Ormond Street Hospital, London, UK

Rachel Bryant-Waugh BSc (Hons), MSc, PhD, FAED, Consultant Clinical Psychologist and Lead Clinician of the National CAMHS ARFID Service at the Maudsley Centre for Child and Adolescent Eating Disorders (MCCAED), Maudsley Hospital, London, UK

Sarah Cawtherley MNutr, MSc, RD, MBDA, Paediatric Dietitian, Great Ormond Street Hospital, London, UK

Elaine Chung MBBS, MA, MRCPsych, Locum Consultant Child and Adolescent Psychiatrist, and Clinical Lead, Feeding and Eating Disorders Service, Great Ormond Street Hospital, London, UK

Lucy Cooke BSc, MSc, PhD, Research Psychologist, Freelance Researcher and Author, London, UK

Christine E. Cooper-Vince, PhD, Senior Research Associate, University of Geneva, Geneva, Switzerland

Eleanor Conway BSc, MRes, MRCSLT, Speech and Language Therapist, Great Ormond Street Hospital, London, UK

Catherine Frogley BSc (Hons), DClinPsy, Clinical Psychologist, The Lighthouse Arabia Centre for Well-being, Dubai, UAE

Claire Higgins BSc (Hons), MSc, DClinPsy, Clinical Psychologist and Associate Clinical Tutor, Feeding and Eating Disorders Service, Great Ormond Street Hospital, and University of East London, London, UK

Lee Hudson MBChB, PhD, MRCPCH, FRACP, Clinical Associate Professor and Honorary Consultant, Great Ormond Street UCL Institute of Child Health and Great Ormond Street Hospital, London, UK

Nadia Micali MD, PhD, MRCPsych, FAED, Professor of Child and Adolescent Psychiatry, University of Geneva & Geneva University Hospitals, Geneva, Switzerland

Úna McCrann RN, RN Child, Systemic Practitioner. Feeding Disorders Practitioner, Feeding and Eating Disorders Service, Great Ormond Street Hospital, London, UK

Sara Milne BSc (Hons), MSc, DClin Psy, Clinical Psychologist, Feeding and Eating Disorders Service, Great Ormond Street Hospital, London, UK

Emma Parish MBChB, BMSc, MRCPCH, Specialist Trainee in Paediatrics, Great Ormond Street Hospital, London, UK

Prabashny Pillay Dip HE, BSc, MSc, Systemic Family Therapist, DCAMH and Psychological Services, Great Ormond Street Hospital, London, UK

Karen Ray BSc (Hons), Occupational Therapist, Neurodisability Team, Great Ormond Street Hospital, London, UK

Heather Scott BSc (Hons), PGdipOT, Clinical Lead Occupational Therapist, Hackney ARK, Homerton University Hospital, London, UK

Amy Siddall BSc, DipHE, PgDip CBT for CYP, Clinical Nurse Specialist, Feeding and Eating Disorders Service, Great Ormond Street Hospital, London, UK

Karen Taylor, Playworker, Feeding and Eating Disorders Service, Great Ormond Street Hospital, London, UK

Preface

This book sets out to provide the clinician with a comprehensive overview of the wide range of considerations to be taken into account when working with children and young people with avoidant restrictive food intake disorder, more commonly referred to as ARFID. This is not a "new" disorder in the sense that the clinical presentations it covers did not exist previously; they certainly did, and in many respects have been well described in the literature. However, the terms that people have used to describe eating difficulties we now recognise as characteristic of ARFID, have been numerous, with multiple definitions and understandings about their origins and nosology. This has had a number of consequences, and has arguably held back the development of knowledge and expertise relating to ARFID to the detriment of wider patient care. When researchers do not have a formally agreed and defined diagnostic categories, it becomes difficult to compare and share findings, and to develop targeted treatments that can be rigorously tested across settings with the full range of individuals who may develop the condition in question. Clinicians using different descriptive terms to refer to patients with similar types of difficulty, can result in valuable opportunities to exchange expertise being lost, and clinical collaboration, so vital to pushing boundaries of patient care forwards, remaining limited. Most importantly, the lack of common language to describe specific, well-recognised, difficulties that have an adverse effect on health, wellbeing and functioning, creates confusion in referral and treatment pathways, potentially exacerbating the burden on individuals and family members even further.

This book, therefore, represents an attempt to draw together what we know about ARFID and to present this in a manner that is accessible to a wide range of clinicians. As will be apparent by the disciplines of the contributing authors and the breadth of topics discussed in the chapters that follow, ARFID is a multi-facetted disorder that requires careful assessment and management across a wide range of parameters.

The book is primarily written for clinicians, by clinicians, with an overarching aspiration that it might contribute to improving the consistency of appropriate care for children and young people with ARFID and their families. The material is based on existing research findings, widely accepted clinical practice and expertise, and our own experiences working and talking with families affected by ARFID. We hope that it will serve as a useful go-to volume and provide guidance where needed. The content is not aimed at any one group of practitioners, as ARFID generally requires multi-disciplinary involvement. Our hope is that clinicians will read all the chapters, not just those relevant to their own discipline, as in this way they are most likely to develop a comprehensive understanding of children's potential difficulties as well as those faced by their families.

A brief word about our use of language throughout the chapters; important given the potential for confusion we know can arise from differences in choice of words. Chapter 4 includes further discussion about the introduction of ARFID as a diagnostic category, including its definition. We conceptualise ARFID as an "umbrella term", covering a range of different manifestations of avoidant or restrictive eating behaviour. In the literature, in particular in published material predating ARFID's inclusion as diagnosis, general terms used to describe ARFID-like clinical presentations include "selective eaters", "extreme picky eating", "selective eating disorder", "restrictive eaters", "sensory food aversions", "eating phobia", "food refusal", and many more. The key point is that none of these "labels" were formally recognised as diagnostic categories in the main classification systems of the World Health Organization or the American Psychiatric Association. In this book, we might mention some of these terms, particularly when referring to studies where authors have used them. As studies with individuals formally diagnosed with ARFID remain limited in number, it is appropriate to refer to some of these other studies; however, we do not wish to perpetuate the plethora of confusing and overlapping terms in doing so.

Finally, to keep things simple, we use the term "child" to refer to anyone up to the age of 18, unless clear from the text that we are specifically talking about younger individuals. In places the reader might therefore encounter the phrase "children and young people", followed by subsequent reference to children only. This can be taken to include teenagers up to 18 years. Similarly the phrase "parents and carers" is often shortened to "parents" and intended to include all those with a primary parenting role. In order to be as inclusive as possible in relation to sex and gender identity an individual child is referred to as "they".

Our main hope is that this book is easy to follow, informative, useful, and supports all those who read it in the delivery of timely, appropriate, and effective care. The chapter contents are not intended to represent the final word on any of the topics discussed; ARFID is the focus of a now rapidly developing field and change is to be expected as a consequence. As new research evidence emerges, clinical expertise accumulates, and the voices of those affected by ARFID are heard, we hope that many positive developments and improvements will ensue. In the meantime, we firmly hold the view that sharing knowledge and experience can promote beneficial change in clinical care delivery, to reduce burden and enhance wellbeing in the families we encounter in the course of our clinical work.

Rachel Bryant-Waugh and Claire Higgins
July 2019

Acknowledgements

We would like to extend our heartfelt thanks to all our contributing authors for being willing to share their views, experiences, and learning with others, in the form of their contributions to this book. They have made time to do so along-side busy jobs and their own full lives, and we are very grateful to them for their hard work on this collective project.

As ever, we acknowledge the significant contribution of the many children, young people, and families we have met over the years in the course of our work, who have taught us so much. We recognise that information can only take us so far; without clinical encounters with real people who share so much about their experience with us, we actually know very little.

Part I

Perspectives

Chapter 1

Young people's perspectives

Louise Bradbury

Introduction

This chapter considers a range of aspects of the experience of children with avoidant restrictive food intake disorder (ARFID) and their difficulties with food, eating, and accessing help. At the time of writing there are no published research studies reporting on, or seeking to understand, the lived experience of children with ARFID. Similarly, only one paper to date has explored the experiences of adults identifying as picky eaters (Fox et al., 2018). Whilst there are several qualitative studies investigating the experience of care in young people with other eating disorders such as anorexia nervosa and bulimia nervosa, there was no inclusion of those with a diagnosis of ARFID even in the most recent of these (Mitrofan et al., 2019). An earlier literature review of research on patient perspectives of treatment of eating disorders predominantly focussed on anorexia nervosa, however this was carried out prior to the introduction of ARFID as a diagnosis (Bell, 2003). Therefore much of what we know about the day-to-day experience of those with a diagnosis of ARFID and their experience of the treatment they have received is gleaned from clinical contact or obtained informally.

When considering the definition of evidence-based practice in developing treatment for young people with a diagnosis of ARFID, it is important to integrate the key components of patient values and preferences alongside clinical expertise and research evidence (Sackett et al., 1996). Qualitative research into young people's perspectives of their mental health difficulties can be particularly helpful in this respect, and going forward should be taken into account to appropriately develop and improve services to fit the needs of those who access them (Buston, 2002). The importance of patient perspectives provides the rationale for opening this book with a chapter addressing this topic. Chapter 3, which addresses information from qualitative research, will further highlight the importance of hearing about the young person's experience of their difficulties.

It is clear from working clinically with children with a diagnosis of ARFID that they often appear to find it very difficult to express how they feel about their situation, and many struggle to offer details about their experiences of being asked to eat. Many are unable to articulate their thoughts and feelings about this. Often the impact of ARFID can only begin to be understood through starting to work on the associated difficulties and observing how these affect a child. It is therefore somewhat challenging to capture the viewpoints of children with this diagnosis, highlighting the importance of sharing what is known and understood from experiences in a clinical setting.

In seeking to obtain more detail to inform the content of this chapter, a group of children with a diagnosis of ARFID were approached informally to talk about their experiences. The views and experiences described here were collated from these discussions, as well as from clinical experience of working with children with ARFID. The quotes woven throughout the text attempt to convey recurring themes derived from those sharing their views. These perspectives have been set out to illustrate the experience of the treatment journey of a child with a diagnosis of ARFID, beginning with them accessing services, and subsequently setting out their experience of the assessment process, including their goals and hopes. This is followed by discussion of their experience of treatment, and their observations about the impact of ARFID on their day-today lives.

It is important to note that experiences are likely to differ between individuals, and that the information presented here is not designed to be exhaustive or necessarily representative of the wider population of people with ARFID. The majority of the perspectives shared here are from boys, with the age of the individual concerned placed in brackets alongside a pseudonym. The aim is to give some context to experiences of ARFID at different stages of childhood. All views represented here have been given with consent and are anonymised to respect confidentiality. This chapter does not attempt to explore parent and carer views and experiences, as these are discussed in Chapter 2.

What is it like for a young person to have ARFID?

Any one child's experience of ARFID is likely to differ from another depending on several factors such as their history, functioning, and family background. In addition to this, their experience may be influenced by whether their difficulties with eating are based on their sensory issues, concerns about the aversive consequences of eating, or as a result of their lack of interest in food.

Whilst many children in clinic may struggle to say what it is like to experience a diagnosis of ARFID, some may simply say it can feel as though there is nothing that can be done to help them,

> You don't want to have it but you've got it, so that's it really.
>
> (Matthew, 8)

Others, who are able to say a little more, will highlight a multitude of overwhelming concerns in relation to food, for example,

It might not even be the type of food, it could just be the way it's cooked. It could be that if one little thing is different, then I want to throw it away. Sometimes it's the look, sometimes it's the texture, sometimes it's the taste. Most of the time it's my brain telling me I don't like this and I won't go near it.

(David, 11)

For many, the feelings associated with confronting their difficulties with food are extremely powerful, and can generally be inferred by witnessing the observable features of anxiety that appear when you present a child with a feared food. Alex (10) was able to express that

... it looks like a monster to me. All the foods that I have not been able to try before seem like a big monster.

and most strikingly for Alex,

Trying food is so overwhelming it feels as though I am being stabbed.

For many children who can't articulate exactly what it is like for them, sometimes an understanding of their experiences can be gleaned through other means. One young boy conveyed the distress and disgust he experiences, through demonstrating this within a computer game in a session. In this game the child was challenged with feeding a character some dinner made from a selection of unpleasant ingredients. If the food was deemed too revolting the character would turn green, vomit, and pass out on the floor. The comments made after playing the game were an indication of what ARFID was like for this young boy when he said:

You see that, that's exactly how I feel when people ask me to eat something.

(Craig, 9)

For this child, the image on the screen appeared to accurately convey the feelings of disgust that he had towards food which he found almost impossible to convey in words.

The assessment process

Children with a diagnosis of ARFID often appear unsure about why they have been brought for an assessment or clinic appointment, with almost all saying that they had not known what to expect from the process. Many are terrified attending the clinic as they have the idea that the process might involve them being asked to try and eat something during the appointment. It is apparent that not being asked to do so initially, is extremely important in allowing them to build up trust and takes away some of the pressure. Nevertheless, anxiety levels are generally spoken of as very high at the outset of the process:

> I was scared and my anxiety was through the roof. I thought – I don't want any help.
>
> (David, 11)

However, in David's case, this progressed to:

> ... after a few sessions I became more confident as I learnt about more tips to help me, which made coming for treatment feel worthwhile.
>
> (David, 11)

For others, a complicated referral pathway has been followed before attending a service specialising in treating ARFID:

> It was just another appointment, I'd already been to so many by that point in my life.
>
> (John, 16)

Seeing a range of different professionals before getting to what was felt to be the right place for help was echoed by many, and can add to the perception of not feeling understood. John also spoke about his journey through the process admitting that:

> At first I found it dull, but eventually I grew to understand why I was coming and began to enjoy taking time to discuss my eating.
>
> (John, 16)

Hopes and goals for treatment

Children and young people may experience high levels of ambivalence about making changes to their eating behaviours, and, in turn, this can create some difficulty in establishing shared goals for treatment. Some children bring a range of different ideas, with some explaining that they want to "fit in" and be like everyone else, or just hoping to be "normal". This often becomes more apparent as children grow older and the difficulties associated with ARFID start to have more of a social impact. Birthday parties and other social events involving eating are often perceived as impossible to attend due to the food that is present, and the absence of foods or circumstances that allow the child to eat in their preferred manner. This experience of not fitting in or being different to peers can motivate some children to want to make changes so that they do not miss out. For many children their difficulties with eating can significantly negatively impact on a range of activities such as their attendance at school, sleepovers, school trips, holidays, as well as visits to relatives.

On the whole, relatively few younger children identify improved physical health as a motivator for engaging in treatment, despite the level of concern that is likely to have been raised by their parents. Some boys may identify wanting to "get stronger" or to grow taller; however, motivation relating to health and wellbeing seems to become more apparent when children approach adolescence. Younger children who do express some concerns about their health may have been influenced by listening to concerns expressed by their caregivers or by something they have learned about at school. Some may start to associate "not eating proper food" with being ill and vice versa. Comments made by others about appearance can also influence children as some might speak of wanting to be "a healthy weight so that everyone will leave me alone". This suggests that for these children a primary motivation to change may be in relation to reducing the level of conflict present in their interactions, rather than a primary concern about required weight status.

The experience of treatment and trying new foods

When talking about their experiences of treatment and describing what it is like to try and eat something new and potentially experienced as terrifying, most children will firstly highlight the importance of the choice of food to try. Some speak positively about the concept and process of "food chaining", confirming that it is best to pick something with a "similar taste and a similar look". In fact, this idea is echoed by many children who give examples of picking foods such as:

> ... different types of chicken nuggets which are kind of like the ones I already eat, so they are a bit less scary.
>
> (Matthew, 8)

For others, food selection is all about choosing something that really matters to them; for example:

> Trying a burger seemed like an ok idea because we talked about needing to be able to eat something when I go on my camping trip which I really want to go on.
>
> (Natalie, 10)

When increasing the variety of accepted foods is not really the child's goal, focussing on a food that could facilitate something they really want to do can be highly motivating. For these children, picking a food such as the burger in

Natalie's example, provides them with a far greater rationale for challenging themselves.

One aspect of a child's treatment for ARFID may include elements of "tasting times". The thought of this process can be accompanied by a variety of feelings, for example:

> When I come to sessions I have mixed feelings about trying new things. There is a part of me that feels regretful if I try something new and then I don't like it, but then I also feel really happy if I try something new and then I do like it.
>
> (Alex, 10)

This comment highlights well the perceived risks of potential negative outcomes from trying new food. However, despite these concerns, the process may also become valued, with Alex also saying:

> When I do try things, whether I like them or not, my confidence goes right up. Part of this is because I start to like more things than I expected to.

John (16) also conveyed his concern about the risk of trying something new:

> If I do enjoy the food, I'll be happy for a long while. Vice versa and I'll be incredibly disappointed – trying new foods is a big thing for me.

From experience in clinic it is often difficult for a child to articulate the fear present when asked to try new foods, as has been expressed so well by Alex and John. It is more likely that this is something they will come to reflect on later through the experience of successfully challenging themselves with feared foods.

When children are asked about what advice they would give to others about engaging in treatment it is interesting that they often give similar tips. David (11) suggested that he would tell others that persistence is really important:

> ... don't stress about it too much, because even if trying it might make you feel ill the first time, after 10–15 tries it tastes better.

Even at a young age there can be recognition and great importance placed on learning from the experience of trying new foods:

> When I try different food I get more confident about other food, even if I don't like it.
>
> (Sally, 6)

In fact, many young people with a diagnosis of ARFID talk about the need to "just try" something, with Matthew (8) suggesting that his advice for others was to:

> Just keep going. You have to follow the advice to check if it works. I was scared at first and it can be hard to start, but keep going. Try and see how it is, because you might like it.

Many young people seem to share this same piece of advice for others attending for treatment; however, it is apparent in a clinical setting that in reality this advice can be very difficult to follow when their own anxiety takes over. It is clear that "advising" and actually "doing" are two very different things.

Children's experiences outside of their home environment

Outside of the treatment process, many children with a diagnosis of ARFID frequently talk about the wider impact of their eating difficulties on their lives and their relationships with others. Significant difficulties with eating appear to continually have a negative impact on their social lives, a reflection of the fact that in many cultures food is an integral part of social occasions. For many children, birthday parties or similar occasions are viewed as their "nemesis", whether due to the overwhelming sensory characteristics of the food and situation, or the lack of available "safe" options that would enable them to join in. What may seem like a minor detail to many about a birthday cake, can be a complete barrier to attending a party for a child with ARFID,

> I just wish that they didn't have jam in them.

> (Sanna, 7)

As children grow older and approach adolescence it is common to hear that the impact of their eating difficulties has a significant impact on them gaining more independent social lives. Christopher (15) expressed hope that things might change as he:

> … would like to be able to go out to a town and just have some lunch or have some fun with friends.

In working clinically with adolescents, it often seems that identifying a goal to work on which might have positive social benefits can represent a starting point to build on motivation to make a change to their eating.

For those with sensory issues, there may be a wish, as in Jack's case, to be able to

> … sit next to people and not be worried about their food, like the smell …

with the idea that the experience of being near food is so aversive that it can be hard to imagine how to overcome this. Again, young people often talk about their difficulties with eating, leading them to becoming more socially withdrawn, although for some avoiding these situations seems far preferable than facing them head on.

For many young people the pressure at home to make change with their eating is experienced as extremely challenging and difficult to manage. Children are often acutely aware how worried their parents are about their eating and how much they want them to change. This level of pressure may be viewed as impeding rather than promoting change. David (11) spoke of the importance of being able to try things in a different setting other than home, where the pressure of expectation to change was less keenly felt. He mentioned the importance of having a good relationship with his teacher and described how being able to try things in the environment of school helped to facilitate the process as there was "no big fuss". This idea was similarly talked about by Simon (10) who said:

> When I do try something and they make a big deal about it, this just means that they expect me to do it again and the pressure goes up. It's easier to try something somewhere else.

Indifference and what others think

Whilst many of the views shared so far have demonstrated that for some children with ARFID there is recognition of difficulty and a desire for things to be different, it is important to acknowledge that some talk about not being bothered by their eating difficulties and demonstrate a lack motivation to make any changes. In some respects, children often seem more able to articulate clearly when they are not interested in making a change and want to be left alone, rather than articulate what they do want to change. A number of children comment on their frustration that they are constantly being asked to change, almost disbelieving that others would think they can do it,

> Why are you asking me to do something you know I can't do?
>
> (Simon, 10)

This may lead to children with ARFID feeling poorly understood by those around them.

Many children do not consider the physical health risks of the impact of ARFID and in this way there can be frequent conflict between them and their primary caregivers. Older children may be able to acknowledge that when their difficulties were significant, they had not attended to the concerns that everyone else had raised, such as John (16) who said:

To be honest, I didn't fully understand the severity of the situation regarding my weight.

There can be a constant battle between children and those around them in terms of the discrepancy in levels of worry about the situation with their eating. Alex (10) said:

I know that my family worry if I don't eat enough or the right things. Lots of people have told me that things need to change, but a lot of the time I disagree with this and I don't feel the same.

This can commonly be heard in a clinic setting and it is important to recognise this pressure to change, as many will say they are willing to work on their eating difficulties because "I wish my mum would worry less". This can be heard from both those that experience high levels of anxiety around food, and from those who have a lack of interest in food. Where there is little or no motivation present from the perspective of the child, this can be very challenging to work with therapeutically. However, some children are able to acknowledge that this can change over time and that a shift may occur, such as in the case of Alex (10) who advised that,

… what helps me to keep working on my eating and coming to sessions is that I didn't feel like I could change but now I feel like people know what I have and understand it.

This statement brings alive the importance of working collaboratively with a child with ARFID and developing an understanding of their difficulties through the process of formulation (see further Chapters 11 and 13). This is crucial not only in terms of initially engaging a child in treatment, but also in developing a treatment plan, and helping others around them to also understand their difficulties. For many, feeling understood and knowing that what they struggle with is "actually a real thing" can have a truly significant impact on the treatment process.

Conclusions

Children with a diagnosis of ARFID share many similarities in terms of their experiences and perspectives, but understandably there are also differences. It is essential to fully explore an individual child's experience of ARFID and associated difficulties with eating. This allows for a better understanding of the particular issues that are relevant for the individual, which need to be understood in order to think about appropriate treatment plans. From listening to the children's views shared in this chapter, the importance of others understanding what it is like to be in their shoes, in order to be best placed to support them, is evident. It seems clear that an exploration of children's lived experience of ARFID should be at the forefront of future research to inform our practice. Improved understanding of what it is like to have ARFID may encourage help-seeking in the young person, as well as facilitate greater engagement in the treatment process. This is particularly important in situations where there may be low levels of motivation and high levels of anxiety. The important process of arriving at a shared understanding of the child's situation may help to alleviate feeling misunderstood and invalidated. It may also empower children with ARFID to feel able to make some changes. The identification of goals that are meaningful to the individual and important to them can play an important part in achieving a willingness to confront the anxiety they experience in relation to food. It is also essential that professionals have a level of empathy for and understanding of the genuine difficulties with eating that are present, particularly when it can be so hard for a child to describe what it is like for them. All the children involved in sharing their stories in this chapter were remarkable in their ability to talk about their diagnosis and their experiences; however, it is important to be aware that many young people, with a diagnosis of ARFID, may struggle to articulate this.

Summary points

- The perspectives and experiences of young people with a diagnosis of ARFID are important in the development and implementation of evidence-based practice in this area
- The individual experience of a young person is key in developing a formulation of their difficulties and supporting understanding
- It is important to consider the systemic implications of ARFID for the young person as the diagnosis can have wide reaching impact
- Many young people with a diagnosis of ARFID will say "I'm OK as I am" and that it is other people who want them to change
- Young people's goals for treatment may be quite varied, often less likely to be focussed on physical health benefits, and more likely to be targeted around the social implications of their difficulties
- Experiences are varied and for many it can be hard to convey how they feel about food
- Future research focussing on exploring young people's experiences of their difficulties is likely to be helpful in directing interventions appropriately and ultimately more effectively

References

Bell, L. (2003) What can we learn from consumer studies and qualitative research in the treatment of eating disorders? *Eating and Weight Disorders* 8(3), 181–87.
Buston, K. (2002) Adolescents with mental health problems: what do they say about health services? *Journal of Adolescence* 25(2), 231–42.

Fox, G., Coulthard, H., Williamson, I., & Wallis, D. (2018) "It's always on the safe list": Investigating experiential accounts of picking eating in adults. *Appetite* 130, 1–10.

Mitrofan, O., Petkova, H., Janssens, A., Kelly, J., Edwards, E., Nicholls, D., McNicholas, F., Simic, M., Eisler, I., Ford, T., & Byford, S. (2019) Care experiences of young people with eating disorders and their parents: qualitative study. *British Journey of Psychiatry Open* 5(1), e6. doi: 10.1192/bjo.2018.78.

Sackett, D.L., Rosenberg, W.M.C., Gray, J.A.M., Haynes, R.B., & Richardson, W.S. (1996) Evidence based medicine: what it is and what it isn't. *British Medical Journal* 3(12), 71–72.

Chapter 2

Parent and carer views and experiences

Sara Milne

Introduction

Along with listening to young people's views, as detailed in Chapter 1, it is also important to hear parents' and carers' unique concerns about their child, their expectations, and their values. This enables clinicians to consider how best to support individual children and the family system around them. It has been proposed that good evidence-based practice involves the integration of clinical expertise, patient values, and the best research evidence into the decision making process for patient care (Sackett et al., 1996). Espousing this model therefore suggests that research-derived evidence alone should not be the only component in determining this decision making process; rather it suggests that full integration of all of these three components enhances opportunities for the best clinical care.

The aim of this chapter is to capture a range of experiences regularly reported by parents and carers of children with avoidant restrictive food intake disorder (ARFID). It begins by presenting experiences often talked about at initial clinical appointments about parenting a child with significant eating difficulties. It then tracks the family's journey through assessment and diagnosis to parents' experiences of treatment. Broad themes are used to group commonly reported experiences, which are illustrated with quotes. All the views presented in this chapter have been gathered from parents attending a clinic specialising in the assessment and treatment of ARFID. Parents and carers were eager to participate in order for others, particularly professionals, to better understand what it is like to parent a child with an extremely restricted diet.

What it is like to be a parent of a child with ARFID?

A number of themes emerge from discussions and reflections on the experience of parenting a child with ARFID, which are set out below with examples:

A lonely experience

Many parents report that having a child with ARFID "is lonely and no one understands". There can also be a sense of frustration in response to other people not understanding that their child is not "just a picky eater". Parents often find others' descriptions of more developmentally typical food-faddiness unhelpful,

> It is especially hard when others call their children fussy for refusing some vegetables on a random day

One parent said,

> She is so specific, I mean it has to be a certain pizza, plain cooked to a specific colour … people just do not get it and I have stopped trying to explain.

Many parents describe feeling that others minimise the extent of their child's eating difficulties, for example, through describing their child as a "fussy eater" or saying "they will just grow out of it". It seems that such statements are experienced as invalidating how serious and longstanding their child's avoidant and restrictive eating has been. One parent noted,

> It's very hard when friends say just let them go hungry and they'll eventually eat, because our kid will starve himself if we did that.

Such statements are often not only experienced as frustrating, but seem to add to parent and carers' sense of isolation.

Another experience often described, relates to the negative judgment that parents and carers may pick up from others. Some parents describe being acutely aware of the looks they receive from members of the general public, for example, when they try to encourage their child to eat on a day out,

> … the stares and judgment you get when you eat out is just horrendous

Parents regularly comment on others' negative reactions to their child's eating,

> I can remember she started to have issues seeing everyone eating different foods, then she began refusing foods, gagging at the table, and all the family looking on in horror.

Repeated occurrences like this seem to lead many parents to avoid social events and occasions involving eating.

Guilt and stress

A number of parents describe feeling that they are not nurturing their child through food and express a wish to be able to feed their child a healthy meal. They may seek help hoping that it will be possible to reduce their child's dependency on a nutritional supplement, for example through being able to eat fruits and vegetables,

> I would just love him to be able to sit and eat a Sunday dinner with us all, instead of being stuck on these milk drinks which cannot be good for him.

Some parents and carers will also comment on feeling frustrated or hopeless that they cannot move their child on to eat something else. For example,

> It would just be lovely to see him sit down with his friends and eat some dinner rather than just this milk. I cannot help feeling this although I know he is nowhere near this.

It seems understandable that a sense of not having been able to achieve change in their child's eating may be experienced as challenging and stressful; tolerating lack of progress can often feel very difficult.

Impact on family functioning

A frequent goal or aim expressed by parents is to be able to have a "normal family mealtime" or the ability to go on holiday without the worry that their child may not eat when away from home. In order to take holidays or breaks, many parents describe needing to pack preferred foods or pay for extra luggage to bring enough of their child's preferred foods with them. One carer reported that they,

> ... pack hundreds of bottles of milk supplement drinks to take to Spain, just in case she will not eat there ... also we split these between all of the luggage cases just in case a case did not turn up or was confiscated.

Many families report having experienced their child not eating, or only eating a minimal amount on holiday, which deterred them from planning further holidays. One mother said,

> We just do not go on holiday now; instead we go and visit my mother who can accommodate his needs.

Parents frequently describe detailed food planning and preparation necessary to enable their family to go out for a day trip. One parent said that caring for a child with ARFID,

> ... is more than food, it's the logistics of it all.

Many will carry highly specific foods around with them to ensure their child has something to eat when they are out. For example, one parent commented,

> I am always packing my handbag full of their foods – custard creams in particular, just in case we are stuck somewhere and I can't get her anything. It used to bother me but now it's just a habit.

Others describe carefully researching restaurants in the area to make sure there is somewhere that might have something they can order which their child might accept. One father reported that,

> ... if we ever wanted to go out to dinner, we could only pick a place that had French fries or pizza.

It is evident that many parents and carers of children with ARFID take great care in preparing their child's food when it comes to mealtimes, which can be experienced as exhausting on an ongoing basis. For example, one carer said that,

> It's unbelievable how careful I have to be whilst cooking the burger. If there is just slightly too much black they will not eat it and I have to start again.

One mother reported that,

> It's hard, one day I had to go to four different supermarkets just to find a particular brand he wanted ... and then I stockpiled them in case we ran out or they changed the brand

Despite parents often going to great lengths to obtain and prepare their child's food many seem to carry a constant worry that it could easily be rejected, or they may not be able to continue to obtain specific preferred foods.

Often parents and carers outline concerns that their other children without ARFID may pick up on "bad habits" from their affected sibling. They describe finding it difficult to explain why one child has different rules around eating to all the others in the family,

> It's hard with my older son because he eats everything, unlike his sister, but also likes the chicken nuggets and smileys too, but I would not give them to him every day. I know it's hard for him to understand why his sister gets these foods each time

When parents and carers describe such experiences about the wider impact of their child's eating it becomes clear that ARFID it is not just about the child's restricted diet, but also about the significant effects such restriction can have on many aspects of parenting and family life.

An uncertain path to receiving a diagnosis of ARFID

Growing concern and help-seeking

There seem to be a number of key moments and triggers that lead parents and carers to seek more specialised help for their child's eating. Some report that one of the most difficult realisations is noticing that as their child gets older they are clearly not expanding the range or amount of food they are willing to eat; in other words, a realisation that this is not a phase that will pass. Some parents report that they began to feel more concern, frustration and stress as their child grew older and it seemed that no one could help them. They also report frustration and concern that advice they may have read or received to manage a normally "fussy" child has not helped,

> She was always picky, I thought when she was younger she might grow out of it a bit like everyone was saying. I realise now that is not happening and actually she seems worse, she doesn't like to sit at the table, she gags and we have to coax her to eat the few foods she will have.

Parents may report having seen a dietitian who may have offered sound nutritional advice but did not appear to have an understanding that their child would be unlikely to be able to try any of the suggested options. For example, one parent said:

> I think I saw a dietitian and she had lots of suggestions how to get his diet to be healthier, however she had no concept that none of these options would be acceptable to my son, so I just thanked her and then did not attend any more of these appointments.

Parents and carers often report that they have seen multiple professionals over lengthy periods of time about their child's eating but describe never having felt properly listened to and understood:

> I have seen many different professionals over the years and no one seemed to take it seriously.

Often parents report being aware that their child has continued to eat only their "preferred" foods for prolonged periods and that the child does not seem to be bothered by this. Some describe an innate feeling that something is "going on" with their child's eating, even though in many cases the child may not have been losing weight,

> There has to be something to explain this selectivity, no other child eats just five foods that have to come in a specific wrapper or packet, it's not right for him to go on like this.

Many describe feeling as if they are perceived as "neurotic" because they have continued to highlight how concerned they are about their child's eating, despite some professionals being reported as telling them,

> It's ok, just continue as you are, it's nothing to be concerned about at this stage.

In spite of such advice most parents and carers describe continuing to search for something, either physical or psychological, to explain their child's eating difficulty.

Diagnosis

When a diagnosis of ARFID is confirmed, some parents describe feeling a sense of relief. One of the sentiments they may share is feeling that their child's longstanding issues with eating have been validated, and they are not just imaging it,

> Hearing about ARFID made me really realise I was not just a neurotic mother; that what my child has is an actual thing, a serious thing and I was not crazy to keep thinking it is not just fussiness.

Other parents may have different opinions and reactions; for example, those who may have understood their child's restricted intake as more of a medical or physical issue may initially be uncertain about a psychological explanation for their child's eating difficulties. One parent said,

> I thought it was more medical and she had problems with the muscle tone in her chewing, however then I started to learn she had the skills to chew but not the interest or desire.

How one family may understand their child's eating difficulties can understandably be different to another family; however, it is apparent that almost all parents and carers will have questions about the meaning of the diagnosis and its prognosis.

A number of families report challenges when trying to communicate news about the diagnosis to others who know the child. This is perhaps unsurprising as ARFID is a relatively new term. For example, one parent asked,

> How can I get the school to understand that this is not behavioural and she needs the calories from the Nutella bars to keep her safe and healthy?

Chapter 17 provides more information about how children and families can be supported in their interactions with others beyond the treatment team.

Risk and crisis

One of the more difficult periods for many parents and carers is when a child drops one of their few preferred foods, or in more severe cases, when a child has drastically restricted their intake or stops accepting food and water for a couple of days. Some parents notice that there may have been another issue impacting on their child at such times, for example, the sensory impact of a loose tooth, which disrupts the normal pattern of eating. In some instances the child is unable to articulate any reasons or explanations, which can make it hard for parents to understand why they have further restricted their intake. At times such as these, some parents report the need to attend local doctors or emergency departments for urgent medical attention. Many experience a high amount stress around these times due to concern about their child's minimal intake.

A parallel issue, or as some parents and carers describe it, "a nightmare", is that their child can find the idea of taking any supplement or medication that may be required very distressing and refuse outright. Parents usually understand that the supplement or medication is like a "new taste" and very challenging for their child to accept, with the lack of understanding that may be shown by clinicians about their child's relationship with food very difficult to bear under such stressful circumstances. They often describe how they try their hardest to encourage their child to eat something at these times, to prevent the need to use more invasive procedures, such as a nasogastric tube, or for medication. Another experience described by some parents as very difficult, is watching their child becoming more distressed during a hospital admission as medical teams seek to promote eating or drinking,

> We have to resort to intravenous treatment for my daughter to get fluid into her, it took a long time but we now have special arrangements for her to have this rather than the offer of oral food or fluid initially

Parents and carers often mention how administering medication to their child, even in less acute situations, is very difficult, if not impossible. One parent reported that they,

> ... have given up on oral medication because as soon as it touches his mouth he will vomit.

Some parents and carers describe how they regularly balance the advantages and disadvantages of giving medication, and only resort to hospitals as a last resort,

> It is about balancing is it worth the stress, the last time he fainted after three members of staff tried to pin him down to give him medication.

Treatment

Managing expectations

Parents and carers of children with ARFID will often express aspirations that many other parents might take for granted, such as,

> My dream is to go into a coffee shop and for him to just eat a sandwich.

> I would like him to eat ANY fruit and vegetables.

Managing parental expectations during treatment is essential. Shared, realistic goals need to be created. For example, if a child is only accepting dry packet food, which is usually very predictable in terms of taste and texture, starting off by aiming to introduce a fruit or vegetable maybe highly challenging for them as the shape, texture and flavour of fresh items vary slightly every time. The clinician may advise starting on something more similar to the food already accepted; however, without explanation of the rationale for this, parents' expectations of what should be happening may be not be met,

> It's hard to think that introducing another beige food from a packet is us making progress when I really just want them to sit and eat a roast dinner.

Expectations about how mealtimes "should" be can also a factor for some parents and carers. Distraction is often a tool used to facilitate mealtimes,

> The only way I can get him to eat is if I put the laptop as a barrier so he cannot see my food and he is distracted.

Often parents would like to be able to have family meals without distractions being needed; however, for some children presenting with ARFID, the use of tablets, DVDs, and other screen-related distractions may be the only way that they are able to ensure their child eats.

Strategies previously tried

When families attend for treatment, many parents report having tried a number of different strategies to improve the situation, but have been unsuccessful in making any progress. For example, they may describe making food into special characters, taking their child to the supermarket to choose food items, promising rewards if their child will eat something new. Some report how they have tried to hide nutritional supplements or other foods, such as vegetables, in the foods their child will accept,

> We have hidden drops of multivitamin in his juice in a closed cup but he can smell it from a mile off.

Whilst this approach can be useful for some children, it is not always successful for a child with a keen sense of smell or taste, or heightened sensitivity to texture or appearance. Often the slightest change can be detected. Hiding foods in familiar foods can also lead to the child mistrusting the "safe" food or mealtimes in general and risks the child dropping even preferred food items. In addition, the child's trust in the parents may be adversely affected. Most parents describe realising that hiding foods in others may not work; however, their own desperation or advice from professionals may lead them to trying a number of pressurising approaches,

> I sat there for two hours with him and a bowl of porridge just to see if he would have a spoon, he ended up crying and I ended up crying, it was just awful ... I know that this approach just is not for him

This theme of experiencing a sense of desperation and hopelessness because their attempts to help their child to eat better have not worked is one echoed by many parents.

Treatment interventions

Many parents are highly motivated to find or do something to help improve their child's ARFID-related difficulties. Families can be resourceful and may be able to generate their own ways to respond to, manage, and work on making changes. Parents and carers are understandably often trying to expand a child's range of foods and it can be frustrating to hear that perhaps before this is considered, it may be important in some cases to improve the child's relationship with food by taking a "no pressure" approach. Alternatively, the treatment may focus more on desensitising to sensory difficulties with food, by touching or exploring foods through play. Some parents report that it can be frustrating to wait for their child to be more ready to actually try to taste new foods,

> It was a relief to hear his diet was ok but it took us time to realise we needed to stop offering him foods at mealtimes and allow him to just explore food on his terms.

It is not uncommon for children to be more willing to engage in food play or try new foods in another setting, such as a clinic, school, or elsewhere, and then not be able to transfer this home. This can be understandably frustrating or difficult for parents,

I feel like they will play with it here so there must be something I am doing not as well as you.

Such statements reflect how parents may be deeply concerned about their own level of skill to support their child and how their confidence to explore food with their child may have been affected by so many negative feeding experiences. With guidance, families may go onto develop their own style of food exploration, play, and tasting,

> Learning to be playful with food and using indirect play to support my child in forming a more positive relationship with food ... this gave me confidence in supporting my child with feeding and I felt more like we are doing a good enough job and as family.

During treatment sessions focused on exposing a child to different food textures through play, parents may express worries that their child is just learning to play with food and this may not improve on their feeding. It is certainly true that food play approaches are not always indicated, in particular in children whose difficulties are predominantly characterised by low interest in eating, or anxieties around swallowing or vomiting. However, in those for whom it is indicated, food play represents a first step in a process of desensitisation. Progress can be slow and it may be difficult to tolerate the uncertainty about when a child may actually taste a food or begin to accept this into their diet. Some parents report constantly watching for change or hoping for a "eureka moment" when their child begins to change. Keeping expectations realistic about pace of change, adopting a low-pressure approach, and acknowledging small changes can all be an important part in supporting the child to move on. One parent noted how,

> ... with the laid back approach Jane eventually tried a new sweet, and I went upstairs and secretly celebrated so she did not see me.

On their journey towards treatment, parents and carers will often meet several professionals offering advice and tips to try, which can feel helpful but for some may feel overwhelming. There can at times be a mismatch in priorities, for example professionals may see a need for a child to gain weight whereas the family may wish to work on expanding a child's range. A discussion about short- and long-term goals can help to consider the initial priority of treatment. Some parents and carers can be surprised that there may be a need to think about food in a different way for their child. One parent reported that, for her,

> It was key to realising that I needed to approach their diet in a different way, for example my daughter did not need the typical healthy food pyramid, instead she needed as many calories as possible ... it took me a while to get my head around that.

Parents often comment on the impact of assessment and treatment in helping them to understand the difficulties from their child's perspective. Some parents describe being somewhat taken aback by hearing their child speak about their food issues, and realising things are harder for them or the problem was more severe than they thought,

> He doesn't really tell us much but I realise we have got into a habit of not asking and actually we as parents want to know more about how he finds things so we can adapt.

Treatment for ARFID often includes a specific focus on working with parents, supporting them to reflect on patterns they think they have got stuck with in their child's eating and to generate ideas how they might change this. Some parents report finding this helpful in allowing them to put things into perspective and find the means to make progress. For example,

> ... realising we had got into a habit of accommodating his selectivity and never approached the anxiety and avoidance. There are small things we could do to make changes and improve family mealtimes.

Post-treatment experiences

Many parents raise understandable and realistic worries at the end of treatment, such as concern that their child may regress or drop foods in the future. Some describe feeling a sense of loss related to knowing that they will no longer have easy access to a team that they feel understands their child's struggles,

> I am worried when we leave this specialist team that if she finds it hard again we will find ourselves right back at the beginning and we do not want to go back to that place.

Although many parents will articulate how much they feel they have gained in terms of their own confidence to manage their child's eating, there may be ongoing concerns about feeling alone and misunderstood in relation to their child's difficulties once again. In families where significant improvements have been achieved, there may be an element of disbelief that their child's eating, previously experienced as overwhelmingly challenging, has improved to such an extent.

Reflection

From listening to these parent and carer experiences about living with and seeking help for their child with ARFID, it is clear that these are markedly different from those parenting a child who goes through a phase of more developmentally normal "picky eating". As clinicians, we hear multiple accounts of the mental, and sometimes physical, distress that parents and carers can go through trying to find ways to feed their child with ARFID. We know that the accommodations that parents and carers make to feed their child, can impact on the wider family functioning. Any one family is never alone in their experience of difficulty, yet this is not always felt to be the case. It is important for clinicians to be aware that for some parents, the sense that they are alone in their struggles can be an acutely painful experience. ARFID in children continues to be little known and poorly understood by the general public and in some cases not believed to be a real difficulty. This can increase parental and carer distress and there is a great need to challenge and change this situation.

Many parents and carers talk about difficulties accessing appropriate help for their child with ARFID. Certainly, services for children with ARFID are currently not as common or as easy to identify as those for other, better known mental health difficulties. However, most parents and carers have an innate sense when something is not right, and more support is needed for their child. This feeling often gets stronger as the child gets older and their eating does not improve. It is to be hoped, that over time more families may be able to access help sooner, so that distress and impairment in all concerned, can be minimised.

When parents and carers arrive at treatment they often hold high expectations of themselves in relation to feeding their child a wider range of foods. They may, understandably, experience difficult feelings when changes in treatment are slower than they might hope for. The majority of parents of children with ARFID are highly resourceful, and most are skilled in finding fine-tuned ways to feed their child. Parents and carers generally seem to value and appreciate accessible information to help them make sense of their child's ARFID. Many benefit from the opportunity to develop a more comprehensive understanding of their child's difficulties and to receive support to create new possibilities around food with their chid.

Summary points

- Parenting a child with ARFID can be experienced as an isolating and lonely
- Typically, when a child presents with ARFID, this difficulty can impact on parenting and many aspects of family life
- The availability of information and services who can recognise and support children with ARFID feels scarce amongst parent and carers
- Parents and carers can find receiving an ARFID diagnosis helpful
- Many families experience situations where children drop foods or stop food intake as highly alarming; under such circumstances parents report finding it unhelpful when clinical staff do not understand their child's difficulties with eating

- Intervention approaches vary depending on the underlying problem causing and or maintaining the issue; treatment for ARFID can be slow, and tolerating lack of progress can feel very difficult for parents and carers
- Parents and carers often find it beneficial to have a facilitated space to understand why their child presents with ARFID and an opportunity to consider what they can try to do next to support their child's eating

Reference

Sackett, D.L., Rosenberg, W.M.C., Gray, J.A.M., Haynes, R.B., & Richardson, W.S. (1996) Evidence based medicine: what it is and what it isn't. *British Medical Journal* 3 (12), 71–72.

Chapter 3

Information from qualitative research

Lucy Cooke

Introduction

Alongside clinical expertise and the application of the best available research evidence, consideration of the individual patient's values and preferences is the third element in Sackett's model of evidence-based practice (Sackett et al., 1996). Consideration of the patient's voice can contribute to improving patient-centred care by enabling clinicians to assess and subsequently target areas identified as mattering most by those affected. Attention to these areas at the start, during, and at the end of treatment can provide information as to whether outcomes that matter to children and families have been achieved through clinical intervention, but also whether families have received the type of treatment they feel would be most appropriate. Limited evidence of the impact of patient-centred approaches to treatment outcomes is currently available, but it has been suggested that engaged patients use less healthcare resources (Wennberg et al., 2010), and that more personalised management and care can increase retention (Hawley & Weisz, 2005) and lead to faster improvement (Bickman et al., 2011) in young people with emotional and behavioural difficulties.

In recent years, a greater emphasis on the experience of the patient has emerged in the design and delivery of health care systems around the world (Australian Commission on Safety and Quality in Health Care, 2011; Delaney, 2018; US Department of Health and Human Services, 2008; World Health Organisation, 2007). In the UK, the National Health Service strategy document, the *Five Year Forward View*, proposes a "more engaged relationship with patients, carers and citizens", giving them greater involvement in their own care and breaking down the traditional divide between patients and health professionals (NHS England, 2014, p. 2). Likewise, the publication of *Future in Mind* promoted a sea change in mental health care for children and young people, emphasising the importance of their involvement and that of their parents and carers in "making choices about what they regard as key priorities" (Department of Health, 2015, p. 12). At a service level, this means that treatments must not only be evidence-based but also must align with service users' stated preferences and must addresses the issues that are most salient to them.

Quantitative research in feeding and eating

Traditionally, clinicians have administered standardised questionnaire measures to aid assessment of the current mental or physical state of an individual at the beginning and end of treatment. Together with expert clinicians' own assessment, these can provide a straightforward quantitative measure of the person's mental wellbeing, for example, which may indicate the presence or absence of a clinically significant problem. These types of data, whilst objective and reliable, reduce the individual's experience to a numeric value and fail to address their subjective experience. In contrast, qualitative methods seek to understand people's values, beliefs, experiences, attitudes, and behaviours and how these are affected by their health. The two, of course, are complementary – qualitative data can put flesh on the bones of questionnaire data, adding a dimension that cannot be measured by a prescribed set of questions generated by researchers and clinicians alone. Three main methods of qualitative research exist: observational studies, interview studies, and textual analysis of written records, choice of which will depend on the aims of the project concerned (Pathak et al., 2013). Whatever method is employed, qualitative approaches can provide the unique perspective of the individual, alerting clinicians to important areas for attention and highlighting treatment priorities.

Avoidant restrictive food intake disorder (ARFID) is a relatively new diagnostic category and the specific experiences of affected individuals and their families are relatively underexplored. However, feeding and eating difficulties in childhood are relatively common and existing quantitative research indicates that at the clinical end of the spectrum these difficulties can have an extremely negative impact on family wellbeing and functioning. Parents of children with feeding difficulties describe the experience as stressful and distressing (Garro, 2004; Greer et al., 2008; Singer et al., 1990), and many report that a lack of empathy and understanding by health professionals may compound the problems for parents (Budd et al., 1992; Singer et al., 1990). Family functioning can be negatively affected (Ammaniti et al., 2004; Gilmore, 2006; Sanders et al., 1993), parents may experience anxiety, frustration, and self-doubt (Chatoor et al., 2000; Didehbani et al., 2011), and parenting can be adversely affected with associated risks for the child (Feldman et al., 2004; Stein et al., 1994). In addition, family mealtimes can become a battleground (Aviram et al., 2015), and disagreements about how to manage feeding difficulties can produce family tension and conflict (Atzaba-Poria et al., 2010). Childhood feeding and eating difficulties are associated with increased risk in a number of areas in addition to risk related to the child's health, such as being subjected to inappropriate disciplining behaviours (Chatoor et al., 1997; Chatoor & Macaoay, 2008). Parents and carers of children with clinically significant feeding or eating difficulties may experience feelings of isolation and high levels of anxiety and depression (Jones & Bryant-Waugh, 2013).

Qualitative research in feeding and eating

Qualitative research into the experiences of individuals with ARFID and their families is lacking. However, the findings of a substantial body of qualitative research in eating disorders may be relevant. A meta-synthesis of qualitative studies into the experiences of caregivers of individuals with eating disorders documented a significant amount of guilt and distress amongst family members (Fox et al., 2015). For example, an Australian study of parents of children and young adults who were living with, or had recovered from an eating disorder (type unspecified), used semi-structured interviews to explore the impact of the eating disorder on family life from the parents' perspective (Hillege et al., 2006). The age at onset of the eating disorder ranged from 10–19 years. Several major themes emerged. A lack of understanding amongst friends and family left parents feeling judged and socially isolated, and sourcing treatment resulted in financial difficulties for some. Whilst some families felt united by their struggle, family disintegration was not uncommon and many parents felt unable to cope. Parents in another study described their experiences as "devastating" and a "nightmare" (Cottee-Lane et al., 2004). Siblings can also be profoundly affected by the experience of living with an individual with an eating disorder with in one study, many expressing feelings of "loss" and "sacrifice", and 80% reporting that their quality of life was negatively impacted by the onset of their sibling's eating disorder (Areemit et al., 2010). Some of these themes also appear in research into younger children's feeding and eating problems. Receiving negative judgments from family members and friends was a problem also reported by the parents of 18–38-month-old "picky" eaters who took part in focus groups conducted by Rubio and Rigal (2017). Parents expressed feelings of guilt and failure about their children's poor diet and worried about their future health and growth. For these families, mealtimes were described as stressful involving conflict and disruption. This was echoed in an interview study of 88 parents of "picky eaters" in the United States who reported considerable disruption to family mealtimes and food-related stress (Trofholz et al., 2017). Bearing in mind that the latter two studies had recruited children with only mild and developmentally appropriate levels of fussy eating, it is likely that the families of children with clinically significant feeding and eating difficulties experience considerably higher levels of stress and distress. This is certainly borne out by studies of the families of children with severe physical disabilities affecting their feeding, such as cerebral palsy. Orally feeding such children has been described as "battleground" or "war" (Craig et al., 2003; Rollins, 2006), and family life can suffer enormous disruption as a consequence (Rouse et al., 2002). A recent meta-analysis of qualitative research into the impact of tube-feeding on mothers' emotional wellbeing concluded that "… food refusal and tube-feeding go to the core of a mother's identity and can trigger maternal

PTSD [post-traumatic stress disorder]" (Wilken, 2012). A further recurring theme in much of the research in this area is a lack of understanding and empathy from health professionals, leaving families feeling dismissed and without the support that they need to cope with the challenges that a significant feeding problem can bring (McKee et al., 2010; Rogers et al., 2012; Rouse et al., 2002; Sleigh, 2005).

Other potential sources of insight into the experiences of parents of children with significant feeding difficulties are the numerous blogs and parent-run support groups to be found online. Posts and comments on these forums testify to the stress and distress experienced by many of these families,

> The doctors didn't see how every time we tried to get her to eat anything different, there would be drama and tears. They didn't see that my daughter declined invitations to birthday parties or sleepovers because of the fear of someone asking her why she didn't eat, or worse, forcing her to eat something she wasn't comfortable eating
>
> (www.thefix.com; posted 3 January 2018)

The use of outcome measures to improve understanding of patient views

In order to better understand the concerns and priorities of patients themselves and their families, there has been increasing interest in patient-centred outcomes research and in developing Patient- (or Person-) Centred Outcome Measures (PCOMS) (Concannon, 2015). PCOMs are a relatively new concept, placing patients, and their families and carers, at the heart of deciding which treatment goals are important to them, rather than these decisions being made by clinicians. Because the concerns and impact of different conditions are so varied, PCOMs need to be constructed and tailored so as to be relevant to the particular patient group in question. Examples of existing PCOMs include: The Multiple Sclerosis Impact Scale (MSIS-29), (Hobart et al., 2001) and The Profile of Neuropsychiatric Symptoms (PONS) (Santosh et al., 2015). These outcome measures differ from Patient Reported Outcome Measures (PROMs), Patient Reported Experience Measures (PREMs) and Clinician Reported Outcome Measures (CROMS): PROMs are mostly questionnaires measuring patients' views of the current status of their health (e.g. The Peptic Ulcer Patient Reported Outcome Measure (PU-PROM; Liu et al., 2017); PREMs measure patients' perceptions of their healthcare experience (e.g. Quality of Trauma Care Patient-Reported Experience Measure (QTAC-PREM; Bobrovitz et al., 2016); and CROMs measure clinician ratings of patient outcomes (e.g. The Health of the Nation Outcome Scales for Children and Adolescents (HoNOSCA;

Gowers et al., 1999). All these three types of measure are typically constructed by clinicians or researchers, whereas the content of a PCOM comes directly from service users themselves.

The development of a PCOM for ARFID: "What Matters to Me"

A recent project sought to develop a PCOM relevant to ARFID and related feeding and eating disorders in children that was evidence-based, systematically derived and had high face validity (i.e. relevant to affected families). The intention was to facilitate a standardised approach to the assessment of concerns and wishes commonly expressed by parents of children with ARFID and related feeding and eating disorders, with the aim of improving patient-centred care delivery. Carried out in a service specialising in ARFID at a paediatric tertiary care hospital in the UK, the project involved the participation of over 200 parents of attending patients. In a four-stage iterative process participants took part in interviews and focus groups, and completed questionnaires.

The first stage comprised a broad survey of parents/carers attending the service asking for their views in four target areas:

1. **Concerns:** what aspect(s) of their child's feeding or eating difficulty were they most worried about.
2. **Impact:** what impact the feeding or eating difficulty was having on the child's health and wellbeing, and that of the family as a whole.
3. **Service Elements**: what they would find the most useful elements of an effective service for children with feeding and eating difficulties.
4. **Desired outcome:** what they would like to achieve through treatment.

Themes identified from survey responses were extracted and were subsequently discussed in focus groups, supplemented by individual in-depth interviews to ensure comprehensive and correct understanding, and to establish the salience of the issues raised to this patient population.

Informed by this first stage, a draft questionnaire was prepared listing the recurring themes emerging from the first stage with a scale on which to rate the importance of each item on a scale from one to ten. A further group of parents completed this and provided feedback and suggestions for improvement. A final version of a parent-completed PCOM for ARFID and related childhood feeding and eating disorders was then produced. Entitled "What Matters to Me?", the measure has been subjected to further testing and refinement in response to the comments and suggestions of families as well as clinicians working in the field. The final version is a 48-item checklist of major concerns, impact on family life and functioning and goals for treatment (see Appendix).

Qualitative findings obtained in the development of "What Matters to Me?"

Concerns

As expected, the major concerns expressed by participating parents and carers were the amount, the variety and the nutritional quality of the foods that their children consumed,

> He won't try new foods at all. His eating speed is so slow that he wouldn't even finish a sandwich and a Frube [type of yogurt in a squeezable tube] at lunchtime at school. Mealtimes are fraught ... the variety of food he eats is down to virtually nothing

Many children were reliant on nutritional supplements and some were being fed via nasogastric tube or a gastrostomy tube in order to maintain their weight and growth. Many parents were very worried about their child's apparent fear of food and eating, especially when foods were unfamiliar, and many were saddened by their child's lack of interest or enjoyment in food.

Impact

The negative impact of eating difficulties on children as well as the wider family was profound. The child's health, growth, mood, energy, and learning, were all mentioned as negatively affected. Children experienced teasing and sometimes bullying in school and were unable in some cases to go on school trips. In common with the research discussed previously, participating parents and carers of children with clinically significant eating difficulties reported experiencing feelings of isolation and high levels of stress, anxiety, and depression,

> I was an absolute mess.

Relationships within the family were often strained and parents described struggling to cope emotionally or financially. Other children in the family were affected too; some were worried about their sibling's health, others imitated their poor eating habits, and still others complained that they were not allowed to eat the same food,

> His siblings have all got an issue around food. I suppose they've grown up with it with him being the eldest. They've watched him and learned from him, it's very sad

The social lives of all family members were sometimes affected and going on holiday, to friend's houses, or out to a restaurant was out of the question for some,

> The impact on him and his social life was the most, the worst thing really for him because obviously he couldn't eat at friend's houses without preparation being done ... we did try play dates years ago, but I stopped doing it because the children would make comments and they were negative comments.

Service elements

Parents confirmed that feelings such as those expressed above can be exacerbated by a lack of understanding of the severity and impact of feeding disorders in the general population and from health professionals. Many families expressed frustration with their previous experiences of care, describing it as fragmented, unhelpful or inconsistent,

> We went to CAMHS [Child and Adolescent Mental Health Service] and we were pretty much told ... he's just a fussy eater – you're not going to see a psychologist

Having their child's problem taken seriously and feeling supported and reassured was rare.

In the UK, many patients and their families travel significant distances to attend specialist clinics although most would prefer to be treated locally. The facility to contact and share information with other affected families is something that many said they would welcome.

Desired outcomes of treatment

Findings suggest that the ultimate goals of treatment are often modest, with some parents acknowledging that there is no "magic wand", but that small improvements could dramatically improve quality of life in affected families,

> I just wanted him to be a little bit more normal. I didn't have high expectations to be honest

For example, being able to eat out as a family or to enjoy a "normal" mealtime at home was often mentioned. Most parents simply wanted their child to eat more, but many also wished that their child could be less anxious and derive some pleasure out of eating,

> I just want him to say to me one day, the words "When is dinner ready? I'm starving"

Conclusions

A growing body of research into the assessment, course, and treatment of ARFID is emerging, but the patient's voice is rarely heard, at least in the published literature to date. We know from other related literatures, notably in the field of eating disorders, that the negative impact of serious feeding and eating problems on the affected individual and their family is profound. The importance of hearing the voice of the patient has been recognised globally and initiatives are starting to emerge to develop more patient-centred measures.

The new parent-report PCOM, *What Matters to Me?* is a step in the right direction, providing insight into the particular experiences, expectations, and priorities of individual families. Attending to the voice of the patient and their family in this way can contribute to improving patient-centred care in this population by enabling clinicians to assess and subsequently target areas identified as mattering most by those affected. Routine use of PCOMs at the start of treatment can facilitate engagement and assist in guiding treatment options. Used post-treatment, PCOMs can provide information as to whether outcomes that matter to children and families have been achieved through clinical intervention, but also whether families have received the type of treatment they feel would be most appropriate. Such measures can additionally make a tangible contribution to service evaluation and to guiding outcomes-based commissioning or purchasing of services, as well as patient choice, by identifying the vital elements of an effective service.

ARFID and related feeding and eating difficulties often emerge in very early childhood when it may not always be possible to elicit the patients' own perspective, and parental report provides an appropriate alternative. However, these difficulties can occur and/or persist across the lifespan and a goal for future research must be the development of parallel PCOMs to explore the views, experiences, priorities and expectations of patients themselves.

Summary points

- Having a child with significant feeding or eating difficulties can negatively affect the whole family
- Attending to the voice of the child and other family members can improve patient engagement and facilitate treatment planning
- Involving patients in their own care has been shown to contribute to improved outcomes
- Using person- or patient-centred outcome measures before and after treatment can reveal whether the outcomes that matter most to patients and their families have been addressed
- Such information can contribute to guiding outcomes-based commissioning or purchasing of services as well as patient choice.

References

Ammaniti, M., Ambruzzi, A.M., Lucarelli, L., Cimino, S., & D'Olimpio, F. (2004) Malnutrition and dysfunctional mother-child feeding interactions: clinical assessment and research implications. *Journal of the American College of Nutrition* 23, 259–71.

Areemit, R.S., Katzman, D.K., Pinhas, L., & Kaufman, M.E. (2010) The experience of siblings of adolescents with eating disorders. *Journal of Adolescent Health* 46, 569–76.

Atzaba-Poria, N., Meiri, G., Millikovsky, M., Barkai, A.Z., Dunaevsky-Idan, M., & Yerushalmi, B. (2010) Father–child and mother–child interaction in families with a child feeding disorder; the role of paternal involvement. *Infant Mental Health Journal* 31, 682–98.

Australian Commission on Safety and Quality in Health Care (2011) *Patient-centred care: improving quality and safety through partnerships with patients and consumers.* Sydney: ACSQHC.

Aviram, I., Atzaba-Proia, N., Pike, A., Meiri, G., & Yerushalmi, B. (2015) Mealtime dynamics in child feeding disorder: the role of child temperament, parental sense of competence and paternal involvement. *Journal of Pediatric Psychology* 40, 45–54.

Bickman, L., Kelley, S.D., Breda, C., de Andrade, A.R., & Riemer, M. (2011) Effects of routine feedback to clinicians on mental health outcomes of youths: results of a randomised trial. *Psychiatric Services* 62, 1423–29.

Bobrovitz, N., Santana, M.J., Kline, T., Kortbeek, J., Widder, S., Martin, K., & Stelfox, H. T. (2016) Multicenter validation of the quality of trauma care patient-reported experience measure (QTAC-PREM). *Journal of Trauma & Acute Care Surgery* 80, 111–18.

Budd, K.S., McGraw, T.E., Farbitz, R., Murphy, T.B., Hawkins, D., Heilman, N., & Werle, M. (1992) Psychosocial concomitants of children's feeding disorders. *Journal of Pediatric Psychology* 17, 81–94.

Chatoor, I., Ganiban, J., Hirsch, R., Borman-Spurrell, E., & Mrazek, D.A. (2000) Maternal characteristics and toddler temperament in infantile anorexia. *Journal of the American Academy of Child & Adolescent Psychiatry* 39, 743–51.

Chatoor, I., Hirsch, R., & Persinger, M. (1997) Facilitating internal regulation of eating: a treatment model for infantile anorexia. *Infants & Young Children* 9, 12–22.

Chatoor, I., & Macaoay, M. (2008) Feeding development and disorders. In M.M. Haith & J.B. Benson (eds) *Encyclopedia of infant and early childhood development*, 524–33. New York, NY: Academic Press.

Concannon, T.W. (2015) Can patient centred outcomes research improve healthcare: we believe it can; now we should put it to the test. *British Medical Journal* 351, h3859.

Cottee-Lane, D., Pistrang, N., & Bryant-Waugh, R. (2004) Childhood onset anorexia nervosa: the experience of parents. *European Eating Disorders Review* 12, 169–77.

Craig, G.M., Scambler, G., & Spitz, L. (2003) Why parents of children with neurodevelopmental disabilities requiring gastrostomy feeding need more support. *Developmental Medicine and Child Neurology* 45, 183–88.

Delaney, J.L. (2018) Patient-centred care as an approach to improving health care in Australia. *Collegian* 25, 119–23.

Department of Health, UK Government, & NHS England (2015). Future in mind: promoting, protecting and improving our children and young people's mental health and wellbeing. https://assets.publishing.service.gov.uk/government/uploads/system/uploads/attachment_data/file/414024/Childrens_Mental_Health.pdf - accessed 9 July 2019.

Didehbani, N., Kelly, K., Austin, L., & Wiechmann, A. (2011) Role of parental stress on pediatric feeding disorders. *Children's Health Care* 40, 85–100.

Feldman, R., Keren, M., Groos-Rozval, O., & Tyano, S. (2004) Mother–child touch patterns in infant feeding disorders: relation to maternal, child and environment factors. *Journal of the American Academy and Adolescent Psychiatry* 43, 1089–97.

Fox, J.R.E., Dean, M., & Whittlesea, A. (2015) The experience of caring for or living with an individual with an eating disorder: a meta-synthesis of qualitative studies. *Clinical Psychology and Psychotherapy* 24, 103–25.

Garro, A. (2004) Coping patterns in mothers/caregivers of children with chronic feeding problems. *Journal of Pediatric Health Care* 18, 138–44.

Gilmore, L. (2006) "You're not leaving the table until you're finished": problem eating behaviours and mother-child conflict during early and middle childhood. In Katsikitis, M. (ed.) *Psychology bridging the Tasman: science, culture & practice*, 135–39. Melbourne, Australia: The Australian Psychological Society Ltd.

Gowers, S., Harrington, R., Whitton, A., Lelliott, P., Beevor, A., Wing, J., & Jezzard, R. (1999) Brief scale for measuring the outcomes of emotional and behavioural disorders in children: Health of the Nation Outcome Scales for Children and Adolescents (HoNOSCA). *British Journal of Psychiatry* 174, 413–16.

Greer, A.J., Gulotta, C.S., Masler, E.A., & Laud, R.B. (2008) Caregiver stress and outcomes of children with pediatric feeding disorders treated in an intensive interdisciplinary program. *Journal of Pediatric Psychology* 33, 612–20.

Hawley, K.M., & Weisz, J.R. (2005) Youth versus parent working alliance in usual clinical care: distinctive associations with retention, satisfaction, and treatment outcome. *Journal of Clinical Child and Adolescent Psychology* 34, 117–28.

Hillege, S., Beale, B., & McMaster, R. (2006) Impact of eating disorders on family life: individual parents' stories. *Journal of Clinical Nursing* 15, 1016–22.

Hobart, J., Lamping, D., Fitzpatrick, R., Riazi, A., & Thompson, A. (2001) The Multiple Sclerosis Impact Scale (MSIS – 29): a new patient-based outcome measure. *Brain* 124, 962–73.

Jones, C.J., & Bryant-Waugh, R. (2013) The relationship between child feeding problems and maternal mental health: a selective review. *Advances in Eating Disorders* 1, 119–33.

Liu, N., L., J., Liu, J., & Zhang, Y. (2017) The PU-PROM: a patient reported outcome measure for peptic ulcer disease. *Health Expectations* 20, 1350–66.

McKee, M.D., Maher, S., Deen, D., & Blank, A.E. (2010) Counseling to prevent obesity among preschool children: acceptability of a pilot urban primary care intervention. *Annals of Family Medicine* 8, 249–55.

NHS England, Care Quality Commission, Health Education England, Monitor, Public Health England, Trust Development Authority (2014) *NHS five-year forward view.* London: NHS England.

Pathak, V., Jena, B., & Kalra, S. (2013) Qualitative research. *Perspectives in Clinical Research* 4 (3), 192.

Rogers, L.G., Magill-Evans, J., & Rempel, G.R. (2012) Mothers' challenges in feeding their children with autism spectrum disorder – managing more than just picky eating. *Journal of Developmental and Physical Disabilities* 24, 19–33.

Rollins, H. (2006) The psychosocial impact on parents of tube feeding their child. *Paediatric Nursing* 18, 19–22.

Rouse, L., Herrington, P., Assey, J., Baker, R., & Golden, S. (2002) Feeding problems, gastrostomy and families: a qualitative pilot study. *British Journal of Disabilities* 30, 122–28.

Rubio, B., & Rigal, N. (2017) Parental concerns and attributions of food pickiness and its consequences for the parent-child relationship: a qualitative analysis. *Journal of Child Health Care* 21, 404–14.

Sackett, D.L., Rosenberg, W.M.C., Gray, J.A.M., Haynes, R.B., & Richardson, W.S. (1996) Evidence based medicine: what it is and what it isn't. *British Medical Journal* 3 (12), 71–72.

Sanders, MR, Patel, RK, Le, GB, & Shepherd, R.W. (1993) Children with persistent feeding difficulties: an observational analysis of the feeding interactions of problem and non-problem eaters. *Health Psychology* 12, 64–73.

Santosh, P., Gringras, P., Baird, G., Fiori, F., & Sala, R. (2015) Development and psychometric properties of the parent version of the Profile of Neuropsychiatric Symptoms (PONS) in children and adolescents. *BMC Pediatrics* 15, 62.

Singer, L.T., Song, L.Y., Hill, B.P., & Jaffe, A.C. (1990) Stress and depression in mothers of failure-to-thrive children. *Journal of Pediatric Psychology* 15, 711–20.

Sleigh, G. (2005) Mothers' voice: a qualitative study on feeding children with cerebral palsy. *Child Care, Health and Development* 31, 373–83.

Stein, A., Woolley, H., Cooper, S.D., & Fairburn, C.G. (1994) An observational study of mothers with eating disorders and their infants. *Journal of Child Psychology and Psychiatry* 35, 733–48.

Trofholz, A.C., Schutte, A.K., & Berge, J.M. (2017) How parents describe picky eating and its impact on family meals: a qualitative analysis. *Appetite* 110, 36–43.

US Department of Health and Human Services (2008) *Personalized health care: pioneers, partnerships, progress.* Washington DC: US Department of Health and Human Services, 1–302.

Wennberg, D.E., Marr, A., Lang, L., O'Malley, S., & Bennett, G. (2010) A randomized trial of a telephone care-management strategy. *New England Journal of Medicine* 363, 1245–55.

Wilken, M. (2012) The impact of child tube feeding on maternal emotional state and identity: a qualitative meta-analysis. *Journal of Pediatric Nursing* 27, 248–55.

World Health Organization (2007) *People-centred health care: a policy framework.* Geneva and Switzerland: World Health Organization.

Part II

Diagnosis and presentation

Chapter 4

Overview of diagnosis and presentation

Rachel Bryant-Waugh

Introduction

This chapter describes the background to the introduction of avoidant restrictive food intake disorder (ARFID) as a diagnostic category and provides an overview of the main features which form part of its current formal definition and description. Inclusion and exclusion criteria are discussed, useful sources of further information highlighted, and clinically informed examples presented by way of illustration. ARFID is an extremely heterogeneous disorder which, in some instances, can contribute to confusion in decision-making about the appropriateness of the diagnosis for a particular individual. This chapter sets out to explain the ways in which ARFID presentations can vary, and how best to use information gained in the process of considering a diagnosis to enhance patient care. Perhaps unsurprisingly for a relatively newly introduced diagnostic category, there is some variability, both in the interpretation of the diagnostic criteria and in their application, as well as a number of myths and misconceptions about ARFID more generally. These issues are highlighted and the reader oriented to relevant literature for further inspection.

The introduction of ARFID as a diagnostic category

ARFID first appeared as a diagnostic category in the 5th edition of the *American Psychiatric Association's Diagnostic and Statistical Manual*, published in 2013 (DSM-5; American Psychiatric Association, 2013). It was included as one of the "feeding and eating disorders", which, alongside ARFID, include pica, rumination disorder, anorexia nervosa, bulimia nervosa, and binge eating disorder. A number of other variants of significant eating disturbance, less well characterised than these six, have been included under one diagnostic category called 2other specified feeding or eating disorder". From being a clinical presentation itself often included in a "residual" category in terms of diagnostic classification, ARFID is now recognised as a separate condition.

The process of reviewing the old diagnostic categories in DSM-IV (American Psychiatric Association, 1994) began in 1999. Work Groups were appointed to consider the evidence supporting all existing categories and criteria, to determine whether revisions, replacements or deletions should be recommended in line with emerging knowledge. The Eating Disorders Work Group, charged with reviewing the DSM-IV Eating Disorders as well as the Feeding Disorders of Infancy and Early Childhood, proposed that ARFID should be included in DSM-5 (Attia et al., 2013). The rationale for this proposal is well described in two key papers. The first described the outcome of a literature review relating to the three DSM-IV "feeding disorders": feeding disorder of infancy or early childhood, pica and rumination disorder. From this it became clear that the study of feeding and eating disturbances in childhood had been hampered by inconsistent use of terminology, but also that a number of specific presentations appeared to be reasonably consistently described across this age range (Bryant-Waugh et al., 2010). The second paper discussed the poor clinical utility of the then existing categories across both the feeding and eating disorders, and supported the proposal that feeding and eating disorders should be merged into one group, with diagnoses applicable to children, adolescents and adults (Uher & Rutter, 2012). Both papers highlighted the well-documented clinical presentation of patients with significant avoidant or restrictive eating behaviour in the absence of weight or shape concerns. Together, these papers include the main discussion points at the time, highlighting the variability in factors that can drive avoidant and restrictive food intake behaviours, as well as the variability in clinical features at presentation resulting from these behaviours. The papers also refer to the continuity between manifestations of such eating disturbances across the entire age range, which led ARFID to be put forward as a replacement and extension of feeding disorder of infancy or early childhood. This had been little used in research and was widely regarded as too narrow through its emphasis on weight loss or a failure to gain weight as a necessary clinical determinant and its specification that onset must be before the age of six years (Kenney & Walsh, 2013). The newly proposed category was duly scrutinised by the relevant internal and external committees and eventually accepted as a diagnosis applicable to children, adolescents and adults.

Since its introduction in DSM-5, ARFID has become internationally adopted as a meaningful diagnosis by clinicians, researchers and the general public. It has been included in the updated diagnostic and classification system of the World Health Organization, the International Classification of Diseases (ICD-11; World Health Organization, 2019), further extending its reach to all member countries around the world. The debate about whether ARFID is a feeding disorder or an eating disorder (Kennedy, Wick, & Keel, 2018; Sharp & Stubbs, 2019) will hopefully recede as it comes to be recognised as one of the feeding and eating disorders alongside the others.

Definition and diagnosis

ARFID is characterised by a disturbance in feeding or eating behaviour resulting in the individual's energy needs, their nutritional needs, or both, failing to be met. In other words the person fails to eat enough in terms of variety, over-all amount, or both. If energy needs are not met, normal weight gain in child-hood will falter or weight will drop. Insufficient energy intake can also have a negative impact on growth, which can falter. If nutritional needs are not met through a limited diet, the individual will be at risk of developing nutritional deficiencies, with related medical and physical consequences (see further Chap-ters 8 and 9). In some instances, these aspects of the disorder will lead to dependence on tube feeding or on oral nutritional supplements to ensure phys-ical requirements are met. Children with ARFID may become stuck on this type of assisted feeding, which will need to be addressed in treatment (see Chapter 12). It is important to be clear that the avoidance and restriction of food intake characteristic of ARFID does not necessarily result in weight loss or low weight. Some individuals may only accept a very restricted range of foods, but if these have a high energy content (for example, a diet of crisps, chocolate biscuits, and a sweet drink), weight may be normal or high, yet the individual is likely to present with significant nutritional deficiencies. Some may not be low weight or nutritionally deficient, but have become completely dependent on prescribed nutritional supplements that maintain their weight. However, some children with ARFID do present with extremely low weight, and some with nutritionally related stunting. The important point here is to rec-ognise that ARFID is not a low weight disorder per se.

Both the DSM-5 criteria for ARFID and the ICD-11 guidance mention three main reasons that may underlie the avoidance and restriction of food intake. These are the presence of a lack of interest in food or eating; avoidance based on certain sensory characteristics of food; and concern about possible negative consequences of eating (American Psychiatric Association, 2013; World Health Organization, 2019). This is not intended to be an exclusive list, and represents the reasons most commonly described in the literature.

The definition of ARFID further includes the required presence of a level of impairment. This can be physical impairment in terms of weight loss, growth faltering, nutritional deficiencies, reliance on assisted intake, as discussed above, but it can also include interference with everyday functioning. Some children with ARFID are unable to manage to eat with the family or at school, requiring special accommodations and resulting in interference with social and emotional development. Mealtimes may be fraught with strained relationships and arguments, impacting negatively on relationships. Children may be unable to participate as expected with their peers, being unable to go on outings, school trips, parties or other social occasions. In most instances both physical and psychosocial impairment will be present, but in some, just one of these areas may be affected.

Exclusion criteria include the presence of significant weight or shape concerns (which suggest that anorexia or bulimia nervosa should be considered); lack of available food (for example, related to neglect or poverty); avoidance or restriction associated with an accepted practice (for example, due to food allergies); or the presence of another medical condition or mental disorder that adequately explains the eating behaviour. There are a number of useful discussions in the literature focussing on the diagnostic criteria of ARFID and using case examples to illustrate the range of presentations seen in clinical practice (e.g. Bryant-Waugh, 2013; Katzman, Stevens, & Norris, 2014; Kreipe & Palomaki, 2012).

The clinical utility of ARFID as a diagnosis

One of the aims contributing to the introduction of ARFID as a diagnosis was to reduce the number of people attending clinical services assigned to a "not otherwise specified", "atypical", or other residual diagnostic category (Call, Walsh, & Attia, 2013; Al-Adawi et al., 2013). An important reason for this is because it is difficult to develop evidence-based approaches to assessment and intervention for people experiencing particular difficulties as long as there is poor agreement about the characteristics they share. A number of studies have demonstrated that this hoped-for effect has indeed occurred. Claudino and colleagues describe a detailed study involving 2288 mental health professionals registered with the World Health Organization's Global Clinical Practice Network who were asked to assign patient vignettes to ICD-11 feeding and eating disorder categories. They found that the introduction of ARFID reduced the use of residual diagnoses and that 85% of participants rated the introduction of ARFID in ICD-11 positively compared to ICD-10 (Claudino et al., 2019).

Two other studies, carried out in child and adolescent eating disorder treatment centres, also demonstrate a reduction in the number of patients assigned to a not otherwise specified category. Fisher and colleagues found that in their clinic sample, 64.6% of 309 patients (N = 198) received a diagnosis of eating disorder not otherwise specified based on DSM-IV criteria, whereas only four patients had a diagnosis of unspecified feeding or eating disorder based on the DSM-5 criteria. Reassigned diagnoses included 60 individuals who received an ARFID diagnosis (Fisher, Gonzalez, & Malizio, 2015). Similarly, Ornstein and colleagues reported that 14% of their clinic population of 215 adolescent patients, moved from eating disorder not otherwise specified to a diagnosis of ARFID using the DSM-5 criteria (Ornstein et al., 2013).

Another aspect of clinical utility is whether a diagnostic category reliably includes individuals who differ in specific ways to others, preferably in both clinical and non-clinical populations. Data from a surveillance study involving 436 children across Australia, Canada, and the United Kingdom were analysed using descriptive and latent class analyses. In each country, two distinct clusters were revealed, both of which presented with food avoidance. One cluster presented with greater weight preoccupation, fear of being fat, body image distortion, and over exercising, whilst the other did not, but had higher rates of co-morbidities. The authors conclude that the clusters closely resembled anorexia nervosa and ARFID respectively. They observed that as symptomatology and distribution were very similar across the three countries their findings add support to the two separate diagnoses (Pinhas et al., 2017). Similarly, Schmidt and colleagues found a three cluster solution using latent class analysis on data from a population-based study of 799 seven to 14 year old children. The three clusters included an asymptomatic class, one with restrictive eating behaviours without shape concern, and one with restrictive eating behaviours with prominent shape concern. Children with ARFID symptoms were predominantly in the second cluster, again suggesting differences in the trajectories of ARFID and anorexia nervosa (Schmidt et al., 2018).

Izquierdo and colleagues also reported distinct differences in their clinical population study of 94 adolescent patients, between those with anorexia nervosa and those with ARFID. Differences were reported in relation to scores on questionnaire-based implicit assumption tests categorising statements as pro-dieting or non-dieting, and as true or false between the two diagnostic groups (Izquierdo et al., 2019). Thus primary evidence continues to emerge in support of the diagnostic differentiation between restrictive eating disorders.

Differential and co-morbid (or concurrent) diagnoses

An important aspect of confirming any diagnosis is the process of adequately considering whether there could be any other explanation or condition that might account for the presenting symptoms or reported characteristics. This process of considering differential diagnoses is particularly important in ARFID given the variability in its presenting features. If there is no one immediately recognisable pathway with universally shared features at presentation, it is even more necessary to be sure that another condition is not being missed.

The text accompanying the DSM-5 ARFID criteria and the ICD-11 guidance both list a number of potential differential diagnoses as well as possible co-morbidities (American Psychiatric Association, 2013, pp. 336–38; World Health Organization, 2019). These, as well as other differential and co-occurring conditions reported in the literature, are set out in Table 4.1. Any one disorder can, in general, be either a differential diagnosis or a co-morbid condition. The former means that it adequately explains the presenting symptoms and that an additional diagnosis of ARFID is not appropriate; the latter means that the two conditions are both present, that is, that ARFID can be diagnosed as the eating disturbance is over and above that usually expected and requires treatment in its own right. In Table 4.1 differential and co-morbid conditions are listed together.

It is important to note that pica is the only feeding and eating disorder diagnosis that can be assigned at the same time as an ARFID diagnosis. All of the other categories are regarded as mutually exclusive. For example, if a young person presents with anorexia nervosa overlaid on pre-existing ARFID type eating behaviour, anorexia nervosa would be the primary diagnosis. It is also important to note that some diagnoses can be both exclusion criteria and common co-morbidities. Autism is perhaps a good example. Many children with autism have idiosyncratic eating behaviours that may account for a certain

Table 4.1 Differential diagnoses and co-morbid conditions mentioned in the literature

Differential diagnosis/co-morbid condition	Sources where relevant examples are given
Other eating disorders (e.g. anorexia nervosa, bulimia nervosa, binge eating disorder)*	Maertens et al., 2017; APA**, 2013, pp. 337–38; WHO***, 2019
Autism spectrum disorder/pervasive developmental disorder	Nicely et al., 2014; Lucarelli et al., 2017; Sharp et al., 2018; APA, 2013, pp. 337–38; WHO, 2019
Anxiety disorders (e.g. specific phobia; social anxiety disorder; generalised anxiety disorder; illness anxiety disorder)	Fisher et al., 2014; Nicely et al., 2014; King, Urbach, & Stewart, 2015; Maertens et al., 2017; Okereke, 2018; APA, 2013, pp. 337–38; WHO, 2019
Attention deficit hyperactivity disorder	Pennell et al., 2016; APA, 2013, p. 338
Obsessive compulsive disorder	Maertens et al., 2017; APA, 2013, p. 338; WHO, 2019
Intellectual disability	APA, 2013, p. 338
Internet gaming disorder	Hadwiger, Middleman, & Pitt, 2019
Major depressive disorder and other depressive disorders	APA, 2013, p. 338; WHO, 2019
Schizophrenia spectrum disorders	Westfall, Mavrides, & Coffey, 2018; APA, 2013, p. 338; WHO, 2019
PANDAS/PANS (paediatric autoimmune neuropsychiatric disorder associated with streptococcus/paediatric acute-onset neuropsychiatric syndrome)	Toufexis et al., 2015
Factitious disorder	APA, 2013, p. 338
Factitious disorder imposed upon another	APA, 2013, p. 338
Reactive attachment disorder	APA, 2013, p. 337
Specific neurological, neuromuscular, structural, or congenital disorders and conditions	APA, 2013, p. 337
Other medical conditions (e.g. irritable bowel syndrome; gastroesophageal reflux disease; allergies; malignancies; hyperthyroidism; infectious disease)	Fisher et al., 2014; Lucarelli et al., 2017; Chey, 2019; APA, 2013, p. 336–7; WHO, 2019

* The only feeding and eating diagnosis that can be assigned concurrently with ARFID is pica;
** American Psychiatric Association;
*** World Health Organization

amount of avoidance or restriction in their diet. Not all such children will meet the diagnostic threshold for ARFID as their eating behaviours may be adequately explained by their autistic traits and not associated with significant impairment as described in the previous section. However, some children with autism will present with eating disturbances that do meet diagnostic threshold for ARFID; here, both diagnoses may be applicable concurrently.

Subtyping, variability and presentation in different settings

One common misconception is that individuals with ARFID can be assigned to specific subtypes. At present, the examples given in the diagnostic criteria are not subtypes as such, but commonly identified reasons behind the avoidance or restriction of food intake; lack of interest in food or eating, sensory based avoidance, and avoidance stemming from concern about the possible consequences of eating, are not necessarily mutually exclusive. However, this is not to say that with further investigation, clear subtypes may not begin to emerge. For example, Norris and colleagues conducted a case note review of 77 patients with ARFID aged eight to17 years and reported that they did identify three subtypes which aligned well with the examples given in DSM-5: 30 (39%) presented with weight loss and/or medical compromise associated with apparent lack of interest in eating; 14 (18%) presented with sensory based restriction; and 33 (43%) had food avoidance and/or fear of the consequences of eating (Norris et al., 2018). Here again, the patient cohort studied, which was predominantly female (73%), may not be representative of the ARFID population as whole, so that the relative percentages of different presentations and characteristics of the proposed different subtypes may be an artefact of the specific treatment setting. This seems to be confirmed by the findings of a study investigating the existence of distinct variants of eating behaviour characterised by avoidance or restriction in a non-clinical population, which in contrast to the above findings, identified fear-based avoidance as the least commonly occurring variant (Kurz et al., 2016; see further Chapter 5).

Another case note review study of 59 patients with ARFID in a partial hospitalisation programme for eating disorders reported that the "sensory sensitivity phenotype" was the most common, frequently co-occurring with the two other "phenotypes". The study authors conclude that this provides evidence that what they refer to as "multiple functions for food avoidance" may be present in any one individual (Reilly et al., 2019). Similarly a case note study of 83 patients with ARFID, also admitted to a partial hospitalisation eating disorder programme and aged eight to 17 years, also found presentations were characterised predominantly by sensory based avoidance, lack of interest in eating or low appetite, and fear of aversive consequences from eating, in that order. However, a fourth group of patients with both sensory-based avoidance and limited interest/appetite was identified, and all four groups were found to differ in terms of core ARFID criteria, symptom trajectory, illness duration, mood, medical comorbidities, age, gender, and parent-reported symptoms of psychopathology. The authors conclude that their findings suggest that there may be meaningful subtypes (Zickgraf et al., 2019b). At present therefore, it seems prudent to hold open the possibility that there can be overlap between different factors contributing to the avoidance and restriction of intake in any one individual and to continue to observe and record the presence or absence of characteristic features in terms of profiles (Bryant-Waugh et al., 2019).

It also seems likely that, at present, different variants of ARFID may predominantly present in different settings. For example, a significant amount of the existing literature specifically relating to ARFID has been conducted by those working in the field of child and adolescent eating disorders. In these settings, the characteristics of ARFID have been explored, documented and compared to those of anorexia nervosa and other eating disorders. Norris and colleagues report that in their retrospective, descriptive study, conducted in an eating disorders setting, the most commonly identified features of ARFID were food avoidance, loss of appetite, abdominal pain, and fear of vomiting (Norris et al., 2014). Cooney and colleagues described the characteristics of 28 patients diagnosed with ARFID, also in an eating disorder programme, and reported that weight loss (or failure to achieve appropriate weight gain) was present in all but one. They noted additionally that all 28 individuals presented with at least two physical symptoms, that 20 (71.4%) had an acute onset of ARFID with an identifiable trigger, and that 16 (57.1%) had a co-occurring psychiatric disorder (Cooney et al., 2018). Authors from the same setting further reported that children with ARFID had a history of abdominal pain and infections preceding their diagnosis, and were more likely to be diagnosed with a comorbid anxiety disorder (Lieberman et al., 2019). Although useful in highlighting the types of ARFID presentation seen in specific contexts, such findings should not be considered representative of the ARFID population as a whole. It seems likely that clinics seeing children with autism or learning disability may capture different variants of ARFID presentations, for example, those with longstanding difficulties and a significant sensory avoidance component.

There has not yet been a great deal of detailed description in the literature about variation in cultural expressions of ARFID, leading to calls for further work in this area (Schermbrucker et al., 2017). Most of the work to date has been carried out in the United States, Canada, the United Kingdom and other European countries, and Australia, with only a handful of papers from Japan, Taiwan, and Singapore. For example, a small case series of eight adolescent and adult patients with ARFID in Singapore found that all had developed ARFID symptoms in early childhood, and presented at low weight with long standing difficulties (Lai, Chee, & Kwok, 2019).

Boundaries and variability in application of criteria

One pointer whether an individual's presentation meets threshold for "caseness" or clinical significance, has long been to identify the presence of associated distress or impairment (Bolton, 2013). There has thus far been limited focussed work measuring the extent of these features in children and adolescents with ARFID. For example, Krom and colleagues found that health related quality of life was lower in young patients with ARFID (aged 0–10 years) attending a paediatric feeding clinic compared to healthy controls across an number of domains, and also that the school aged children included in the study (those aged 6–10 years) had significantly lower reported school functioning (Krom et al., 2019). Clearly more work is required in this respect.

There is also ongoing debate about which clinical presentations meet criteria for ARFID and which do not. One aspect of this has been the discussion relating to "orthorexia nervosa" (Cena et al., 2019). This term, not currently recognised as a formal disorder, is used to describe individuals who are excessively focussed on eating a "healthy" diet, which in some cases leads to clinically significant restriction of intake. Some argue that it warrants a new diagnostic category in its own right (e.g. Moroze et al., 2015), whilst others comment that most presentations of "orthorexia" can be appropriately captured by anorexia nervosa (where weight/shape concerns are the underlying motive driving the restricted eating behaviour) or by ARFID (where "unhealthy" foods are avoided because of concern for health and general well-being). For example, in a study of 449 adults, orthorexia nervosa symptoms were found to be more strongly related to anorexia nervosa and bulimia nervosa than to ARFID, but recognised as overlapping with both (Zickgraf, Ellis, & Essayli, 2019a). Similar research has not yet been conducted with children and adolescents.

Another area of discussion in relation to ARFID diagnostic criteria is how these should best be operationalised for research purposes. The interpretation of criteria tends to vary in clinical practice, with diagnostic systems generally set up in the knowledge that a degree of clinical judgement will be exercised. The aim of diagnostic categories is usually to achieve good levels of clinical utility; however, greater precision is needed in relation to research. Clearly specified inclusion and exclusion criteria are extremely helpful in determining the comparability of patients across different studies. In ARFID there are two main issues at play; first the variability in presentations inherent in the definition; and second evidence that there is some degree of variability in the way clinicians are interpreting the criteria (Eddy et al., 2019).

What lies ahead?

It is important to recognise that any diagnostic category is not fixed in relation to its definition or conceptualisation. As evidenced by the work leading to the DSM-5 and ICD-11 classification systems, diagnostic categories may be "retired", introduced, or altered in line with emerging evidence. At the time of writing, a change is being considered to the DSM-5 criteria for ARFID; namely that psychosocial impairment alone could be considered sufficient for a diagnosis without the requirement that the eating disturbance in ARFID is "manifested by persistent failure to meet appropriate nutritional and/or energy needs" (American Psychiatric

Association, 2013; Becker et al., 2018; Walsh, 2019; Zickgraf et al., 2019b). Clearly this might be helpful in enabling some patients to access services when they might otherwise be unable to do this. One note of caution, however, is the observation that DSM-5 lists factitious disorder, or factitious disorder imposed on another, in its list of differential diagnoses for ARFID. The absence of the "harder" markers of impact, in the form of nutritional inadequacies or impact on weight or growth, places an additional responsibility on clinicians to ensure genuine distress and impairment secondary to the avoidance and restriction of food intake are indeed present. In the majority of situations, patients will reliably report their experience, yet in a small number there may be falsification of symptoms and even deliberate deception. In the case of younger children, clinicians are reliant on parental report; confirming impressions through observation and comprehensive assessment of functioning with information derived from a number of sources can be very helpful.

Strand and colleagues' systematic scoping review of the diagnostic validity of ARFID concludes that current criteria are unable to ensure optimal diagnostic validity, with related negative impact on their usefulness in clinical practice and epidemiological research. They put forward a number of suggestions to improve matters, including placing a stronger emphasis on the three identified "subdomains" and working to clarify more specific boundaries of ARFID (Strand, von Hausswolff-Juhlin, & Welch, 2019). The further characterisation of individuals presenting with singular versus multiple phenotype characteristics and the need to develop a subtype taxonomy has also been proposed by others (Reilly et al., 2019; Sharp & Stubbs, 2019).

Time will tell, therefore, whether the diagnostic category of ARFID as currently conceptualised and formulated, proves to be valid and useful. It seems likely, indeed, to be hoped, that as clinical expertise increases, research evidence builds, and we learn from those directly affected by ARFID, that updates and changes will be made. As with all diagnostic categories, ARFID is not a fixed entity; it is a construct representing a collective best effort to capture current knowledge. As we find out more, revisions may be required.

Summary points

- Although ARFID is a newly introduced diagnostic term, the clinical presentations it includes are not
- ARFID is a diagnosis that can be applied to children, adolescents and adults, who may present with low, normal or high weight
- There can be significant variation in presenting features in different people with ARFID, particularly in terms of:
  - whether eating difficulties are long standing or have an acute onset
  - the reasons behind the avoidance or restriction
  - the impact of the disorder on physical and mental health and everyday functioning

- As ARFID includes heterogeneous presentations, comprehensive, multi-disciplinary assessment is indicated in the majority of cases
- It is anticipated that diagnostic guidelines and specific criteria will be updated and amended in line with emerging evidence.

References

Al-Adawi, S., Bax, B., Bryant-Waugh, R., Claudino, A., Hay, P., Monteleone, P., Norring, C., Pike, K., Pilon, D., Rausch Herscovici, C., Reed, G, Rydelius, P., Sharan, P., Thiels, C., Treasure, J., & Uher, R. (2013) Revision of ICD – status update on feeding and eating disorders. *Advances in Eating Disorders* 1(1), 10–20.

American Psychiatric Association. (1994) *Diagnostic and statistical manual of mental disorders* (4th ed.) Washington, DC: Author.

American Psychiatric Association. (2013) *Diagnostic and statistical manual of mental disorders* (5th ed.) Arlington, VA: Author.

Attia, E., Becker, A.E., Bryant-Waugh, R., Hoek, H.W., Kreipe, R.E., Marcus, M.D., Mitchell, J.E., Striegel, R.H., Walsh, B.T., Wilson, G.T., Wolfe, B.E., & Wonderlich, S. (2013) Feeding and eating disorders in DSM-5. *American Journal of Psychiatry* 170(11), 1237–39.

Becker, K.R., Keshishian, A.C., Liebman, R.E., Coniglio, K.A., Wang, S.B., Franko, D.L., Eddy, K.T., & Thomas, J.J. (2018) Impact of expanded diagnostic criteria for avoidant/restrictive food intake disorder on clinical comparisons with anorexia nervosa. *International Journal of Eating Disorders* 52(3), 230–38.

Bolton, D. (2013) Overdiagnosis problems in the DSM-IV and the new DSM-5: can they be resolved by the distress-impairment criterion?. *Canadian Journal of Psychiatry* 58(11), 612–17.

Bryant-Waugh, R. (2013) Avoidant restrictive food intake disorder: an illustrative case example. *International Journal of Eating Disorders* 46(5), 420–23.

Bryant-Waugh, R., Markham, L., Kreipe, R.E., & Walsh, B.T. (2010) Feeding and eating disorders in childhood. *International Journal of Eating Disorders* 43(2), 98–111.

Bryant-Waugh, R., Micali, N., Cooke, L., Lawson, E.A., Eddy, K.T., & Thomas, J.J. (2019) Development of the Pica, ARFID, and Rumination Disorder Interview, a multi-informant, semi-structured interview of feeding disorders across the lifespan: A pilot study for ages 10-22. *International Journal of Eating Disorders* 52(4), 378–87.

Call, C., Walsh, B.T., & Attia, E. (2013) From DSM-IV to DSM-5: changes to eating disorder diagnoses. *Current Opinion in Psychiatry* 26(6), 532–36.

Cena, H., Barthels, F., Cuzzolaro, M., Bratman, S., Brytek-Matera, A., Dunn, T., Varga, M., Missbach, B., & Donini, L.M. (2019) Definition and diagnostic criteria for orthorexia nervosa: a narrative review of the literature. *Eating and Weight Disorders* 24(2), 209–46.

Chey, W.D. (2019) Elimination diets for irritable bowel syndrome: approaching the end of the beginning. *American Journal of Gastroenterology* 114(2), 201–03.

Claudino, A.M., Pike, K.M., Hay, P., Keeley, J.W., Evans, S.C., Rebello, T.J., Bryant-Waugh, R., Dai, Y., Zhao, M., Matsumoto, C., Rausch Herscovici, C., Mellor-Marsa, B., Stona, A-C., Kogan, C.S., Andrews, H.F., Monteleone, P., Pilon, D.J., Thiels, C., Sharan, P., Al-Adawi, S., & Reed, G.M. (2019) The classification of feeding and eating disorders in the ICD-11: results of a field study comparing proposed ICD-11 guidelines with existing ICD-10 guidelines. *BMC Medicine* 17(93), https://doi.org/10.1186/s12916-019-1327-4 – accessed 14 July 2019.

Cooney, M., Lieberman, M., Guimond, T., & Katzman, D.K. (2018) Clinical and psychological features of children and adolescents diagnosed with avoidant/restrictive food intake disorder in a pediatric tertiary care eating disorder program: a descriptive study. *Journal of Eating Disorders* 27(6), 7. 10.1186/s40337-018-0193-3 accessed 14 July 2019.

Eddy, K.T., Harshman, S.G., Becker, K.R., Bern, E., Bryant-Waugh, R., Hilbert, A., Katzman, D.K., Lawson, E.A., Manzo, L.D., Menzel, J., Micali, N., Ornstein, R., Sally, S., Serinsky, S.P., Sharp, W., Stubbs, K., Walsh, B.T., Zickgraf, H., Zucker, N., & Thomas, J.J. (2019) Radcliffe ARFID workgroup: toward operationalization of research diagnostic criteria and directions for the field. *International Journal of Eating Disorders* 52(4), 361–66.

Fisher, M., Gonzalez, M., & Malizio, J. (2015) Eating disorders in adolescents: how does the DSM-5 change the diagnosis?. *International Journal of Adolescent Medicine and Health* 27(4), 437–41.

Fisher, M.M., Rosen, D.S., Ornstein, R.M., Mammel, K.A., Katzman, D.K., Rome, E.S., Callahan, S.T., Malizio, J., Kearney, S., & Walsh, B.T. (2014) Characteristics of avoidant/restrictive food intake disorder in children and adolescents: a 'new disorder' in DSM-5. *Journal of Adolescent Health* 55(1), 49–52.

Hadwiger, A.N., Middleman, A.B., & Pitt, P.D. (2019) Case series: gaming vs. eating-comorbidity of ARFID and IGD. *Eating and Weight Disorders* Feb 20. doi: 10.1007/s40519-019-00639-2. [Epub ahead of print] accessed 14 July 2019.

Izquierdo, A., Plessow, F., Becker, K.R., Mancuso, C.J., Slattery, M., Murray, H.B., Hartmann, A.S., Misra, M., Lawson, E.A., Eddy, K.T., & Thomas, J.J. (2019) Implicit attitudes toward dieting and thinness distinguish fat-phobic and non-fat-phobic anorexia nervosa from avoidant/restrictive food intake disorder in adolescents. *International Journal of Eating Disorders* 52(4), 419–27.

Katzman, D.K., Stevens, K., & Norris, M. (2014) Redefining feeding and eating disorders: what is avoidant/restrictive food intake disorder?. *Paediatrics and Child Health* 19(8), 445–446.

Kennedy, G.A., Wick, M.R., & Keel, P.K. (2018) Eating disorders in children: is avoidant-restrictive food intake disorder a feeding disorder or an eating disorder and what are the implications for treatment?. *F1000Research* 7(88), 10.12688/f1000research.13110.1 accessed 14 July 2019.

Kenney, L. & Walsh, B.T. (2013) Avoidant/restrictive food intake disorder (ARFID). *Eating Disorders Review* 24(3), https://eatingdisordersreview.com/avoidantrestrictive-food-intake-disorder-arfid/ – accessed 14 July 2019.

King, L.A., Urbach, J.R., & Stewart, K.E. (2015) Illness anxiety and avoidant/restrictive food intake disorder: cognitive-behavioral conceptualization and treatment. *Eating Behaviours* 19, 106–09.

Kreipe, R.E. & Palomaki, A. (2012) Beyond picky eating: avoidant/restrictive food intake disorder. *Current Psychiatry Reports* 14(4), 421–31.

Krom, H., van der Sluijs Veer, L., van Zundert, S., Otten, M.A., Benninga, M., Haverman, L., & Kindermann, A. (2019) Health related quality of life of infants and children with avoidant restrictive food intake disorder. *International Journal of Eating Disorders* 52(4), 410–18.

Kurz, S., van Dyck, Z., Dremmel, D., Munsch, S., & Hilbert, A. (2016) Variants of early-onset restrictive eating disturbances in middle childhood. *International Journal of Eating Disorders* 49(1), 102–06.

Lai, D., Chee, A., & Kwok, V. (2019) A case series on the clinical profile of avoidant–restrictive food intake disorder in Singapore. *Proceedings of Singapore Healthcare* First Published 17 March 2019, https://doi.org/10.1177/2010105819838290 – accessed 14 July 2019.

Lieberman, M., Houser, M.E., Voyer, A.P., Grady, S., & Katzman, D.K. (2019) Children with avoidant/restrictive food intake disorder and anorexia nervosa in a tertiary care pediatric eating disorder program: A comparative study. *International Journal of Eating Disorders* 52(3), 239–45.

Lucarelli, J., Pappas, D., Welchons, L., & Augustyn, M. (2017) Autism Spectrum Disorder and Avoidant/Restrictive Food Intake Disorder. *Journal of Developmental and Behavioral Pediatrics* 38(1), 79–80.

Maertens, C., Couturier, J., Grant, C., & Johnson, N. (2017) Fear of vomiting and low body weight in two pediatric patients: diagnostic challenges. *Journal of the Canadian Academy of Child and Adolescent Psychiatry* 26(1), 59–61.

Moroze, R.M., Dunn, T.M., Craig Holland, J., Yager, J., & Weintraub, P. (2015) Microthinking about micronutrients: a case of transition from obsessions about healthy eating to near-fatal "orthorexia nervosa" and proposed diagnostic criteria. *Psychosomatics* 56(4), 397–403.

Nicely, T.A., Lane-Loney, S., Masciulli, E., Hollenbeak, C.S., & Ornstein, R.M. (2014) Prevalence and characteristics of avoidant/restrictive food intake disorder in a cohort of young patients in day treatment for eating disorders. *Journal of Eating Disorders* 2(1), 21.

Norris, M.L., Robinson, A., Obeid, N., Harrison, M., Spettigue, W. & Henderson, K. (2014) Exploring avoidant/restrictive food intake disorder in eating disordered patients: a descriptive study. *International Journal of Eating Disorders* 47(5), 495–99.

Norris, M.L., Spettigue, W., Hammond, N.G., Katzman, D.K., Zucker, N., Yelle, K., Santos, A., Gray, M., & Obeid, N. (2018) Building evidence for the use of descriptive subtypes in youth with avoidant restrictive food intake disorder. *International Journal of Eating Disorders* 51(2), 170–73.

Okereke, N.K. (2018) Buspirone treatment of anxiety in an adolescent female with avoidant/restrictive food intake disorder. *Journal of Child and Adolescent Psychopharmacology* 28(6), 425–26.

World Health Organization. (2019) *International classification of diseases – 11th revision* https://icd.who.int/browse11/l-m/en#/http://id.who.int/icd/entity/1242188600 - accessed 14 July 2019.

Ornstein, R.M., Rosen, D.S., Mammel, K.A., Callahan, S.T., Forman, S., Jay, M.S., Fisher, M., Rome, E., & Walsh, B.T. (2013) Distribution of eating disorders in children and adolescents using the proposed DSM-5 criteria for feeding and eating disorders. *Journal of Adolescent Health* 53(2), 303–05.

Pennell, A., Couturier, J., Grant, C., & Johnson, N. (2016) Severe avoidant/restrictive food intake disorder and coexisting stimulant treated attention deficit hyperactivity disorder. *International Journal of Eating Disorders* 49(11), 1036–39.

Pinhas, L., Nicholls, D., Crosby, R.D., Morris, A., Lynn, R.M., & Madden, S. (2017) Classification of childhood onset eating disorders: a latent class analysis. *International Journal of Eating Disorders* 50(6), 657–64.

Reilly, E.E., Brown, T.A., Gray, E.K., Kaye, W.H., & Menzel, J.E. (2019) Exploring the cooccurrence of behavioural phenotypes for avoidant/restrictive food intake disorder in a partial hospitalization sample. *European Eating Disorders Review* 27(4), 429–35.

Schermbrucker, J., Kimber, M., Johnson, N., Kearney, S., & Couturier, J. (2017) Avoidant/restrictive food intake disorder in an 11-year old South American boy: medical and cultural challenges. *Journal of the Canadian Academy of Child and Adolescent Psychiatry* 26(2), 110–13.

Schmidt, R., Vogel, M., Hiemisch, A., Kiess, W., & Hilbert, A. (2018) Pathological and non-pathological variants of restrictive eating behaviors in middle childhood: A latent class analysis. *Appetite* 127, 257–65.

Sharp, W.G. & Stubbs, K.H. (2019) Avoidant/restrictive food intake disorder: a diagnosis at the intersection of feeding and eating disorders necessitating subtype differentiation. *International Journal of Eating Disorders* 52(4), 398–401.

Sharp, W.G., Postorino, V., McCracken, C.E., Berry, R.C., Criado, K.K., Burrell, T.L., & Scahill, L. (2018) Dietary intake, nutrient status, and growth parameters in children with autism spectrum disorder and severe food selectivity: an electronic medical record review. *Journal of the Academy of Nutrition and Dietetics* 118, 1943–50.

Strand, M., von Hausswolff-Juhlin, Y., & Welch, E. (2019) A systematic scoping review of diagnostic validity in avoidant/restrictive food intake disorder. *International Journal of Eating Disorders* 52(4), 331–60.

Toufexis, M.D., Hommer, R., Gerardi, D.M., Grant, P., Rothschild, L., D'Souza, P., Williams, K., Leckman, J., Swedo, S.E., & Murphy, T.K. (2015) Disordered eating and food restrictions in children with PANDAS/PANS. *Journal of Child and Adolescent Psychopharmacology* 25(1), 48–56.

Uher, R. & Rutter, M. (2012) Classification of feeding and eating disorders: review of evidence and proposals for ICD-11. *World Psychiatry* 11(2), 80–92.

Walsh, B.T. (2019) Diagnostic categories for eating disorders: current status and what lies ahead. *Psychiatric Clinics of North America* 42(1), 1–10.

Westfall, N.C., Mavrides, N.A., & Coffey, B.J. (2018) Multidisciplinary management of adolescent early-onset, treatment-resistant schizophrenia complicated by avoidant/restrictive food intake disorder and catatonia in acute exacerbations. *Journal of Child and Adolescent Psychopharmacology* 28(9), 663–66.

Zickgraf, H.F., Ellis, J.M., & Essayli, J.H. (2019a) Disentangling orthorexia nervosa from healthy eating and other eating disorder symptoms: relationships with clinical impairment, comorbidity, and self-reported food choices. *Appetite* 134, 40–49.

Zickgraf, H.F., Lane-Loney, S., Essayli, J.H., & Ornstein, R.M. (2019b) Further support for diagnostically meaningful ARFID symptom presentations in an adolescent medicine partial hospitalization program. *International Journal of Eating Disorders* 52(4), 402–09.

Chapter 5

Aetiology and epidemiology

Nadia Micali and Christine E. Cooper-Vince

Aetiology

Introduction

As a recently defined diagnosis, there are limited data available on the aetiology of avoidant restrictive food intake disorder (ARFID), though avoidant and restrictive eating in early childhood has been studied using a variety of inconsistently defined terms, including "picky/fussy eating", "food neophobia", "feeding disorder", and "feeding difficulty" (Goday et al., 2019). The term picky/fussy eating has been used inconsistently to describe a range of behaviours, including the rejection of a significant number of familiar foods, fear of new foods (neophobia), rejection of food based on sensory properties, and/or inadequate volume of food intake, without reliably differentiating between clinically impairing and developmentally typical behaviours (see Cardona Cano, Hoek, & Bryant-Waugh, 2015 for a review). Feeding disorder/difficulty has more often described behaviours with a clinical level of impairment, but also at times described children with feeding skills dysfunction (e.g. impaired swallowing, oral-motor dysfunction). Therefore, these terms cannot be used synonymously with ARFID. However, relevant data from these complementary literatures can inform our preliminary understanding of what may drive clinically impairing avoidant and restrictive food intake in childhood. A recent attempt to inform the pathophysiology of ARFID has been made through the three-dimensional neurobiological model of ARFID (Thomas et al., 2017), which is currently under evaluation among adolescents. This chapter briefly reviews evidence for this model within a preliminary biopsychosocial framework of ARFID aetiology.

Biological factors

Three-dimensional model of neurobiology

Thomas and colleagues argue that a single individual ARFID can present with multiples of the prototypic presentations (i.e. sensory sensitivity, low interest/

low appetite, and concern about aversive outcomes), which are rooted in dimension-specific biological vulnerabilities (Thomas et al., 2017).

The sensory dimension of ARFID encompasses the rejection of food based on its sensory qualities (e.g. taste, smell, texture, temperature, sound, appearance) and is one of the most commonly presenting clinical features of ARFID (Reilly et al., 2019). Biologically driven differences in sensory perception likely play a role, given that one study found that 67.5% of children presenting to a feeding clinic had clinically elevated sensory processing difficulties (Davis et al., 2013). Data from non-clinical samples of pre-schoolers indicate that enhanced detection of bitter and sweet flavours is correlated with picky/fussy eating and rejection of bitter vegetables (Keller et al., 2002), which is consistent with the avoidance of vegetables often reported in children with ARFID.

The low appetite/low interest dimension of ARFID likely captures symptoms previously described as "infantile anorexia" and "food avoidance emotional disorder" (Higgs, Goodyer, & Birch, 1989; Zero to Three, 2005). Within this model, the low appetite observed in some individuals with ARFID is hypothesised to be in part due to low levels of an orexigenic (appetite stimulating) hormone ghrelin, as seen in low-weight women with ARFID, and decreased activation of the hypothalamus and anterior insula (brain regions responsible for integrating appetite signals, visceral signals, and housing the primary taste cortex) (Thomas & Eddy, 2019; Thomas et al., 2017).

Within this model, the third dimension is characterised by restrictive eating due to fear of its consequences, such as choking, vomiting, or abdominal discomfort. The primary aetiology of this feature is thought to be rooted in conditioned food aversion following a distressing eating experience, although it can also develop through vicarious learning. Conditioned aversion occurs when a previously innocuous food is followed by an aversive stimulus (e.g. vomiting), causing future presentations of the food to be associated with vomiting, driving food avoidance (Logue, 1985). Thomas and colleagues hypothesise that an underlying biological vulnerability toward anxious responding, specifically neurological and physiological hyperactivation of the defence motive system (i.e. amygdala, anterior cingulate, and ventral prefrontal cortex) seen in other phobic disorders, may play a key role in determining which children will go on to develop an impairing fear of aversive eating consequences and subsequently engage in food restriction following an aversive eating experience (Thomas et al., 2017).

Genetic risk

Genetic risk for ARFID has yet to be explicitly evaluated, although findings from twin studies show moderate to high heritability for infant and child appetite (53%–84%), toddler food fussiness (78%), and food neophobia among four–seven-year-olds (72%) (Faith et al., 2013; Llewellyn et al., 2010). Importantly, associations between higher food fussiness and lower liking of vegetables/fruits among toddlers is largely explained by shared genetic influences, possibly in part due to the inherited enhanced detection of bitter flavours (Fildes et al., 2016; Keller et al., 2002).

Temperament

Temperamental traits of negative affectivity (e.g. heightened sadness, irritability, and reactivity) and behavioural inhibition are associated with feeding problems and picky eating among community samples of infants and toddlers, particularly when parents are less responsive to child feeding cues (Hagekull, Bohlin, & Rydell, 1997; Moding, Birch, & Stifter, 2014). Similarly, negative affectivity has been linked to infantile anorexia, whilst behavioural inhibition is a well-established risk for child anxiety disorders (Chatoor et al., 2000; Fox & Pine, 2012). Clinically, children with ARFID are often described as temperamentally anxious and reactive to change, further suggesting these temperamental traits, in interaction with social influences, may contribute to the development of ARFID.

Medical conditions

Medical comorbidities known to affect oral feeding skill development and comfort are associated with impairing avoidant and restrictive eating in infancy and early childhood, including child premature birth, oral feeding delays, prolonged tube feeding, gastrointestinal problems, oesophageal atresia, and dysphagia (Galloway, Lee, & Birch, 2003; Hawdon et al., 2000; Mathisen et al., 1999; Micali et al., 2011a; Samara et al., 2010). Importantly, a diagnosis of ARFID is only indicated if the avoidant and restrictive eating difficulties are in excess of that expected for the medical condition. Accordingly the majority of children and adolescents with probable ARFID treated in feeding/eating disorder clinics have medical conditions, most commonly presenting with gastrointestinal problems, food allergies, and pulmonary problems (Fisher et al., 2014; Williams et al., 2015). Conditions that place children at risk for aversive feeding experiences, such as abdominal discomfort, may contribute to the development of concern of aversive consequences of eating and low interest in food through conditioned aversion.

Psychological factors

Anxiety and disgust

Anxiety disorders are often comorbid with ARFID symptoms among children presenting for treatment (Fisher et al., 2014; Nicely et al., 2014). As described in the three-dimensional model discussed above, the process of conditioned aversion is thought to play an important role in the aetiology of the concern for aversive consequences feature of ARFID. Children with an anxious/

inhibited temperament and family factors known to reinforce child anxiety (e.g. parental modelling of anxiety and accommodation, see *Parent feeding behaviour* below), may be most susceptible to developing conditioned food aversion or food neophobia following a mildly aversive feeding experience, such as gagging on a pizza crust or seeing a classmate vomit at lunch (Pliner & Loewen, 1997).

Disgust may also play an important role in the aetiology of sensory-based restrictive eating. Although disgust is believed to be an adaptive emotional response to avoid or expel poisons/pathogens, heightened sensory perception may trigger a disgust in response to safe foods (e.g. gagging), leading to conditioned food aversion and avoidance (Rozin & Fallon, 1987; Menzel et al., 2019). Accordingly, in non-clinical adult samples, disgust correlates with food texture aversion and restriction of food variety, and in one study explains the relationship between anxiety and self-reported ARFID symptoms (Egolf, Siegrist, & Hartmann, 2018; Harris et al., 2019). However, as disgust is thought to develop across childhood (Rottman, 2014), longitudinal data are needed to understand how sensory perception, disgust, and anxiety drive avoidant and restrictive eating across childhood.

Attention and impulsivity

Attention and impulsivity may also play a role in the restricted food intake features of ARFID. Feeding problems are found at higher rates among children with attention deficit hyperactivity disorder (ADHD) relative to peers, and linked to hyperactivity and impulsivity ADHD symptoms in boys (Råstam et al., 2013). Children with ADHD not on stimulant medication, therefore without the side-effect of decreased appetite, have been shown to have a more irregular eating schedule (>5 meals day), eat fewer fruits and vegetables, and leave the table more often (Ptacek et al., 2014). Clinical observations also reveal that parents of children with ARFID and comorbid ADHD often note struggling to maintain child focus on eating during meals due to excessive talking, frequent distractions, and difficulty remaining seated.

Arousal

High emotional arousal states, such as tension and fear, are known to reduce food intake (i.e. emotional undereating), and may drive increased neophobic behaviour in an attempt to down-regulate arousal (Pliner & Loewen, 2002; Macht, 2008). The contribution of such high arousal states to low volume and range of food intake may be most prominent among children with comorbid anxiety or autism, given the high baseline arousal experienced by children with these disorders, and potential for over-arousal during feeding due to sensory processing difficulties, particularly among children with autism (Kushki et al., 2013; Chistol et al., 2018).

Social factors

Parent feeding behaviour

Beyond the effect of parental sensitivity on temperamental risk for feeding problems in infancy and toddler years, parent feeding behaviour likely plays a role in the development of impairing, restrictive eating in childhood. Clinically, it is often observed that parents of children with ARFID engage in a range of accommodating to pressuring behaviours due to concern for their child's impaired nutrition. Examples include preparing separate meals, allowing grazing, prompting each bite, extending mealtimes, or allowing the child to eat alone in an attempt to increase the child's food intake. These behaviours are similar to those reported by parents of picky eaters (Mascola, Bryson, & Agras, 2010). Such parent–child interactions may contribute to the low food interest feature of ARFID by reducing the opportunities for social modelling of foods and social reinforcement of meal participation (Lafraire et al., 2016). They may also lead to a negative-coercive cycle of parent–child mealtime interactions that drive challenging mealtime behaviours (e.g. leaving the table, spitting out food, crying) and promote the child's conceptualisation of eating as a chore.

Parental accommodation of food avoidance may also contribute to persistent concern about the aversive consequence of eating in ARFID. It is well established that parental accommodation contributes to the maintenance of child anxiety symptoms by limiting the child's ability to face their fear and recognise that the feared outcome is unlikely and/or tolerable (Lebowitz et al., 2013). Parental accommodation of child restrictive eating can be longstanding in families of children with ARFID and likely contributes to further food variety restriction by reinforcing the child's belief about the feared consequence of eating. (Lock et al., 2019). Preliminary evidence from adolescents with ARFID supports this hypothesis, suggesting that graduated food exposure within an anxiety treatment framework leads to a greater range of food acceptance through extinguishing the conditioned fear response (Thomas, Wons, & Eddy, 2018).

Parent psychiatric distress

Parent eating pathology, anxiety and depression are associated with early childhood feeding problems, including child emotional undereating (Micali et al., 2011b). Though this is partly explained by genetic hereditability, emotional undereating is also heavily influenced by environmental learning (Herle et al., 2017). Parental modelling of emotional reactivity and coping has a strong influence on child threat perception and emotion regulation (Morris et al., 2007). Therefore, parental modelling of restrictive range or volume of foods, or anticipation of and/or strong emotional response to negative consequence of eating, may contribute to the child's restrictive eating behaviour.

Cultural feeding practices

The majority of data that informs the aetiology of ARFID has been collected from the global north. As feeding is a culturally-based practice, parents from different cultural backgrounds often rely on different feeding practices, such as pressure to eat and accommodation of child food requests (Gu et al., 2017). However, it remains unclear if and how these behaviours interact with the family's cultural context in the development of clinically impairing avoidant and restrictive child eating behaviour.

Conclusions

There is compelling preliminary evidence for the interaction of biological, psychological, and social factors in the aetiology of ARFID, supporting a biopsychosocial conceptualisation of ARFID. As the majority of children with ARFID present with features in multiple domains, we must also consider how feature-specific vulnerabilities interact with each other in the development of ARFID. Additionally, as most work has been conducted in speciality medical settings in the global north, longitudinal research in diverse cultural contexts is needed to clarify the aetiology of this heterogeneous disorder.

Epidemiology

Given its status as a recently defined disorder, ARFID has not been included in any large-scale epidemiological studies, nor is ARFID included in register-based studies. Therefore, its incidence and prevalence in the general population remain to be established. The majority of studies available on the epidemiology of ARFID or related presentations have focused on child and adolescent populations.

Prevalence

A questionnaire-based study investigated the prevalence of ARFID features in a primary school setting amongst 8–13 year olds in Switzerland, finding that 3.2% self-reported features of ARFID (Kurz et al., 2015). In a two-phase school-based study on the prevalence of eating disorders amongst adolescents (n = 2,230) three had ARFID, corresponding to a lifetime prevalence of about 0.3% (Smink et al., 2014). A recent Australian population-based survey of adolescents and adults aged >15 years similarly found the three-month prevalence of ARFID to be 0.3% (Hay et al., 2017). A nationally representative sample of Taiwanese school children in grades 3 to 7 (n=4816), assessed with a structured clinical interview, also found prevalence rates of ARFID <1% (Chen et al., 2019). All these studies have limitations relating to assessment methods used, leaving the question of what the true prevalence of ARFID is in the general population still open.

A recent population-based study of over 10,000 children from the UK Avon Longitudinal Study of parents and Children (ALSPAC) followed up from birth to ten years of age, demonstrated that 2% of the sample had parentally reported under-eating that was persistent over the first ten years of life, and 8% of the children had parentally reported fussy eating that was persistent over the first ten years of life (Herle et al., 2019). Although identifying a diagnosis of ARFID in this cohort was not possible, as assessments were selected before ARFID was defined, these figures provide a broad estimate of what the prevalence of ARFID might be in the general population.

The prevalence of ARFID in health care settings has been generally shown to be higher. For example, a series of case reviews and clinical studies across eating disorder treatment programmes in North America found that between 5 and 14% of children and adolescents in outpatient treatment met diagnostic criteria for ARFID (Ornstein et al., 2013; Fisher et al., 2014; Forman et al., 2014; Norris et al., 2014). In a similar retrospective chart review of individuals aged 15–40, seeking treatment for eating disorders in Japan, 11%, all women, met criteria for ARFID (Nakai et al., 2016). Further, ARFID was even more common (22.5%) among young people aged 7–17 years in a day treatment programme for eating disorders (Nicely et al., 2014). Moreover, amongst children seen in clinics for feeding problems in a retrospective case review, 32% would have met criteria for ARFID (Williams et al., 2015). By contrast, a retrospective review of 2,231 consecutive referrals of individuals aged 8–18 years to paediatric gastrointestinal clinics in the Boston area, showed a 1.5% ARFID prevalence (Eddy et al., 2015). These studies suggest that despite variation in estimates, likely due to the setting under study, ARFID is commonly seen in clinical settings across ages.

Incidence

Drawing on the broader literature on restrictive eating, a recent study combined three similar paediatric surveillance studies, in which paediatricians and child psychiatrists were asked to report on any children <12 years with a newly diagnosed restrictive type eating disorder, across Canada, the United Kingdom and Australia. The findings showed that one of two identified clusters, representing between 25% and 34% of children with incident restrictive type eating disorder, mapped onto symptoms consistent with ARFID (Pinhas et al., 2017). No studies are available on the incidence of ARFID.

Individual characteristics

Socio-demographic characteristics

Overall, the majority of studies that have investigated ARFID in clinical populations, across outpatient, inpatient and day treatment centres, have highlighted a younger age for children and adolescents presenting with ARFID relative to children with other eating disorders, with a mean age of ARFID children closer to 11 years, and a longer duration of illness (Fisher et al., 2014; Forman et al., 2014; Nicely et al., 2014; Strandjord et al., 2015; Pinhas et al., 2017). Age estimates of children with ARFID from eating disorder treatment programmes may however be higher than for children with ARFID seen elsewhere, as such programmes more often treat adolescents.

The findings on sex distribution of identified cases with ARFID have been inconsistent, with population-based or community studies identifying either equal prevalence of ARFID across sexes (Kurz et al., 2015); or a higher prevalence amongst males (Hay et al., 2017). In studies of outpatient clinics and day treatment centres in North America, a higher percentage of boys meeting criteria for ARFID (23–35.5%) has been reported relative to classical eating disorders such as anorexia nervosa and bulimia nervosa (Fisher et al., 2014; Forman et al., 2014; Nicely et al., 2014; Cooney et al., 2018). Similarly, among children receiving care in gastrointestinal clinics, children with ARFID were more often boys, relative to the overall clinic sample; 67% of those identified as having ARFID were males (Eddy et al., 2015). The higher percentage of males with ARFID is likely due to the comorbidity between ARFID and neurodevelopmental disorders (see *Illness characteristics and comorbidity* below). In contrast, amongst Japanese individuals aged 15–40 years presenting for eating disorder treatment, all the cases identified with ARFID were female (Nakai et al., 2016).

Race and ethnicity data are limited, as prevalence studies of ARFID have included predominantly Caucasian samples from high-income countries and/or have not reported race ethnicity data in relation to ARFID. However, amongst Australian 15–40-years-olds, those with ARFID had significantly lower annual median household incomes compared to those with no eating disorders (Hay et al., 2017).

A recent review of 32 studies on picky eating in children aged <30 months showed that the majority of studies identify no association between picky eating or food neophobia and sex, or race/ethnicity (Cole et al., 2017). Similarly, this review did not show consistent relationships between picky eating or food neophobia and parent socio-economic status. In a population-based study of Danish children aged five to seven years, a small association between parent immigrant status and picky eating was shown (Micali et al., 2016).

Illness characteristics and comorbidities

Across the population and clinical samples that have included individuals with ARFID, the majority of studies have highlighted that those with ARFID in general have a lower body mass index (BMI) compared to the general population (Kurz et al., 2015; Hay et al., 2017). Features of ARFID were more often reported by underweight children compared to children in the normal or overweight BMI range (Kurz et al., 2015). Similarly, children with ARFID identified amongst those attending gastrointestinal clinics in the Boston area also had a lower BMI compared to all other children presenting to these clinics (Eddy et al., 2015). Mean percentage body weight was similar to that of children with anorexia nervosa, but lower than those with bulimia nervosa, amongst children and adolescents with ARFID attending a day treatment programme between 2008 and 2012 (Nicely et al., 2014). Comparable findings of no differences in BMI in adults with ARFID and anorexia nervosa are reported by Nakai and colleagues (2016). ARFID cannot be diagnosed concurrently with rumination disorder, although pica and ARFID can be diagnosed together (see further Chapter 4). However, both rumination disorder and pica behaviours have been found to be common in children with ARFID (Hartmann et al., 2018).

In relation to medical and psychiatric comorbidities, a large retrospective chart review of 8–18-year-olds carried out across seven adolescent-medicine eating disorder programmes in 2010 in North America, highlighted that more than half of children with a presentation consistent with ARFID, had a medical comorbidity (55%). This percentage was significantly higher than that in children with anorexia nervosa or bulimia nervosa, with gastrointestinal symptoms the most commonly reported medical comorbidity (Fisher et al., 2014). In a recent case review of children and adolescent with ARFID, all those included reported two or more physical symptoms (Cooney et al., 2018).

In relation to psychiatric comorbidities, 57% of children and adolescents with ARFID had a psychiatric comorbidity (Cooney et al., 2018). Anxiety disorders are the most common comorbid psychiatric disorder reported across the studies that included an investigation of psychiatric comorbidity. Fifty-eight percent (58%) of children and adolescent with ARFID in adolescent medicine ED programs had an anxiety disorder (Fisher et al., 2014), and 72% in a North American day programme (Nicely et al., 2014). Consistent with high levels of sensory based feeding problems among children with autism (see review, Cermak, Curtin, & Bandini, 2010), there is some evidence of a high comorbidity with autism, although comorbidity rates are lower among adolescents attending eating disorder treatment (13%) (Nicely et al., 2014).

Only one study to date has investigated quality of life in individuals with ARFID, concluding that overall health related quality of life was lower in those with ARFID compared to individuals without an eating disorder (Hay et al., 2017).

Conclusions

In summary, very few studies so far have investigated the prevalence of ARFID in the general population, however, based on current evidence the prevalence of ARFID amongst children and adolescents is estimated at <5%, and <1% for adults. No studies are available on the incidence of ARFID. Available studies seem to converge on the high percentage of males with ARFID across population-based and clinical samples. Individuals with ARFID in health care settings have also been found to have high levels of medical and psychiatric comorbidities, with anxiety disorders being the most common psychiatric comorbidity. These findings suggest that ARFID is a severe disorder with multiple comorbidities, and that its management is likely to require a multidisciplinary approach. More research is needed at a population level to understand the nature of ARFID across the developmental span and cultural contexts and its impact on the general population.

Summary points

- ARFID is a new, heterogeneous diagnosis, with limited data currently available to inform its aetiology and epidemiology
- ARFID is most often depicted by three major features that are not mutually exclusive; sensory sensitivity, low appetite/low interest, and concern about aversive consequences of eating
- Each core feature is likely rooted in biological vulnerabilities that interact with psychological and social factors
- The prevalence of ARFID amongst children and adolescents is estimated at <5%; and <1% for adults
- A higher percentage of males with ARFID than females has been identified thus far across population-based and clinical samples
- Individuals with ARFID in healthcare settings have high levels of medical and psychiatric comorbidities; anxiety disorders being the most common psychiatric comorbidity

References

Cardona Cano, S., Hoek, H.W., & Bryant-Waugh, R. (2015) Picky eating: the current state of research. *Current Opinion in Psychiatry* 28(6), 448–54.

Cermak, S.A., Curtin, C., & Bandini, L.G. (2010) Food selectivity and sensory sensitivity in children with autism spectrum disorders. *Journal of the American Dietetic Association* 110(2), 238–46.

Chatoor, I., Ganiban, J., Hirsch, R., Borman-Spurrell, E., & Mrazek, D.A. (2000) Maternal characteristics and toddler temperament in infantile anorexia. *Journal of the American Academy of Child and Adolescent Psychiatry* 39(6), 743–51.

Chen, Y.-L., Chen, W.J., Lin, K-C., Shen, L-J., & Gau, SS-F. (2019) Prevalence of DSM-5 mental disorders in a nationally representative sample of children in Taiwan: Methodology and main findings. *Epidemiology and Psychiatric Sciences* 30, 1–9. DOI: 10.1017/S2045796018000793 accessed 14 July 2019.

Chistol, L.T., Bandini, L.G., Must, A., Phillips, S., Cermak, S.A., & Curtin, C. (2018) Sensory sensitivity and food selectivity in children with autism spectrum disorder. *Journal of Autism and Developmental Disorders* 48(2), 583–91.

Cole, N.C., An, R., Lee, S-Y., & Donovan, S.M. (2017) Correlates of picky eating and food neophobia in young children: a systematic review and meta-analysis. *Nutrition Reviews* 75(7), 516–32.

Cooney, M., Lieberman, M., Guimond, T. & Katzman, D.K. (2018) Clinical and psychological features of children and adolescents diagnosed with avoidant/restrictive food intake disorder in a pediatric tertiary care eating disorder program: A descriptive study. *Journal of Eating Disorders* 6(1), 7. DOI: 10.1186/s40337-018-0193-3 accessed 14 July 2019.

Davis, A.M., Bruce, A.S., Khasawneh, R., Schulz, T., Fox, C., & Dunn, W. (2013) Sensory processing issues in young children presenting to an outpatient feeding clinic. *Journal of Pediatric Gastroenterology and Nutrition* 56(2), 156–60.

Eddy, K.T., Thomas, J.J., Hastings, E., Edkins, K., Lamont, E., Nevins, C.M., Patterson, R. M., Murray, H.B., Bryant-Waugh, R., & Becker, A.E. (2015) Prevalence of DSM-5 avoidant/restrictive food intake disorder in a pediatric gastroenterology healthcare network. *International Journal of Eating Disorders* 48(5), 464–70.

Egolf, A., Siegrist, M., & Hartmann, C. (2018) How people's food disgust sensitivity shapes their eating and food behaviour. *Appetite* 127, 28–36.

Faith, M.S., Heo, M., Keller, K.L., & Pietrobelli, A. (2013) Child food neophobia is heritable, associated with less compliant eating, and moderates familial resemblance for BMI. *Obesity* 21(8), 1650–55.

Fildes, A., Van Jaarsveld, C.H.M., Cooke, L., Wardle, J., & Llewellyn, C.H. (2016) Common genetic architecture underlying young children's food fussiness and liking for vegetables and fruit. *American Journal of Clinical Nutrition* 103(4), 1099–104.

Fisher, M.M., Rosen, D.S., Ornstein, R.M., Mammel, K.A., Katzman, D.K., Rome, E.S., Callahan, S.T., Malizio, J., Kearney, S., & Walsh, B.T. (2014) Characteristics of avoidant/restrictive food intake disorder in children and adolescents: a "new disorder2 in DSM-5. *Journal of Adolescent Health* 55(1), 49–52.

Forman, S.F., McKenzie, N., Hehn, R., Monge, M.C., Kapphahn, C.J., Mammel, K.A., Callahan, S.T., Sigel, E.J., Bravender, T., Romano, M., Rome, E.S., Robinson, K.A., Fisher, M., Malizio, J.B., Rosen, D.S., Hergenroeder, A.C., Buckelew, S.M., Jay, M.S., Lindenbaum, J., Rickert, V.I., Garber, A., Golden, N.H., & Woods, E.R. (2014) Predictors of outcome at 1 year in adolescents with DSM-5 restrictive eating disorders: report of the national eating disorders quality improvement collaborative. *Journal of Adolescent Health* 55(6), 750–56.

Fox, N.A. & Pine, D.S. (2012) Temperament and the emergence of anxiety disorders. *Journal of the American Academy of Child and Adolescent Psychiatry* 51(2), 125–28.

Galloway, A.T., Lee, Y., & Birch, L.L. (2003) Predictors and consequences of food neophobia and pickiness in young girls. *Journal of the American Dietetic Association* 103(6), 692–698.

Goday, P.S., Huh, S.Y., Silverman, A., Lukens, C.T., Dodrill, P., Cohen, S.S., Delaney, A.L., Feuling, M.B., Noel, R.J., Gisel, E., Kenzer, A., Kessler, D.B., Kraus de Camargo, O., Browne, J., & Phalen, J.A. (2019) Pediatric feeding disorder: consensus definition and conceptual framework. *Journal of Pediatric Gastroenterology and Nutrition* 68(1), 124–29.

Gu, C., Warkentin, S., Mais, L.A., & Carnell, S. (2017) Ethnic differences in parental feeding behaviors in uk parents of preschoolers. *Appetite* 113, 398–404.

Hagekull, B., Bohlin, G., & Rydell, A.M. (1997) Maternal sensitivity, infant temperament, and the development of early feeding problems. *Infant Mental Health Journal* 18(1), 92–106.

Harris, A.A., Romer, A.L., Hanna, E.K., Keeling, L.A., LaBar, K.S., Sinnott Armstrong, W., Strauman, T.J., Wagner, H.R., Marcus, M.D., & Zucker, N.L. (2019) The central role of disgust in disorders of food avoidance. *International Journal of Eating Disorders* 52(5), 543–53.

Hartmann, A.S., Poulain, T., Vogel, M., Hiemisch, A., Kiess, W., & Hilbert, A. (2018) Prevalence of pica and rumination behaviors in german children aged 7–14 and their associations with feeding, eating, and general psychopathology: a population-based study. *European Child & Adolescent Psychiatry* 27(11), 1499–508.

Hawdon, J.M., Beauregard, N., Slattery, J. & Kennedy, G. (2000) Identification of neonates at risk of developing feeding problems in infancy. *Developmental Medicine and Child Neurology* 42(4), 235–39.

Hay, P., Mitchison, D., Collado, A.E.L., González-Chica, D.A., Stocks, N. & Touyz, S. (2017) Burden and health-related quality of life of eating disorders, including avoidant/restrictive food intake disorder (ARFID), in the Australian population. *Journal of Eating Disorders* 5(1), 21.

Herle, M., De Stavola, B., Hübel, C., Abdulkadir, M., Santos Ferreira, D., Loos, R.J.F., Bryant-Waugh, R., Bulik, C., & Micali, N. (2019) Eating behaviours in childhood and later eating disorder behaviours and diagnoses: A longitudinal study. *British Journal of Psychiatry* 1–7. DOI: 10.1192/bjp.2019.174.

Herle, M., Fildes, A., Steinsbekk, S., Rijsdijk, F., & Llewellyn, C.H. (2017) Emotional over- and under-eating in early childhood are learned not inherited. *Scientific Reports* 7(1), 9092.

Higgs, J.F., Goodyer, I.M., & Birch, J. (1989) Anorexia nervosa and food avoidance emotional disorder. *Archives of Disease in Childhood* 64(3), 346–51.

Keller, K.L., Steinmann, L., Nurse, R.J., & Tepper, B.J. (2002) Genetic taste sensitivity to 6-n-propylthiouracil influences food preference and reported intake in preschool children. *Appetite* 38(1), 3–12.

Kurz, S., Vandyck, Z., Dremmel, D., Munsch, S., & Hilbert, A. (2015) Early-onset restrictive eating disturbances in primary school boys and girls. *European Child and Adolescent Psychiatry* 24(7), 779–85.

Kushki, A., Drumm, E., Pla Mobarak, M., Tanel, N., Dupuis, A., Chau, T., & Anagnostou, E. (2013) Investigating the autonomic nervous system response to anxiety in children with autism spectrum disorders. *PLoS ONE* 8(4), e59730. DOI: 10.1371/journal.pone.0059730 accessed 14 July 2019.

Lafraire, J., Rioux, C., Giboreau, A., & Picard, D. (2016) Food rejections in children: cognitive and social/environmental factors involved in food neophobia and picky/fussy eating behavior. *Appetite* 96, 347–57.

Lebowitz, E.R., Woolston, J., Bar-Haim, Y., Calvocoressi, L., Dauser, C., Warnick, E., Scahill, L., Chakir, A.R., Shechner, T., Hermes, H., Vitulano, L.A., King, R.A., & Leckman, J.F. (2013) Family accommodation in pediatric anxiety disorders. *Depression and Anxiety* 30(1), 47–54.

Llewellyn, C.H., Van Jaarsveld, C.H.M., Johnson, L., Carnell, S., & Wardle, J. (2010) Nature and nurture in infant appetite: Analysis of the gemini twin birth cohort. *American Journal of Clinical Nutrition* 91(5), 1172–79.

Lock, J., Robinson, A., Sadeh Sharvit, S., Rosania, K., Osipov, L., Kirz, N., Derenne, J., & Utzinger, L. (2019) Applying family based treatment (FBT) to three clinical presentations of avoidant/restrictive food intake disorder: Similarities and differences from fbt for anorexia nervosa. *International Journal of Eating Disorders* 52(4), 439–46.

Logue, A.W. (1985) Conditioned food aversion learning in humans. *Annals of the New York Academy of Sciences* 443(1), 316–29.

Macht, M. (2008) How emotions affect eating: a five-way model. *Appetite* 50(1), 1–11.

Mascola, A.J., Bryson, S.W., & Agras, W.S. (2010) Picky eating during childhood: a longitudinal study to age 11 years. *Eating Behaviors* 11(4), 253–57.

Mathisen, B., Worrall, L., Masel, J., Wall, C., & Shepherd, R. (1999) Feeding problems in infants with gastro-oesophageal reflux disease: a controlled study. *Journal of Paediatrics and Child Health* 35(2), 163–69.

Menzel, J.E., Reilly, E.E., Luo, T.J., & Kaye, W.H. (2019) Conceptualizing the role of disgust in avoidant/restrictive food intake disorder: implications for the etiology and treatment of selective eating. *International Journal of Eating Disorders* 52(4), 462–65.

Micali, N., Rask, C.U., Olsen, E.M., & Skovgaard, A.M. (2016) Early predictors of childhood restrictive eating. *Journal of Developmental & Behavioral Pediatrics* 37(4), 314–21.

Micali, N., Simonoff, E., Elberling, H., Rask, C.U., Olsen, E.M., & Skovgaard, A.M. (2011a) Eating patterns in a population-based sample of children aged 5 to 7 years: association with psychopathology and parentally perceived impairment. *Journal of Developmental and Behavioral Pediatrics* 32(8), 572–80.

Micali, N., Simonoff, E., Stahl, D., & Treasure, J. (2011b) Maternal eating disorders and infant feeding difficulties: Maternal and child mediators in a longitudinal general population study. *Journal of Child Psychology and Psychiatry* 52(7), 800–07.

Moding, K.J., Birch, L.L., & Stifter, C.A. (2014) Infant temperament and feeding history predict infants' responses to novel foods. *Appetite* 83, 218–25.

Morris, A.S., Silk, J.S., Steinberg, L., Myers, S.S., & Robinson, L.R. (2007) The role of the family context in the development of emotion regulation. *Social Development* 16(2), 361–88.

Nakai, Y., Nin, K., Noma, S., Teramukai, S., & Wonderlich, S.A. (2016) Characteristics of avoidant/restrictive food intake disorder in a cohort of adult patients. *European Eating Disorders Review* 1(6), 2015–17.

Nicely, T.A., Lane-Loney, S., Masciulli, E., Hollenbeak, C.S., & Ornstein, R.M. (2014) Prevalence and characteristics of avoidant/restrictive food intake disorder in a cohort of young patients in day treatment for eating disorders. *Journal of Eating Disorders* 2(1), 21.

Norris, M.L., Robinson, A., Obeid, N., Harrison, M., Spettigue, W., & Henderson, K. (2014) Exploring avoidant/restrictive food intake disorder in eating disordered patients: a descriptive study. *International Journal of Eating Disorders* 47(5), 495–99.

Ornstein, R.M., Rosen, D.S., Mammel, K.A., Callahan, S.T., Forman, S., Jay, M.S., Fisher, M., Rome, E., & Walsh, B.T. (2013) Distribution of eating disorders in children and adolescents using the proposed DSM-5 criteria for feeding and eating disorders. *Journal of Adolescent Health* 53(2), 303–05.

Pinhas, L., Nicholls, D., Crosby, R.D., Morris, A., Lynn, R.M., & Madden, S. (2017) Classification of childhood onset eating disorders: a latent class analysis. *International Journal of Eating Disorders* 50(6), 657–64.

Pliner, P. & Loewen, E.R. (1997) Temperament and food neophobia in children and their mothers. *Appetite* 28(3), 239–54.

Pliner, P. & Loewen, R. (2002) The effects of manipulated arousal on children's willingness to taste novel foods. *Physiology & Behavior* 76(4–5), 551–58.

Ptacek, R., Kuzelova, H., Stefano, G.B., Raboch, J., Sadkova, T., Goetz, M., & Kream, R.M. (2014) Disruptive patterns of eating behaviors and associated lifestyles in males with ADHD. *Medical Science Monitor* 20, 608–13.

Råstam, M., Täljemark, J., Tajnia, A., Lundström, S., Gustafsson, P., Lichtenstein, P., Gillberg, C., Anckarsäter, H., & Kerekes, N. (2013) Eating problems and overlap with ADHD and autism spectrum disorders in a nationwide twin study of 9- and 12-year-old children. *The Scientific World Journal 2013* 315429. DOI: 10.1155/2013/315429 accessed 14 July 2019.

Reilly, E.E., Brown, T.A., Gray, E.K., Kaye, W.H., & Menzel, J.E. (2019) Exploring the cooccurrence of behavioural phenotypes for avoidant/restrictive food intake disorder in a partial hospitalization sample. *European Eating Disorders Review* 27(4), 429–35.

Rottman, J. (2014) Evolution, development, and the emergence of disgust. *Evolutionary Psychology* 12(2), 417–33.

Rozin, P. & Fallon, A.E. (1987) A perspective on disgust. *Psychological Review* 94(1), 23–41.

Samara, M., Johnson, S., Lamberts, K., Marlow, N., & Wolke, D. (2010) Eating problems at age 6 years in a whole population sample of extremely preterm children. *Developmental Medicine and Child Neurology* 52(2), e16–e22.

Smink, F.R.E., Van Hoeken, D., Oldehinkel, A.J., & Hoek, H.W. (2014) Prevalence and severity of DSM-5 eating disorders in a community cohort of adolescents. *International Journal of Eating Disorders* 47(6), 610–19.

Strandjord, S.E., Sieke, E.H., Richmond, M., & Rome, E.S. (2015) Avoidant/restrictive food intake disorder: Illness and hospital course in patients hospitalized for nutritional insufficiency. *Journal of Adolescent Health* 57(6), 673–78.

Thomas, J.J. & Eddy, K.T. (2019) *Cognitive-behavioral therapy for avoidant/restrictive food intake disorder.* Cambridge: Cambridge University Press.

Thomas, J.J., Lawson, E.A., Micali, N., Misra, M., Deckersbach, T., & Eddy, K.T. (2017) Avoidant/restrictive food intake disorder: A three-dimensional model of neurobiology with implications for etiology and treatment. *Current Psychiatry Reports* 19(8), 54.

Thomas, J.J., Wons, O.B. & Eddy, K.T. (2018) Cognitive-behavioral treatment of avoidant/restrictive food intake disorder. *Current Opinion in Psychiatry* 31(6), 425–30.

Williams, K.E., Hendy, H.M., Field, D.G., Belousov, Y., Riegel, K., & Harclerode, W. (2015) Implications of avoidant/restrictive food intake disorder (ARFID) on children with feeding problems. *Children's Health Care* 44(4), 307–21.

Zero to Three. (2005) *DC:0-3R: Diagnostic classification of mental health and developmental disorders of infancy and early childhood. Revised edition* Washington, DC, US: ZERO TO THREE/National Center for Infants, Toddlers and Families.

Chapter 6

Baseline and outcome measures

Lucy Cooke

Introduction

Despite the inclusion of avoidant restrictive food intake disorder (ARFID) in DSM-5 in 2013 (APA, 2013), comprehensive instruments to measure its severity and clinical features have been slow to emerge. Measures of constructs related to ARFID are available, but until recently, structured assessment tools capable of diagnosing ARFID and, crucially, of providing a continuous index of psychopathology severity and related impairment, had not been forthcoming. Accurate assessment is essential for treatment planning, evaluation of clinical outcomes, and refinement of diagnosis, as well as epidemiological enquiry and research. What follows is an overview of available interview and questionnaire measures with a discussion of their strengths and weaknesses, suitability for this patient population, and their reliability and validity where tested. A summary table has been included (Table 6.1). Subsequent chapters focus on other important elements of psychological, nutritional, and physical assessment by specialist clinicians.

Brief screening measures for ARFID

Problems with feeding and eating are relatively common in infants and young children, in many cases resolving after a short time (Cardona Cano et al., 2015). In children aged nine months to seven years, over 50% of parents have been found to report one problem feeding behaviour and over 20% report multiple problem feeding behaviours (Crist & Napier-Phillips, 2001). Brief screening measures may be useful in distinguishing the wariness of unfamiliar food that represents a normal developmental stage of early childhood, from clinically significant feeding or eating difficulties. For example, the Eating Disturbances in Youth Questionnaire (EDY-Q; Hilbert & van Dyck, 2016) is a 14-item self-report measure for 8–13-year-olds designed to assess early-onset feeding and eating disturbances. The authors state that 12 items in the EDY-Q are based on a combination of the DSM-5 criteria for ARFID, the Great Ormond Street criteria relating to disordered eating patterns without weight or shape concerns

Table 6.1 Baseline and outcome measures for feeding and eating difficulties

	Age range	Evaluates constructs relevant to:			Confers diagnosis of ARFID	Measures severity	Multi-informant	Reliability and validity
		Pica	ARFID	RD				
Brief screening measures								
Nine-item Avoidant Restrictive Food Intake Disorder Screen (NIAS) (Zickgraf & Ellis, 2018)	Adults		×					**Internal reliability:** 0.87–0.93 **Construct validity:** Normative sample had significantly lower scores than clinical sample **Test-re-test reliability:** Adequate (values not reported) **Convergent validity:** Significantly correlated with existing measures of related constructs
Eating Disturbances in Youth-Questionnaire (EDY-Q) (Hilbert & van Dyck, 2016)	8 to 13 years	×	×	×				**Internal reliability:** 0.62 **Convergent validity:** Mean score weakly correlated with established measure – ChEDE-Q. Underweight children scored significantly higher on ARFID items than normal or overweight
Montreal Children's Hospital Feeding Scale (Ramsay et al., 2011)	6 months to 7 years		×					**Internal reliability:** 0.48–0.87 **Test-re-test reliability:** 0.85 (normative sample) 0.92 (clinical sample)

Measure	Age range			Psychometric properties
The Screening Tool of Feeding Problems applied to children (STEP-CHILD) (Seiverling, Hendy, & Williams, 2011)	2 to 18 years	x	x	**Construct validity:** Normative sample had significantly lower scores than clinical sample **Convergent validity:** Specificity = 0.82; Sensitivity = 0.87
General psychiatric assessment measures				
Child & Adolescent Psychiatric Assessment (CAPA) (Angold et al., 1995)	9 to 18 years	x	x	**Internal reliability:** 0.57–0.66 **Convergent validity:** significantly correlated with subscales of CEBQ **Test re-test reliability:** 0.55–1.00 **Reliability:** Children diagnosed via CAPA are at increased risk for impaired functioning at school, home and with peers. High scores on the Child Behavior Checklist externalising items predict CAPA diagnoses in the following 4 years
Preschool Age Psychiatric Assessment (PAPA) (Egger et al., 2006)	2 to 5 years	x		**Test re-test reliability:** 0.56–0.89 **Diagnostic reliability:** 0.36–0.87
	5 to 16 years	x	x	**Convergent validity:** Specificity: 0.89; Sensitivity: 0.92

(Continued)

Table 6.1 (Cont.)

	Age range	Evaluates constructs relevant to:	Confers diagnosis of ARFID	Measures severity	Multi-informant	Reliability and validity
Development and Well-Being Assessment (DAWBA) (Goodman et al., 2000)						In a community sample, individuals with DAWBA diagnoses had more emotional, behavioural or psychiatric difficulties. In a clinical sample, agreement between DAWBA diagnoses and case note diagnoses was moderate
Diagnostic interviews for eating and feeding disorders						
Eating Disorder Assessment for DSM-5 (EDA-5) (Sysko et al., 2015)	8 years to adult	X	X		X	**Test-re-test reliability:** 0.87 **Convergent validity:** Specificity = 0.83–0.98; Sensitivity = 0.65–1.00 Agreement between EDE and EDA-5 diagnoses was high NB: utility of EDA-5 in diagnosing ARFID has not been tested
Structured Clinical Interview for DSM-5 (SCID-5) (First et al., 2015)	Adults	X				No data available
	2 years to adult	X	X	X	X	**Internal reliability:** 0.77–0.89

Measure	Age			Psychometric properties
Pica, ARFID, and Rumination Disorder Interview (PARDI) (Bryant-Waugh et al., 2019)				**Inter-rater reliability:** 0.75 **Convergent validity:** Individuals with ARFID scored higher on all subscales and on ARFID severity than healthy controls or those with restrictive eating without ARFID
Eating Disorder Examination – ARFID module (Schmidt et al., 2019)	8 to 13 years	x	x	**Inter-rater reliability:** 0.62–0.92 **Convergent validity:** Children with ARFID consumed less energy, protein and fat. Scores significantly correlated with those on established measures **Divergent validity:** Children identified as having ARFID scored had low mean scores on weight and shape concern items.
Questionnaire measures of eating behaviour				
Behavioral Pediatrics Feeding Assessment (BPFAS) (Crist et al., 1994)	7 months to 13 years	x		**Internal reliability:** 0.74–0.88 **Test-re-test reliability:** 0.82–0.85 **Construct validity:** Normative sample had significantly lower scores than clinical sample **Convergent validity:** Specificity: 0.80–0.91; Sensitivity: 0.78–0.87

(Continued)

Table 6.1 (Cont.)

	Age range	Evaluates constructs relevant to:	Confers diagnosis of ARFID	Measures severity	Multi-informant	Reliability and validity
Children's Eating Behavior Inventory (CEBI) (Archer, Rosenbaum, & Streiner, 1991)	2 to 12 years	x				**Internal reliability:** 0.58–0.76 **Test-re-test reliability:** 0.84–0.87 **Construct validity:** Normative sample had significantly lower scores than clinical sample
Pediatric Eating Assessment Tool (Pedi-EAT) (Thoyre et al., 2014)	6 months to 7 years	x				**Internal reliability:** 0.83–0.92 **Test-re-test reliability:** 0.95 **Content validity:** Extensive testing by researchers, clinicians and parents **Construct validity:** Normative sample had significantly lower scores than clinical sample. **Convergent validity:** Scores significantly correlated with those on established measure
Mealtime Behavior Questionnaire (Berlin et al., 2010)	2 to 6 years	x				**Internal reliability:** 0.76–0.91 **Convergent validity:** Normative sample had significantly lower scores than clinical sample

Child Eating Behaviour Questionnaire (CEBQ)* (Wardle et al., 2001)	3 to 13 years	x		**Internal reliability:** 0.56–0.84 **Test re-test reliability:** 0.52–0.87 **Convergent validity (FF subscale):** Distinguished normal, moderate and severe pickiness as defined by the PAPA
Child Food Neophobia Scale (CFNS)* (Pliner, 1994)	2 to 11 years	x		**Internal reliability:** (0.72–0.90) **Convergent validity:** Significantly correlated with a behavioural test of food neophobia **Construct validity:** Normative sample had significantly lower scores than clinical sample

* Have also been trialled as screening tools for ARFID

(Bryant-Waugh & Lask, 1995) and "literature on early-onset restrictive eating disturbances". They suggest that these questions "cover the three variants of ARFID": food avoidance emotional disorder (FAED; three items), selective eating (SE; three items), and functional dysphagia (FD; two items) (see Chapter 4 and glossary for descriptions of these terms). The phrasing of the questions relevant to these "variants" suggests that the authors are referring to avoidance or restriction stemming from low interest in food or eating, sensory properties of foods, and concern about possible adverse consequences of eating, respectively. These features are included in current diagnostic criteria, however they do not currently constitute formal, separate subtypes or variants of ARFID (see further Chapter 4). Additional EDY-Q questions assess difficulties in meeting adequate weight growth (n = 2) and distorted cognitions about weight or shape (n = 2). Two final items cover pica and rumination disorder, two other disorders now also included in the feeding and eating disorders section of diagnostic classification. Items are scored from 0 – "never true" to 6 – "always true". A mean score for the ARFID-related items is calculated, and in addition, the authors provide a set of indicators that must be met at specified thresholds in order to detect the presence of ARFID symptoms. For example, an answer of 4 or above in response to the statement "Food/eating does not interest me" is taken to indicate the probable presence of the "FAED variant of ARFID". The EDY-Q has undergone preliminary testing in a community sample of 8–13-year-olds (n = 1444), resulting in 46 children (3.2%) being identified as having features of ARFID (Kurz et al., 2015). The psychometric properties of the questionnaire appear reasonably sound and it may be useful as an epidemiological or screening tool to investigate prevalence of feeding and eating disturbances in middle childhood in the general population, although its diagnostic capability remains to be fully evaluated.

The only other screening measure specifically based on the DSM-5 ARFID criteria is the Nine-Item ARFID Screen (NIAS; Zickgraf & Ellis, 2018) comprising three questions on each of three eating behaviour patterns that are said to lead to symptoms of ARFID; here these are described as "low appetite or limited interest in eating", "avoidance of many foods based on their sensory properties ('picky eating')", and "fear of the consequences such as choking or vomiting, from eating". The measure is designed to produce a total score and three subscale scores. The NIAS has undergone preliminary testing in adults aged 18–65 years with promising results in terms of its factor structure, test-re-test reliability and convergent validity against other measures of problematic eating behaviour. It has not to date been formally validated for use in children and adolescents.

There are a number of other screening tools available but none are specifically designed to screen for ARFID. One such tool, the Montreal Children's Hospital Feeding Scale (MCH-Feeding Scale; Ramsay et al., 2011) is a 14-item parent-report instrument to identify feeding difficulties in children from six months to six years of age and the level of parental concern about these difficulties. Whilst not developed specifically to screen for ARFID, items evaluate related constructs such as appetite, food selectivity and refusal, mealtime behaviour, and problems with chewing, gagging or vomiting. The measure takes approximately five minutes to complete and generates a single score with a clinical cut-off. Score ranges are provided to indicate the magnitude of the difficulty: "mild", "moderate" or "severe". The MCH-Feeding Scale has been subjected to testing in normative and clinical samples and has demonstrated good reliability and validity (Ramsay et al., 2011; Rogers, Ramsay & Blissett, 2018).

Another brief measure is the Screening Tool of Feeding Problems Applied to Children (STEP-CHILD; Seiverling, Hendy, & Williams, 2011). Based on the Screening Tool for Feeding Problems (STEP; Matson & Kuhn, 2001) for adults, the STEP-CHILD is a 15-item parent-report measure with six subscales of child feeding problems: chewing problems, rapid eating, food refusal, food selectivity, vomiting, and stealing food. A score for each of the six subscales is calculated. The STEP-CHILD has been tested in 142 children and young people aged from 2 to 18 years referred to a hospital-based feeding clinic, of whom 43 had an autism diagnosis, 51 had other special needs and 48 had problems restricted to feeding and eating. The scales demonstrated reasonable internal reliability and were associated in the anticipated direction with scores on the well-established Children's Eating Behaviour Questionnaire (CEBQ: Wardle et al., 2001) and with anthropometric and dietary variables.

Whilst not designed for this purpose, two long-established child eating behaviour questionnaires have recently been tested as potential screening tools for ARFID and related feeding and eating difficulties: the Child Food Neophobia Scale (CFNS; Pliner, 1994) and the Child Eating Behaviour Questionnaire (CEBQ; Wardle et al., 2001). The ten-item CFNS principally assesses willingness to try unfamiliar foods but includes items pertaining more to general pickiness. Dovey and colleagues recruited a community sample of over three hundred parents of 2–7-year-old children together with a further 28 parents of children with a diagnosis of ARFID. Participants completed a six-item version of the CFNS and the Behavioral Pediatrics Feeding Assessment Scale (BPFAS; Crist & Napier-Phillips, 2001), a 35-item standardised and validated parent-report questionnaire assessing children's eating behaviours and the extent to which these behaviours are a problem to parents. Both measures differentiated the clinical group with ARFID from the community sample (Dovey et al., 2016). In the case of the CFNS, this might be expected given that a complete refusal to stray outside a tightly prescribed range of "safe" and familiar foods is frequently seen in children with serious feeding or eating difficulties. However, some degree of food neophobia is common in early childhood, and some resistance to trying unfamiliar foods between the ages of 2 and 8 years is usually considered a normal stage in the development of eating behaviour. The difference is one of magnitude, but food neophobia does not, in isolation, indicate a clinically significant feeding or eating problem and its presence is neither necessary nor sufficient to support a diagnosis of ARFID.

The CEBQ contains eight subscales, one of which is "Food Fussiness (FF)" comprising six items assessing reactions to both novel and familiar foods.

Whilst providing a useful measure of pickiness in population samples, no clinical cut-offs have been established that would allow differentiation between normal and clinical levels of food selectivity or avoidance (nor specifically, ARFID). In a large community sample (n = 752) of parents of Norwegian six-year-olds (Steinsbekk et al., 2017), scores on the FF subscale differentiated moderate or severe picky eaters ("moderately restricted intake; child only eats food s/he likes" or "severe pickiness; separate meals must be made for the child") from non-picky eaters ("no restricted intake"), as identified by the Preschool Age Psychiatric Assessment (PAPA; Egger et al., 2006). The PAPA is a lengthy clinical interview and the authors suggest that when time and resources are limited, the CEBQ FF scale may be a useful instrument for identifying non-normative picky eating in population samples (Steinsbekk et al., 2017). Since not all ARFID presentations are characterised by "picky" eating, it would appear however, to have limited utility as a screening tool for treatment-seeking clinical samples.

It should be noted that neither of the comparison measures used in the studies discussed above, the BPFAS nor the PAPA, were developed to provide ARFID diagnoses. Further discussion about their relative merits and utility can be found later in this chapter.

General psychiatric assessment measures

For most people seeking treatment for a mental health difficulty, one-to-one psychological assessment will be necessary. A number of comprehensive measures have been developed to provide a general assessment of children and adolescents in order to generate ICD and DSM mental and behavioural disorder diagnoses. The first of these, the Child and Adolescent Psychiatric Interview (CAPA; Angold et al., 1995), is suitable for use with 9–18-year-old children and their parents, and has been subjected to extensive reliability and validity testing. A complementary instrument, the Preschool Age Psychiatric Assessment (PAPA; Egger et al., 2006) has been developed by the same team for use with 2–5-year-olds. Both are lengthy to administer (up to two hours) and a further half hour is required for the interviewer to code the CAPA/PAPA and input the data into a customised database that uses algorithms to generate diagnoses. Both instruments require assessors to receive formal training and certification by a qualified CAPA/PAPA trainer, with associated costs. An alternative instrument, the Development and Wellbeing Assessment (DAWBA; Goodman et al., 2000), can be completed online or by non-clinical interviewers with minimal online training, although there is a charge for usage (currently £10 per assessment in the UK). A computer programme generates likely ICD and DSM psychiatric diagnoses that can then be further investigated, confirmed or overturned by experienced clinical raters. Parent-report (children aged 2–4 or 5–17 years) and self-report versions (young people aged 11 to 17 years) are available and administration or self-completion of the assessment takes approximately one hour. Both the CAPA/PAPA and the DAWBA include questions relating to feeding and eating, but neither is currently able to generate a diagnosis of ARFID, and may well be too broad, costly, and time-consuming to administer in many clinical settings. The same can be said of a number of other general psychiatric assessment measures, including the National Institute of Mental Health Diagnostic Interview Schedule for Children (NIMH-DISC-IV: Shaffer et al., 2000), the Diagnostic Interview for Children and Adolescents (DICA; Reich, 2000) and the Schedule for Affective Disorders and Schizophrenia for School-Age Children-Present and Lifetime Version (K-SADS-PL; Kaufman et al., 1997). The Spanish version of the last of these has recently been modified to integrate changes made to the DSM-5, including the addition of ARFID as a diagnostic category (K-SADS-PL-5; de la Pena et al., 2018), but an English language version has yet to be evaluated.

Diagnostic interviews for feeding and eating disorders

A handful of structured clinical interviews can be used to diagnose ARFID in clinical or research settings. For example, the Eating Disorder Assessment for DSM-5 (EDA-5; Sysko et al., 2015) is a semi-structured interview that requires minimal training to administer and can produce ARFID diagnoses in adults and in young people from 8–14 years of age (EDA-5 Youth; Sysko et al., 2015). The Structured Clinical Interview for DSM-5 (SCID-5; First et al., 2015) can also be used to diagnose ARFID in adults. However neither of these measures provides a continuous measure of psychopathology severity, which is crucial for treatment planning, evaluation of clinical outcomes, and refinement of diagnosis.

An ARFID module has recently been developed (Schmidt et al., 2019) for the Eating Disorder Examination (EDE: Fairburn et al., Edition 17, 2014) for individuals aged 14 years and older, and for the age-adapted version of the EDE for children, for individuals aged 8–13 years (Bryant-Waugh et al., 1996). The ARFID module takes approximately 20 minutes to complete and was designed to be used in conjunction with either the main or the child format of the full EDE or as a stand-alone tool to diagnose ARFID. In a pilot study, 39 8–13-year-old children with underweight and/or restrictive eating and their parents completed the appropriate versions of the module as well as the full child version of the EDE and a number of other well-established questionnaires relating to quality of life and psychosocial functioning. Seven children received a diagnosis of ARFID and the module showed high reliability, convergent and divergent validity. In addition it was able to distinguish children with and without ARFID in terms of their anthropometric and clinical characteristics, such that children with ARFID were more likely to be underweight and had lower micro- and macro-nutrient intake than those without. However, participant numbers were small and further testing of the module is in progress in both community and clinical settings to evaluate its psychometric properties more robustly. Again, no continuous measure of severity is included.

Another new diagnostic tool has shown promise and has been translated into a number of languages. In an international collaboration between the UK and the USA, the Pica, ARFID and Rumination Disorder Interview (PARDI) was developed (Bryant-Waugh et al., 2019). The PARDI is a standardised measure to aid diagnosis, indicate severity and characterise the presenting features of individuals with difficulties characteristic of pica, rumination disorder and ARFID seeking treatment. There are four versions of the PARDI, enabling it to be used with parents of children of 2–3 years (Parent 2–3); parents of children 4 years and older (Parent 4+); children between 8–13 years (Self 8–13); and individuals aged 14 years and older (Self 14+).

The PARDI contains a screen to assess the possible presence of another eating disorder (anorexia nervosa, bulimia nervosa, or binge-eating disorder) and related sub-threshold disorders. This is because a diagnosis of such an eating disorder "trumps" that of ARFID and thus their presence must be ruled out before other disorders can be identified. Introductory items in the PARDI cover growth and development, current pattern of feeding or eating, and medical history, to provide important context for potential diagnoses of pica, ARFID and rumination disorder, including the ascertainment of potential exclusion criteria (see Chapter 4). The PARDI then assesses the specific diagnostic criteria for pica, ARFID and rumination disorder, as well as associated functional impairment.

The section in the PARDI on ARFID includes profile subscales relating to three common features: food avoidance related to sensory features, lack of interest in food or eating, and avoidance related to concern about aversive consequences of eating. The PARDI is designed to assess the present state of individuals, and so questions are concerned with the situation over the previous month. The interview takes, on average, 45–60 minutes to administer. Algorithms enable diagnoses of the three disorders (pica, rumination disorder, ARFID) to be made and scores on severity items provide a measure of the degree of impairment suffered. Finally, profile scores offer insight into the reasons for restriction and avoidance of foods to aid treatment planning. The PARDI was developed to complement the Eating Disorders Examination, which covers anorexia nervosa, bulimia nervosa, and binge eating disorder (Fairburn et al., Edition 17, 2014). Together the PARDI and the EDE allow detailed assessment of the six main feeding and eating disorder diagnoses.

In an initial pilot study of the PARDI, the Self 8–13 and Self 14+ were administered to 47 individuals with clinically significant feeding and eating difficulties and 10 healthy controls (Bryant-Waugh et al., 2019). Feasibility and acceptability to participants was high, and inter-rater reliability and internal consistency were adequate to good. As predicted, individuals with ARFID scored higher on measures of severity than the controls.

In a further preliminary validation study (manuscript submitted), nearly 100 parents of children with significant feeding and eating difficulties seeking treatment were interviewed using the two parent versions of the PARDI (Parent

2–3 and Parent 4+), in addition to a full assessment by experienced clinicians. The extent of agreement between the PARDI and clinicians in terms of an ARFID diagnosis was high, and scores relating to the three common features underlying the avoidance or restriction of food intake were highly correlated with those on established questionnaires measuring similar constructs. Further testing and use of the instrument is under way.

Questionnaire measures of eating behaviour

A number of questionnaire measures of eating behaviour and feeding problems exist, but none are linked to the DSM-5 ARFID constructs and criteria. However, such measures can provide a rapid assessment of relevant and related constructs to complement a clinical interview. They may also be useful as pre- and post-measures to evaluate treatment outcomes if included constructs have been a particular focus of treatment. The 40-item Children's Eating Behavior Inventory (CEBI; Archer, Rosenbaum, & Streiner, 1991) is a parent-report questionnaire that takes approximately 15 minutes to complete and was developed for use with children from 2 to 12 years of age. Twenty-eight items assess the child's food preferences, motor skills, and eating behaviour, whilst the remainder assess parental feelings about feeding and family interactions around food. Two scores are derived from the measure: a total eating problem score and a percentage of items perceived to be a problem by the respondent. In a sample of over 200 non-clinical and 110 clinical families, the CEBI showed reasonable inter-rater and internal reliability, and construct validity, in terms of distinguishing clinical from non-clinical populations. The CEBI has also demonstrated sensitivity to change post-treatment in two case reports (Archer, Cunningham, & Whelan, 1988; Archer & Szatmari, 1990) and in a study evaluating mealtimes in 46 families of children with autism attending an outpatient feeding program (Laud et al., 2009).

Another instrument, the Behavioral Pediatrics Feeding Assessment Scale (BPFAS; Crist et al., 1994) was developed initially for use with parents of children with cystic fibrosis, who frequently display behavioural difficulties at mealtimes, although it has since been widely used for other patient populations (e.g. Martin, Young & Robson, 2008; Powers et al., 2002). Focusing on refusal to eat, 25 items describe the child's behaviour and ten describe parental feelings and feeding strategies. The BPFAS is perhaps the best-known instrument in the field of feeding difficulties with the most comprehensive reliability and validity data in non-clinical and clinical samples (Crist & Napier-Phillips, 2001). Interestingly, the authors found that basic patterns of problematic mealtime behaviour were similar in clinical and non-clinical groups, fundamentally differing only frequency and severity.

Two further measures of mealtime behaviour warrant mention: the Mealtime Behavior Questionnaire (MBQ; Berlin et al., 2010) and the Pediatric Eating Assessment Tool (Pedi-EAT; Thoyre et al., 2014). The 33-item MBQ was developed for use with the parents of 2–6-year-old typically developing children and focuses solely on the frequency of child mealtime behaviours, not confounded, the author's state, by parental behaviour and feelings, thereby providing a supposedly objective measure of the extent of a child's difficulties. Scores on four factors can be derived from the measure: food refusal, food manipulation, mealtime aggression/distress, and choking/gagging/vomiting. Concurrent validity of the measure has been established in both community and clinical settings (Berlin et al., 2010; Hill et al., 2013) and sensitivity to change post-treatment was demonstrated in tube-dependent children after an intensive behaviour modification programme (Silverman et al., 2013).

More thorough testing has been undertaken of the PediEAT (Thoyre et al., 2014), a 77-item parent-report questionnaire to assess "observable symptoms of problematic feeding in children between the ages of 6 months and 7 years". It is not a diagnostic tool, but is intended to identify children in need of a more in-depth assessment of feeding and eating behaviours. A factor analysis revealed four factors: physiologic symptoms, problematic mealtime behaviours, selective/restrictive eating, and oral processing. Scores on each of these are assigned a level of concern (no concern, concern, or high concern) using age-specific reference values supplied by the authors (Thoyre et al., 2018). The results of reliability and validity testing have been positive, and a version for infants from birth to seven months, the Neonatal Eating Assessment Tool (NeoEAT) has recently been developed for both breastfed and bottle-fed infants (Pados et al., 2017, 2018a, 2018b).

The Children's Eating Behaviour Questionnaire (CEBQ; Wardle et al., 2001) was developed for research into eating behaviour in normal populations rather than for clinical purposes. However, the Food Fussiness (FF) subscale has recently been used to screen for more serious feeding and eating difficulties as discussed earlier in this chapter (Steinsbekk et al., 2017). Suitable for ages 3–13 years, the CEBQ has 35 items and eight subscales, several of which may be relevant to the three common factors underlying food restriction in ARFID – lack of interest in eating or food, avoidance based on sensory characteristics of certain foods, or concern about the aversive consequences of eating. For example, children with ARFID might be likely to score low on the food responsiveness (FR) or enjoyment of food (EF) subscales and high on food fussiness (FF), satiety responsiveness (SR) or slowness in eating (SE). With nearly 900 citations in the academic literature and having undergone extensive validity and reliability testing, the CEBQ, like the Child Food Neophobia Scale (CFNS; Pliner, 1994) might be a useful addition to the clinical toolbox.

Children with severe feeding and eating problems will often present with additional and significant difficulties in distinct but related domains such as depression, anxiety or sensory sensitivity. Specialist assessment instruments exist to measure such constructs, and whilst it is beyond the scope of this chapter to review these, their use is highly recommended to aid treatment planning.

Conclusions

Despite the length of time that has elapsed since ARFID was included in the DSM-5, few valid and reliable measures have emerged to aid its diagnosis and provide an indication of the severity of impact on the child themselves and on the wider family. The PARDI and the EDE-ARFID module are the exception and hold promise for identification of children in need of clinical attention. In addition, the PARDI is able to characterise different types of presentation and to assess severity. A suite of reliable and validated instruments for screening, diagnosing and characterising ARFID could facilitate accurate diagnosis and help with treatment planning by identifying each child's unique pattern of difficulties. In addition, high-quality measures can aid evaluation of clinical outcomes, as well as epidemiological enquiry to establish the prevalence and course of ARFID. Most importantly, well-worked up, comprehensively validated, robust measurement tools with high levels of acceptability and clinical utility can make an important contribution to research into multiple facets of this relatively new and under-studied diagnostic category.

Summary points

- Mild feeding difficulties commonly occur in childhood and these transient episodes need to be clearly distinguished from clinically significant feeding or eating difficulties such as ARFID
- Brief screening measures can help to discriminate those with more serious feeding and eating problems
- A wide variety of questionnaire and interview measures exist to assess feeding and eating difficulties; not all are relevant to ARFID in every individual but may capture idiosyncratic aspects of presentation in some
- Only a handful of measures have been designed for or tested in clinical and community populations with ARFID
- A variety of reliable measures of ARFID could facilitate accurate diagnosis and help with treatment planning by identifying each child's unique pattern of difficulties.

References

American Psychiatric Association. (2013) *Diagnostic and statistical manual of mental disorders* (5th ed.). Arlington, VA: American Psychiatric Association.

Angold, A., Prendergast, M., Cox, A., Harrington, R., Simonoff, E., & Rutter, M. (1995) The Child and Adolescent Psychiatric Assessment (CAPA). *Psychological Medicine* 25, 739–53.

Archer, L., Cunningham, C.E., & Whelan, D. (1988) Coping with dietary therapy in phenylketonuria: a case report. *Canadian Journal of Behavioral Science* 20, 461–66.

Archer, L. & Szatmari, P. (1990) Assessment and treatment of food aversion in a four-year old boy: a multidimensional approach. *Canadian Journal of Psychiatry* 35, 501–05.

Archer, L.A., Rosenbaum, P.L., & Streiner, D.L. (1991) The Children's Eating Behaviour Inventory: reliability and validity results. *Journal of Pediatric Psychology* 16, 629–42.

Berlin, K.S., Davies, W.H., Silverman, A.H., Woods, D.W., Fischer, E.A., & Rudolph, C.D. (2010) Assessing children's mealtime problems with the Mealtime Behaviour Questionnaire. *Children's Health Care* 39, 142–56.

Bryant-Waugh, R. & Lask, B. (1995) Annotation: eating disorders in children. *Journal of Child Psychology & Psychiatry* 36, 191–202.

Bryant-Waugh, R., Micali, N., Cooke, L., Lawson, E.A., Eddy, K.T., & Thomas J.J. (2019) Development of the Pica, ARFID and Rumination Disorder Interview, a multi-informant semi-structured interview of feeding disorders across the lifespan: a pilot study for ages 10-22. *International Journal of Eating Disorders* 52, 378–87.

Bryant-Waugh, R.J., Cooper, P.J., Taylor, C.L. & Lask, B.D. (1996) The use of the Eating Disorder Examination with children: a pilot study. *International Journal of Eating Disorders* 19, 391–97.

Cardona Cano, S., Tiemeier, M.D., Van Hoeken, D., Jaddoe, V.W.V., Hofman, A., Verhulst, F.C. & Hoek, H.W. (2015) Trajectories of picky eating during childhood: a general population study. *International Journal of Eating Disorders* 48, 570–79.

Crist, W., McDonnell, P., Beck, M., Gillespie, C.T., Barrett, P. & Matthews, J. (1994) Behavior at mealtimes and the young child with cystic fibrosis. *Developmental and Behavioral Pediatrics* 15, 157–61.

Crist, W. & Napier-Phillips, A. (2001) Mealtime behaviors of young children: a comparison of normative and clinical data. *Developmental and Behavioral Pediatrics* 22, 279–86.

Dovey, T.M., Aldridge, V.K., Martin, C.I., Wilken, M. & Meyer, C. (2016) Screening Avoidant/Restrictive Food Intake Disorder (ARFID) in children: outcomes from utilitarian versus specialist psychometrics. *Eating Behaviors* 23, 162–67.

Egger, H.L., Erkanli, A., Keeler, G., Potts, E., Walter, B.K. & Angold, A. (2006) Test-retest reliability of the Preschool Age Psychiatric Assessment (PAPA). *Journal of the Academy of Child and Adolescent Psychiatry* 45, 538–49.

Fairburn, C.G., Cooper, Z. & O'Connor, M.E. (2014) Eating Disorder Examination (Edition 17.OD) www.credo-oxford.com/pdfs/EDE_17.0D.pdf - accessed 9 July 2019.

First, M.B., Williams, J.B.W., Karg, R.S. & Spitzer, R.L. (2015) *Structured Clinical Interview for DSM-5 Disorders, Research Version*. Arlington, VA: American Psychiatric Association Publishing.

Goodman, R., Ford, T., Richards, H., Gatward, R. & Meltzer, H. (2000) The Development and Well-Being Assessment: description and initial validation of an integrated assessment of child and adolescent psychopathology. *Journal of Child Psychology and Psychiatry* 41, 645–55.

Hilbert, A. & van Dyck, Z. (2016) *Eating Disorders in Youth-Questionnaire. English version*. University of Leipzig http://nbn-resolving.de/urn:nbn:de:bsz:15-qucosa-197246 accessed 9 July 2019.

Hill, G.D., Silverman, A.H., Noel, R.J., Simpson, P.M., Slicker, J., Scott, A.E. & Bartz, P.J. (2013) Feeding dysfunction in children with single ventricle following staged palliation. *Journal of Pediatrics* 164, 243–46 e1.

Kaufman, J., Birmaher, B., Brent, D., Rao, U., Flynn, C., Moreci, P., Williamson, D. & Ryan, N. (1997) Schedule for Affective Disorders and Schizophrenia for School-Age Children-Present and Lifetime Version (K-SADS-PL): initial reliability and validity data. *Journal of the American Academy of Child and Adolescent Psychiatry* 36, 980–88.

Kurz, S., van Dyck, Z., Dremmel, D., Munsch, S. & Hilbert, A. (2015) Early-onset restrictive eating disturbances in primary school boys and girls. *European Child and Adolescent Psychiatry* 24, 779–85.

Laud, R.B., Girolami, P.A., Boscoe, J.H. & Gulotta, C.S. (2009) Treatment outcomes for severe feeding problems in children with autism spectrum disorder. *Behavior Modification* 33, 520–36.

Martin, Y., Young, R.L. & Robson, D.C. (2008) Feeding and eating behaviors in children with autism and typically developing children. *Journal of Autism and Developmental Disorders* 38, 1878–87.

Matson, J.L. & Kuhn, D.E. (2001) Identifying feeding problems in mentally retarded persons: development and reliability of the screening tool for feeding problems (STEP). *Research in Developmental Disabilities* 22, 165–72.

Pados, B.F., Estrem, H.H., Thoyre, S.M., Park, J. & McComish, C. (2017) The Neonatal Eating Assessment Tool: development and content validation. *Neonatal Network* 36, 359–67.

Pados, B.F., Thoyre, S.M., Estrem, H.H., Park, J. & McComish, C. (2018a) Factor structure and psychometric properties of the Neonatal Eating Assessment Tool – breastfeeding. *Journal of Obstetric and Gynaecologic Neonatal Nursing* 47, 396–414.

Pados, B.F., Thoyre, S.M., Estrem, H.H., Park, J. & McComish, C. (2018b) Factor structure and psychometric properties of the Neonatal Eating Assessment Tool – bottle-Feeding (NeoEAT – bottle-Feeding). *Advances in Neonatal Care* 18, 232–42.

Pliner, P. (1994) Development of measures of food neophobia in children. *Appetite* 23, 147–63.

de la Peña, F.R., Villavicencio, L.R., Palacio, J.D., Félix, F.J., Larraguibel, M., Viola, L., Ortiz, S., Rosetti, M., Abadi, A., Montiel, C., Mayer, P.A., Fernández, S., Jaimes, A., Feria, M., Sosa, L., Rodríguez, A., Zavaleta, P., Uribe, D., Galicia, F., Botero, D., Estrada, S., Berber, A.F., Pi-Davanzo, M., Aldunate, C., Gómez, G., Campodónico, I., Tripicchio, P., Gath, I., Hernández, M., Palacios, L., & Ulloa R.E. (2018) Validity and reliability of the kiddie schedule for affective disorders and schizophrenia present and lifetime version DSM-5 (K-SADS-PL-5) Spanish version. *BMC Psychiatry* 18, 193.

Powers, S.W., Byars, K.C., Mitchell, M.J., Patton, S.R., Standiford, D.A. & Dolan, L.M. (2002) Parent report of mealtime behavior and parenting stress in young children with type 1 diabetes and in healthy control subjects. *Diabetes Care* 25, 313–18.

Ramsay, M., Martel, C., Porporino, M. & Zygmuntowicz, C. (2011) The Montreal Children's Hospital Feeding Scale: a brief bilingual screening tool for identifying feeding problems. *Paediatrics & Child Health* 16, 147–51.

Reich, W. (2000) Diagnostic Interview for Children (DICA). *Journal of the American Academy of Child and Adolescent Psychiatry* 39, 59–66.

Rogers, S., Ramsay, M. & Blissett, J. (2018) The Montreal Children's Hospital Feeding Scale: relationships with parental report of child eating behaviours and observed feeding interactions. *Appetite* 125, 201–09.

Schmidt, R., Kirsten, T., Hiemisch, A., Kiess, W., & Hilbert, A. (2019) Interview-based assessment of Avoidant/Restrictive Food Intake Disorder (ARFID): a pilot study evaluating an ARFID module for the Eating Disorder Examination. *International Journal of Eating Disorders* 52, 388–97.

Seiverling, L., Hendy, H.M., & Williams, K. (2011) The Screening Tool of Feeding Problems applied to children (STEP-CHILD): psychometric characteristics and associations with child and parent variables. *Research in Developmental Disabilities* 32, 1122–29.

Shaffer, D., Fisher, P., Lucas, C.P., Dulcan, M.K., & Schwab-Stone, M.E. (2000) NIMH Diagnostic Interview Schedule for Children Version IV (NIMH DISC – IV): description, differences from previous versions and reliability of some common diagnoses. *Journal of the American Academy of Child and Adolescent Psychiatry* 39, 28–38.

Silverman, A.H., Kirby, M., Clifford, L.M., Fisher, E., Berlin, K.S., Rudolph, C.D., & Noel, R.J. (2013) Nutritional and psychosocial outcomes of gastrostomy tube-dependent children completing an intensive inpatient behavioural treatment program. *Journal of Pediatric Gastroenterology and Nutrition* 57, 668–72.

Steinsbekk, S., Hamre Sveen, T., Fildes, A., Llewellyn, C. & Wichstrom, L. (2017) Screening for pickiness – a validation study. *International Journal of Behavioral Nutrition and Physical Activity* 14, 2 https://doi.org/10.1186/s12966-016-0458-7 accessed 14 July 2019.

Sysko, R., Glasofer, D.R., Hildebrandt, T., Klimek, P., Mitchell, J.E., Berg, K.C. & Walsh, B.T. (2015) The eating disorder assessment for DSM-5 (EDA-5): development and validation of a structured interview for feeding and eating disorders. *International Journal of Eating Disorders* 48, 452–63.

Thoyre, S., Pados, B., Park, J., Estrem, H., Hodges, E., McComish, C., Van Riper, M., & Murdoch, K. (2014) Development and content validation of the Pediatric Eating Assessment Tool (Pedi-EAT). *American Journal of Speech-Language Pathology* 23, 1–14.

Thoyre, S., Pados, B., Park, J., Estrem, H., McComish, C. & Hodges, E. (2018) The Pediatric Eating Assessment Tool (PediEAT): factor structure and psychometric properties. *Journal of Pediatric Gastroenterology and Nutrition* 66, 299–305.

Wardle, J., Guthrie, C.A., Sanderson, S. & Rapoport, L. (2001) Development of the Children's Eating Behaviour Questionnaire. *Journal of Child Psychology and Psychiatry* 42, 963–70.

Zickgraf, H.F. & Ellis, J.M. (2018) Initial validation of the Nine Item Avoidant/Restrictive food intake disorder Screen (NIAS): a measure of three restrictive eating patterns. *Appetite* 123, 32–42.

Part III

Assessment

Chapter 7

Psychological assessment of child and family

Claire Higgins and Prabashny Pillay

Introduction

Comprehensive assessment of children presenting with avoidant restrictive food intake disorder (ARFID) is generally recommended to be multi-faceted, with medical, dietetic, sensory, psychological, and family factors usefully considered together. The focus of this chapter is on individual and family psychological assessment as a key component of a holistic, integrated assessment of the child's eating difficulties. Discussion is structured in line with an assessment model proposed for use in the general field of child and adolescent mental health. Emerging recommendations for assessment specifically in relation to ARFID are highlighted, and reflections from clinical experience and from families' experiences included.

Guidelines for assessment

Goodman and Scott have suggested a useful, general framework for the assessment of mental health and behavioural difficulties in children and adolescents. They propose a five-component focus – using the mnemonic SIRSE – on symptoms, impact, risk, strengths (of the child and family), and explanations the family may have regarding the presenting difficulties (Goodman & Scott, 2012). This framework is used here to structure discussion about potentially important areas for consideration in the psychological assessment of ARFID. Assessment of nutritional, physical and sensory aspects of the child's presentation, and of their feeding and eating ability, are discussed in subsequent chapters.

Symptoms

The model proposes that most mental health difficulties affecting children and adolescents involve symptoms from four main areas of psychological and neurological functioning: behavioural difficulties, emotional symptoms, developmental delays, and relationship aspects of presentation (Goodman & Scott, 2012). Each is discussed below with specific reference to considerations in the context of a possible ARFID diagnosis.

Behavioural difficulties

The main behavioural difficulty in ARFID is the primary presenting eating behaviour, which is characterised by avoidance or restriction of food intake, or a combination of the two. This can be longstanding, or may have a more recent onset, so that enquiring about possible triggers for the behaviour, such as a vomiting illness, or a choking incident, can be helpful. The behavioural element of the psychological assessment usefully not only to covers the parents' and the child's account of how the child behaves in relation to food and mealtimes, which needs to be explored in detail, but also whether there are any wider behavioural difficulties or unusual behaviours. This can help the clinician to understand if the avoidant or restrictive eating behaviours are part of a wider pattern of similar behaviour, perhaps manifest as shyness and withdrawal, rigid or repetitive behaviours, or cautious, safety behaviours, or whether they are related to food and eating alone. Behavioural assessment also helpfully includes asking about attention and activity regulation. Difficulties with attention have been shown to be associated with "selective eating" in preschool aged children (Zucker et al., 2015), and attention difficulty hyperactivity disorder identified as one of the more common co-occurring conditions with ARFID. Knowledge about any areas of functioning affected by identified difficulties can be important when planning intervention, as when isolated to the arena of food and eating, the child may be able to draw on existing skills to manage their behaviour, whereas, if the difficulties are wider, more generalised skills acquisition may be required.

Requesting that a food diary is completed prior to the assessment can not only provide nutritional information, but can also contribute to the assessment of the child's eating behaviour. For example, a list covering a three-day period of exactly what the child has eaten, and when and where, can point to follow-up questions that can help the clinician to understand what might be driving the eating behaviour. The types of food listed, when the food is eaten, and the quantities recorded as eaten, can help to highlight whether the avoidant or restrictive eating behaviour appears to be related to sensory issues, fear of foods, a lack of interest in food, or other contextual factors, as well as allowing any significant preferences to be identified.

Asking parents about their own eating behaviour, particularly when they were younger, can also be helpful; clinical experience suggests that not uncommonly, one or more of the parents may have been quite particular about food choices and some may still have somewhat limited diets. Eliciting patterns of behaviour shared between family members can help greatly with acceptance, as well as response to the child's current difficulties.

Emotional symptoms

Assessment of this aspect of a child's functioning helpfully covers a range of emotions such as sadness, hopelessness, fears and worries, and disgust, experienced both generally and specifically in relation to food and eating. Asking about sleep, appetite, and general enjoyment of life can be helpful in highlighting possible mood disturbances. Engaging the child in discussion about what they like to do when not at school can help the clinician get a sense about their emotional functioning and their level of interest and engagement in life. Highly anxious children, younger children, and develop-mentally delayed children, may struggle to engage fully with this aspect of the assessment process and clinicians may be reliant on parental report. Direct questioning about emotions may be experienced as challenging, and some chil-dren are better able to engage and participate when distracted, for example, with drawing or with a game.

Anecdotally, some children with ARFID are described as "temperamentally anxious" and both social and separation anxiety have been found to be associ-ated with "selective eating" in pre-school children (Zucker et al., 2015). Anx-iety has also been identified as one of the more common co-occurring conditions with ARFID, so certainly represents an important aspect of emo-tional experience to explore. The presence of anxiety may have an influence not only on the child's presenting eating difficulties, but also on the focus of any recommended intervention, which may need to specifically address sup-porting the fearful child to manage their anxiety more generally (Siddaway, Wood, & Cartwright-Hatton, 2014). It is not uncommon for parents to report that their child has wider fears and worries, and a thorough assessment can help to distinguish between anxiety restricted to food and mealtimes, and a more generalised anxiety that may need treating alongside, or where physical risk is low, prior to, any focus on food. It will be important to also ask the parents about their emotions and how they are coping with their child's eating difficulty (Chatoor et al., 2000).

Developmental delay

A thorough history of the child's development, to include feeding development, is needed in order to assess progression from birth through to the current presen-tation, and to identify any areas where the child may be behind their peers. Important components of developmental history will usually include ascertaining timing of meeting major milestones for example, sitting, walking, speech and language development, and toileting. The parent's description of their child's functioning in relation to play and achievement at school can be useful in high-lighting possible delay in cognitive development, and asking about any delay in motor and co-ordination skills is helpful, as these can be associated with difficul-ties self-feeding, accepting a full range of food textures, or managing mealtimes. In children presenting with possible underlying cognitive, motor or co-ordination difficulties, more detailed assessment of these areas of functioning may be help-ful to inform subsequent intervention and support needs and to ensure that these are adapted to an appropriate level of ability.

Developmental delay is often associated with delay in feeding and eating skills (Quitadamo et al., 2016; Rouse et al., 2002), making it important to assess whether a child's eating behaviour represents a difficulty that needs addressing, or is in line with their overall development, as in the case of Suzanna,

> Suzanna (5 years old) was referred for an assessment of her eating as she remained on a diet of smooth purées. Suzanna has Downs syndrome; at her last developmental assessment with her local paediatrician, it was estimated that her developmental age was 22 months. During the assessment of her eating difficulties, Suzanna sat well at the table and enjoyed the social element of the meal. She showed no aversion to being in the presence of food and was happy to explore the food with her hands. She happily ate her purée when her parents fed her. It was observed that she had some co-ordination difficulties with managing the spoon but was happy to attempt to feed herself. She explored a range of finger foods presented to her and put these up to her mouth but did not eat them. It was concluded that Suzanna did not meet the diagnosis for ARFID, as she was at a developmentally appropriate stage for her eating and her diet was meeting her nutritional needs. Her parents were given advice about continuing with the weaning at Suzanna's pace and given reassurance that they were doing well in supporting her development.

When asking about developmental history the clinician should preferably also include a family account of the child's medical history. This is important as medical conditions can not only contribute directly to feeding and eating difficulties, for example through pain or discomfort, but can also contribute indirectly, through emotional and behavioural responses to illness which may arise in both child and parents. Eliciting family beliefs, experiences, and responses regarding any health problems, as well as previous experience of health care delivery, can provide important contextual information about each family member's response to the current difficulties.

Relational factors and relationship difficulties

Children have multiple relationships with others both within and outside the family, which typically change over time as a child develops. Drawing a genogram can help explore wider relationships in the family and consider similarities or degree of proximity between family members. Inviting the child to name or draw a map of their friends can give insight into the richness of social relationships outside the family. Enquiring about the nature of the child's relationships, the child's position in their family and wider context, and interaction with others they encounter, can provide important information relevant to refining an understanding of the presenting eating difficulties. For example, when children experience stress in relationships or their social context, they can become withdrawn or narrower in their focus, which can manifest itself through increased avoidance or restriction of intake. Gently exploring possible links between the child's eating behaviour and other stressful or traumatic circumstances in their social context, such as illness in the family, bereavements, domestic violence, school stresses, can be useful. Developing a time-line of life events or other significant occurrences or situations alongside one of the onset of feeding and eating difficulties may help the family make their own links between the two. Considering any relational changes at such times can also help to establish if there is any suggestion of over-protection, parental accommodation, or coercive management, which may be unintentionally perpetuating the eating difficulties. Such discussions can be helpful in arriving at a shared understanding of the presenting difficulties and moving towards planning intervention.

Information about the child's relationships can come both from the clinical interview, but can also be obtained from observation. For example, the quality of relationships between the child, parents, and any other family members present, can be observed during the assessment or on the family's arrival or departure. The clinician can notice how the child relates to them or other colleagues, and can reflect on their own response to the child, which might mirror commonly elicited responses in others. Staff at the child's school can also provide helpful information about the child's relational style, friendships and interactions with others.

The perspective of both parents and the child should be obtained with regards to the child's functioning socially and relationally, with family and friends. This usually provides insight into the child's ability to form and sustain relationships; the impact of the eating difficulties on their lives; their sense of identity and self-esteem; and the family's role within all of these. This information can be important to take into account when targeting intervention.

Impact

Many young children go through stages of not eating or of being "picky" eaters (Toyama & Agras, 2016). This is sometimes called developmental "neo-phobia" and is most common between the ages of two and four or five years of age (Cardona Cano et al., 2016). This normal, and typically benign, variant of eating behaviour is not usually associated with any significant negative impact on psychological development and functioning; indeed it can be regarded as an important aspect of healthy psychological development, where the young child is asserting their independence and ability to make choices. The situation for children with ARFID and their families is however different; here, the eating difficulty is likely to be associated with impairment to development and functioning across multiple domains, to include in the psychosocial domain.

The possible psychological impact of ARFID includes an increase in distress which can be related to such things as conflict at mealtimes, missing out on age-appropriate activities, not being able to participate in family outings and holidays. Fears and worries can be exacerbated and the child may suffer from embarrassment, shame, and an increasing sense of isolation or "differentness". Social impact can include barriers and impediments to family life, exposure to new places and situations, friendships, and leisure activities. Taken together these areas of possible impact can lead to distress and impairment not only for the child, but can also contribute to distress, disruption or inconvenience for others. For example, some children find it difficult to eat around others as they find the presence of non-preferred foods overwhelming. Such children may require special accommodations at school to ensure they eat at least something during the school day. Others may not be particularly concerned about their limited diet or other people's food, but the impact on their family may be greater as they restrict activities, holidays, and mealtimes to accommodate the child's preferences (Rouse et al., 2002).

Risk

Areas of risk to consider in assessing ARFID are varied, and include physical and psychological risks, social, and family risk, including possible impact on parental mental health. The child's cognitive and academic functioning may suffer through poor nutrition, anxiety, ability to focus, and as discussed above, there can be risk related to impairment to the child's social and emotional development. Children with ARFID may additionally be at risk through force-feeding, pressure to eat, inconsistent parenting, parental loss of temper, and in some instances physical chastisement, verbal or emotional abuse. Parental over-reporting of symptoms and presentation for multiple invasive assessments is also an area of risk to hold in mind.

Strengths

A good assessment will usefully explore the strengths of the child, the family, and the network around them, for example grandparents and school staff. Asking questions about what the family likes doing together, or what they value about being a family, represents a good place to start. Eliciting strengths is important, not only to build confidence in being able to tackle difficulties, but also to inform interventions that are appropriately adapted to the child's level of ability and context. Some clinicians have a tendency to take the reins more than is necessary; it is important to allow and support the family to access and use their own resources where these are appropriate and available. During the assessment it is important to strike a careful balance between gathering information and managing parental emotions and responses to discussing what they may perceive as "failures", or they may think the clinician might regard as their "inadequacies". Parents can often feel guilt and shame about the difficulties and may feel that they have failed their child (Chatoor et al., 2000), or that the clinician is judging them. It is important to be mindful of this and be able to address such sentiments, as they are rarely helpful.

Explanatory model (of the family)

Families attending assessment will often hold a number of explanatory ideas about why their child has difficulties with eating and it is important to elicit these. During the process of the assessment family members' views about explanations for the eating difficulties may change, remain in doubt, or they may become more crystallised. It is often useful to ask the family again towards the end of the assessment whether their thinking has changed. Clinicians should always be aware of any assumptions that they may be making during the assessment process regarding the family, such as assumptions related to socioeconomic status or cultural background. The only way to discover the wider societal, cultural and religious views, beliefs and values of any family is by being curious, and by asking. It can also be helpful to ask about the views, beliefs and values of extended family members and important friends, to include family members' perceptions of what these individuals think about the presenting issues, as there are often many opinions in one network. Families sometimes report feeling judged by others or not believed, to include their concerns being dismissed by professionals (McKee et al., 2010). They may report that members of the wider family make unhelpful suggestions like "… leave him with me for a week, I'll get him eating". Such experiences can contribute to the family's own explanatory model for the child's difficulties.

It is always worth discussing the environmental, social and financial circumstances of the child and family in the event that there may be other underlying difficulties that may explain the presenting feeding or eating problems, such as scarcity of food or a culturally endorsed tradition. Hay and colleagues found that a high percentage of their sample of adolescents and adults presenting with ARFID were from low socio- economic groups (Hay et al., 2017). The use of food banks is increasing and represents a hidden aspect of poverty that does not get widely asked about (Bulman, 2018). It is an area that could potentially have an impact on families managing ARFID, as the child's preferred foods are likely to be more difficult to access. Asking about personal and family circumstances, and remaining curious, may help the family discuss openly some of the wider explanations they may hold about their child's eating. Sometimes, families may be sensitive about some aspects of their situation, but maintaining a straightforward, non-judgmental questioning style is usually best.

Planned observational assessment

Arranging an opportunity to observe a family meal can represent a valuable additional component to the psychological assessment as it can provide useful information about all the areas discussed above. It can illustrate the child's emotional responses, behaviour, developmental level, and relationships in vivo, as well as flag strengths and risks, and highlight the impact of the difficulties. Observation might confirm parental or family descriptions of the presenting issues, but equally might demonstrate discrepancies. Discrepancies in themselves do not mean that that the family's account has been unreliable, as it is well known that children may behave and respond differently in different contexts. Differences observed during an assessment meal may be due to a novel environment, but may also be an indicator of how parental anxiety may contribute to their perception of the magnitude of difficulty and their response to it. An observer may be able to discern the way that the family tolerates, embraces, or discourages any different or unusual responses to food and eating. Observation also allows non-verbal aspects of interaction to be included and the tone, content and flow of conversations to be noted. Family "rules" at the table, such as whether parents allow tactile involvement with food, or games to be played at the table, can be observed. It has been suggested that family meals can play an important role in the promotion of family unity and interactions (Hamilton & Wilson, 2009; Neumark-Sztainer et al., 2004). Therefore it is relevant to investigate the interactional patterns that take place during family meals to form a view whether these are related to or a consequence of eating behaviours, or whether they represent wider patterns of interaction (Godfrey, Rhodes, & Hunt, 2013).

If possible and with family consent, it is often useful to record such an assessment meal, or subsequent mealtimes in clinic or at home, for the purpose of contributing to the multi-disciplinary assessment. Watching the recording may also be useful as a reflective tool with families, in particular to highlight specific areas of emotional, behavioural and interactional functioning and to elicit individual family members' views and experiences of what happened. Some parents will notice things that they otherwise miss, as in Amir's situation,

> Amir (4 years old) came for an assessment lunch with both of his parents. His father is a tall man, and when he stood up to help Amir with his food he looked somewhat intimidating, as the position in which he stood meant that he towered over Amir. The parents were shown the assessment lunch recording and immediately Amir's father noticed his positioning and commented on how threatening he must have seemed to Amir. This enabled him to change how he supported Amir at mealtimes.

Closing reflections

A comprehensive psychological assessment as described above, can act as an intervention in itself as it can enable the child and family to understand difficulties from a different perspective and to identify their own strengths and potential to make positive changes. Detailed exploration of emotions, behaviours, relationships, risks, impact, perspectives, and different people in the family's understanding of the situation, can helpfully lead to revisions to thinking, acceptance, problem-solving, and the development of creative approaches tailored by the family to their own situation which they feel enthusiastic about trying out at home. As Joe's parent commented,

> During the assessment we suddenly became aware, that all of the medical interventions Joe had had were around his face and were incredibly invasive – lots of tubes in his nose and mouth – and we began to understand that his struggle to eat, what we thought was him being awkward, was more about his fear of another thing being pushed into him. This has helped us adapt our expectations of his ability and willingness and allowed us to be more supportive as we have felt that we understand his difficulties more.

Summary points

- Psychological assessment is one part of a comprehensive assessment process that encompasses physical, nutritional, and sensory assessment as well as evaluation of the child's eating skills and abilities
- Psychological assessment includes obtaining information about the child's developmental level, as well as behavioural, emotional and relationship aspects of the child's presentation
- The impact of presenting difficulties should be explored in terms of distress and impairment to psychological development and functioning, as well as any risks specifically in relation to psycho-social functioning
- The child and family members strengths and their understanding and explanation of the presenting difficulties are important to elicit and can contribute usefully to planning and supporting intervention
- Assessment can be a powerful intervention in itself which can allow family members to confirm their understanding of difficulties or form a new one as well as recognise their own strengths and potential to make changes.

References

Bulman, M. (2018) Food bank use in UK reaches highest rate on record as benefits fail to cover basic costs. *Independent Newspaper*, 24 April 2018 www.independent.co.uk/news/uk/home-news/food-bank-uk-benefits-trussell-trust-cost-of-living-highest-rate-a8317001.html - accessed 9 July 2019.

Cardona Cano, S., Van Hoek, H.W., Van Hoeken, D., de Barse, L.M., Jaddoe, V.W.V., Verhulst, F.C., & Tiemeier, H. (2016) Behavioural outcomes of picky eating in childhood: a prospective study in the general population. *Journal of Child Psychology and Psychiatry*, 57(11), 1239–46.

Chatoor, I., Ganiban, J., Hirsch, R., Boorman-Spurrell, E., & Mrazek, D. (2000). Maternal characteristics and toddler temperament in infantile anorexia. *Journal of the American Academy of Child and Adolescent Psychiatry*, Elsevier, 39(6), 743–51.

Godfrey, K., Rhodes, P., & Hunt, C. (2013) The relationship between family mealtime interactions and eating disorder in childhood and adolescence: a systematic review. *Australian and New Zealand Journal of Family Therapy*, 34, 54–74.

Goodman, R. & Scott, S. (2012) *Child and adolescent psychiatry* (3rd ed.). Chichester, UK: Wiley-Blackwell.

Hamilton, S.K. & Wilson, J.H. (2009) Family mealtimes: worth the effort? *Infant, Child and Adolescent Nutrition*, 1, 346–50.

Hay, P., Mitchison, D., Callado, A.E.L., González-Chica, D.A., Stocks, N., & Touyz, S. (2017) Burden and health-related qualify of life of eating disorders, including Avoidant/Restrictive Food Intake Disorder (ARFID) in the Australian population. *Journal of Eating Disorders*, 5, 21.

McKee MD, Maher S., Deen D., & Blank A.E. (2010) Counseling to prevent obesity among preschool children: acceptability of a pilot urban primary care intervention. *Annals of Family Medicine*, 8, 249–55.

Neumark-Sztainer, D., Wall, M., Story M. & Fulkerson, J.A. (2004) Are family meal patterns associated with disordered eating behaviors among adolescents? *Journal of Adolescent Health*, 35(5), 350–59.

Quitadamo, P., Thapar, N., Staiano, A., & Borrelli, O. (2016). Gastrointestinal and nutritional problems in neurologically impaired children. *European Journal of Paediatric Neurology*, 20, 810–15.

Rouse, L., Herrington, P., Assey, J., Baker, R. & Golden, S. (2002) Feeding problems, gastrostomy and families: a qualitative pilot study. *British Journal of Learning Disabilities*, 30(3), 122–28.

Siddaway, A.P., Wood, A.M. & Cartwright-Hatton, S. (2014) Involving parents in cognitive-behavioral therapy for child anxiety problems: a case study. *Clinical Case Studies*, 13(4), 322–35.

Toyama, H. & Agras, W.S. (2016) A test to identify persistent picky eaters. *Eating Behaviours*, 23, 66–69.

Zucker, N., Copeland, W., Franz, L., Carpenter, K., Keeling, L., Angold, A., & Egger, H. (2015) Psychological and psychosocial impairment in pre-schoolers with selective eating. *Pediatrics*, 136(3), 582–90.

Chapter 8

Nutritional and feeding assessment

Sarah Cawtherley and Eleanor Conway

Introduction

This chapter discusses assessment of dietary intake and feeding ability in children with avoidant restrictive food intake disorder (ARFID). It addresses two key questions:

- is the child eating and drinking enough of the right foods to be able to meet their nutritional and growth requirements?
- is the child capable of managing a full oral diet in terms of their oral-motor function and swallow ability?

Dietary intake and eating ability represent two aspects of a child's presentation that are inextricably linked. They are therefore combined in this chapter to demonstrate the importance of assessing these aspects of feeding and eating alongside each other rather than separately. The primary role for a speech and language therapist as part of a multi-disciplinary approach to the assessment of ARFID is to ascertain if a child can eat or drink safely and efficiently enough to sustain an oral diet. This goes hand in hand with the role of the dietitian to determine whether the content of that diet is adequate. Through their specialist skills and knowledge in these respective areas, the dietitian and speech and language therapist can therefore contribute to a comprehensive formulation and appropriately prioritised management plan for a child's feeding or eating difficulties.

This chapter includes guidance for the assessment of what is eaten and how it is eaten, including the importance of determining the adequacy of the intake to meet a child's nutritional and energy requirements and to sustain growth, the child's ability to eat, typical development of feeding and eating skills, and factors that may interrupt a child's progression through the usual stages of feeding development. Common myths about eating skills and abilities are dispelled and the importance of attention to areas of potential risk highlighted.

Nutritional assessment

The nutritional component of a multi-disciplinary approach to the assessment of ARFID is ideally conducted by a dietitian (Kohn, 2016; Taylor & Emmett, 2019). Nutritional assessment involves collecting and interpreting information regarding energy and nutritional intake, in order to make clinical decisions about treatment and monitoring requirements, and to elucidate the reasons that might have led to any nutritional inadequacies identified. It is important to assess whether the child's diet is nutritionally adequate or is deficient in any nutrient(s), as this may need addressing. A comprehensive nutritional assessment is recommended to include information relating to a number of areas alongside the dietary assessment, including anthropometry, biochemistry, clinical and physical assessment, and environmental, behavioural or social factors (British Dietetic Association, 2016).

Anthropometry

Assessment of anthropometry includes weight, height, body mass index (BMI) and percentage median BMI, which allows the clinician to assess whether the child is growing appropriately. Weight and height measurements should be obtained according to standard techniques and measurements plotted on appropriate gender-specific growth charts (e.g. in the UK, as recommended by the Department of Health, 2009, and the Royal College of Paediatrics and Child Health, 2009a, 2009b). This will help to identify whether a child is growing appropriately or if their growth is faltering by tracking their centile lines. Growth faltering can include weight loss, leading to falling centiles, or weight plateauing, therefore crossing centile lines (see also Chapter 9). When assessing a child's growth, it is important to take growth history into account, as well as current weight and height, as this will give a clearer picture of growth over time. It can be of benefit to calculate mid-parental height to help identify where a child's growth is in relation to predicted height centile, particularly if there are concerns that height may have been affected by poor nutrition. Anthropometric measurements are important to be able to calculate whether the child is meeting their nutritional requirements and to help with monitoring growth following dietary interventions. Inaccurate data plotting on growth charts can lead to misdiagnosis or non-identification of nutritional and growth problems.

Biochemistry

Biochemical and haematological indices may be helpful to identify any nutritional deficiencies or abnormalities. Some children with ARFID may require monitoring of biochemical or haematological indices if they demonstrate signs or symptoms of a deficiency. The dietitian's assessment should allow identification of any inadequacies in the diet, with related nutritional deficiencies, or risk of deficiencies, which might indicate a need for nutritional bloods. It is important to note that clinical signs of poor nutrition, from physical examination, often only appear at a late stage in the development of a deficiency disease; absence of clinical signs of deficiency should therefore not be taken as indicators of absence of that deficiency (Shaw, 2015).

Clinical assessment

When conducting a nutritional assessment it is essential to include consideration of the medical and other multi-disciplinary aspects of assessment as well as reviewing other clinical diagnoses of the child, to see whether these have any nutritional implications. Gastro-oesophageal reflux, constipation, food allergies, and iron deficiency/anaemia, are all known to impact a child's nutrition and appetite. It is important also to have up-to-date information about any medication the child might be taking, either prescribed or over-the-counter (to include nutritional supplements), so that the implications for nutritional recommendations can be assessed.

Dietary assessment

Dietary assessment involves the collection of information on food and drinks consumed over a specific time period (Dao et al., 2019). Analysis of this information ascertains whether the nutritional requirements for both macro- and micronutrients are met for the individual. Dietary assessment can include a number of different assessment methods, including a 24-hour diet history or recall, a recorded food diary (preferably for at least three days, including two weekdays and a weekend day), a weighed food intake diary, or a food frequency questionnaire (Gibson, 2005). A combination of these methods is generally preferred as this provides the greatest depth of information. There are advantages and limitations for each of the different methods used in clinical practice (Dao et al., 2019; Gandy, 2016), requiring a dietitian to be skilled in using this knowledge to ensure the data obtained are interpreted as accurately as possible.

When assessing the child's intake it can be useful to determine:

- information regarding meal patterns and times when the child eats and/or drinks
- how much food or fluid is consumed rather than what is offered
- whether weekdays differ to days in the weekend or holidays
- whether the child eats better or eats different foods in different settings
- what a "good day" and a "bad day" look like and how often each occurs
- whether there any foods or food groups that are being avoided, and to ascertain whether this is due to allergies, medical reasons for exclusions, or family preference

- whether any foods are eaten in excess
- how long meal times last.

Conducting a thorough assessment of foods and fluids consumed helps to determine whether the child's nutritional intake regularly incorporates all major food groups i.e. carbohydrates, fruit and vegetables, dairy, protein containing foods, and sources of fat, and whether any specific food types or groups are avoided. It also highlights whether the child's diet is limited in the variety of food consumed or quantities eaten and can highlight potential nutritional risks. There are a range of different tools available to help with assessing the adequacy of a child's intake, for example, pictorial guides to assess whether portion sizes are age-appropriate (Dao et al., 2019), or computer aided dietary analysis packages which compare individual intake to recommended amounts.

Environmental, behavioural or social factors

Any contextual factors that may be impacting on the child's intake, or have implications for any treatment recommended, should be explored, for example, social circumstances, family finances, behavioural considerations, mealtime arrangements, and the child's and family's readiness to change (see further Chapter 7).

Macro- and micro-nutrient requirements

When assessing a child's nutritional status, energy intake, macro-, and micro-nutrient intake should be assessed and compared with national recommendations (for example in the UK, dietary reference values published by the Department of Health, 1991, and the Scientific Advisory Committee on Nutrition, 2011). This will help to determine whether total nutritional intake (i.e. food, drink, and any nutritional supplements) is meeting estimated requirements for growth and development.

Energy and protein requirements

Energy and protein requirements should be individually calculated based on age and gender. If the child is under- or overweight, individual energy and protein requirements should be determined using appropriate national guidelines. In the UK, the Scientific Advisory Committee on Nutrition outlines guidelines for estimated average energy requirements, and the Department of Health has outlined the reference nutrient intake for protein, both for children aged one to 18 years of age (Department of Health, 1991; Scientific Advisory Committee on Nutrition, 2011). Not all children with ARFID have problems consuming sufficient energy, some will consume enough of their preferred or "safe" foods to meet or even exceed their energy requirements. However, some children are unable to consume sufficient food to meet their requirements resulting in faltering growth and/or weight loss. All children should meet at least the minimum safe protein intake (World Health Organization, 1985) from their diet; if they do not then this can affect their optimal growth potential.

Vitamin and mineral requirements

When completing a dietary assessment, the vitamin and mineral content of the diet should be analysed and compared to requirements for age and gender using reference values as above. Computer aided dietary analysis packages can be used to assess the nutritional adequacy of the diet for both macro-nutrients and micro-nutrients, which can then be compared to requirements.

Nutritional deficiencies in children with ARFID

Micro-nutrient deficiencies in the general population have long been reported in the literature, recently being described as a growing public health concern that affects health, with intervention considered essential to improve population micro-nutrient status (Magee & McCann, 2019). Many studies describe micro-nutrient deficiencies in a number of different population and disorder types, including: iron (Taylor & Emmett, 2019), the most common nutritional disorder worldwide (Magee & McCann, 2019); vitamin A (Ali et al., 2014), which can result in vision loss (McAlbee et al., 2009); B vitamins (Baird & Ravindranath, 2015); vitamin C (Hahn, Adams, & Williams, 2019), which can lead to scurvy (Ma, Thompson & Weston, 2016); vitamin D (Keown, Bothwell, & Jain, 2014; Magee & McCann, 2019) leading to rickets (Stewart & Latif, 2008); calcium (Sharp et al., 2013); folate deficiencies (Allen, 2008); and fibre and zinc (Taylor & Emmett, 2019). Further research is required to assess the micro-nutrient status and commonly occurring nutritional deficiencies of children with ARFID, as there are currently limited data available in this area. It is known that individuals with severely restricted diets are at increased risk of micro-nutrient deficiencies (DiBaise & Tarleton, 2019), and being aware of common patterns or deficiencies might allow screening tools to be designed for use with children with ARFID and regular monitoring of specific markers.

It is certainly not unusual to see children with ARFID who have micro-nutrient deficiencies due to their limited dietary range, but conversely children with excessive amounts of certain micro-nutrients may also be seen. Such children tend to consume excessive amounts of one particular food or food group, which can equally result in nutritional impairment.

Sharp and colleagues investigated the dietary intake, nutritional status and growth parameters of children with autism spectrum disorders (n = 70), which is a relatively common co-occurring condition with ARFID. They found that 78% of those included had five or more nutritional inadequacies, with children consuming insufficient amounts of vitamin D (97%), fibre (91%), vitamin

E (83%), and calcium (71%) (Sharp et al., 2018). Children consuming insufficient amounts of key nutrients can be at a healthy weight or even overweight but still have significant nutritional deficiencies that could lead to long term medical complications due to their limited dietary intake (Sharp & Stubbs, 2018). A recent review found that children who restrict their diet to the extent that they develop nutritional deficiencies, are generally unable to alter their eating pattern without intervention (Hahn, Adams, & Williams, 2019).

Oral nutritional supplements and enteral feeding

During the dietetic assessment it will become apparent if the child is on any form of an oral nutritional supplement. This may have been prescribed by a health care professional, bought over the counter, or a homemade high calorie supplement to boost dietary intake. In some instances where a child is unable to consume sufficient calories from preferred foods or oral nutritional supplements, tube feeding may be indicated.

Re-feeding syndrome

During the dietetic assessment, children should be assessed for risk of refeeding syndrome, particularly if they are consuming insufficient calories and have lost weight. This should be taken into consideration when deciding upon appropriate management (see Chapter 9 and 12). The risk of refeeding syndrome is rare but as it can occur in extreme presentations of ARFID, it is important that this is considered where appropriate.

Development of oral skills for eating and drinking

Alongside the dietary assessment it is important to consider a child's skills with eating, including oral skills and swallow safety, typically requiring the specialist input and knowledge of a speech and language therapist. A child's ability to eat and drink requires the complex integration of their neurological, cardio-vascular and sensory-motor systems; difficulties in any of these areas may have contributed to the avoidance or restriction of intake. Disruption in these systems can occur at different times and to differing extents, due to a range of underlying medical or developmental experiences.

The normal swallow

There are many excellent textbooks on swallow function that describe the anatomy and physiology of eating and drinking in detail (e.g. Arvedson & Brodsky, 2019). Most outline how the transition of food from the mouth to the stomach can be broken down into four stages:

- The oral preparatory stage, where food is taken into the mouth and chewed and mixed with saliva in preparation to be swallowed; this is a voluntary stage of swallowing.
- The oral stage, where food or liquid is formed into a bolus (a ball of food or liquid) and transferred to the back of the throat (pharynx) to be swallowed; this is also a voluntary stage.
- The pharyngeal stage, where the bolus moves from the oro-pharynx to the valleculae, laryngeal elevation and excursion cause the opening of the crico-pharyngeal sphincter (also called the upper oesophageal sphincter), and the bolus moves past the airway into the oesophagus; this is an involuntary swallow stage.
- The oesophageal stage, where food passes through the oesophagus in a peristaltic wave through the lower oesophageal sphincter into the stomach; this is also an involuntary stage.

Some children have difficulties with the co-ordination and control of one or more of these stages. This is called "dysphagia" and can cause a range of difficulties including aspiration (when the food or drink enters the airway) or fatigue when eating and drinking. The assessment and management of oro-pharyngeal dysphagia are beyond the remit of this chapter, however if a child is presenting with signs of oro-pharyngeal dysphagia such as regular coughing or choking on swallowing, it is essential that they receive an assessment from an appropriately trained professional.

Oral-motor/oral-sensory development

From birth through to around two years of age a child's feeding skills change from the reflexive sucking and swallowing of bottle or breastfeeding, to volitional control of all the oral structures to eat and drink a range of textures. A child's oral skills are closely interrelated with their motor abilities and sensory development. The focus of assessment of children's oral-motor skills is to determine whether a child has the required underlying oral-motor skills to progress to an age-appropriate diet, or whether they lack the motivation to attempt to eat certain foods, alternatively conceptualised as "can't versus won't" (Silverman, 2010). Many children with ARFID have adequate muscle control and intact oral structures, therefore should be able to ingest a normal diet, but have significant anxiety around certain foods whereby they "won't" accept them. Some children, particularly those with neurological impairment or structural difficulties, "can't" achieve the motor abilities to be able to eat a family diet.

Ages and stages for development of oral skills

The World Health Organization recommends that infants are initially offered smooth blended foods, then progressively move through textures until by approximately 12 months of age would usually be eating family foods. Finger foods are recommended at around eight months of age, alongside purees (World Health Organization, UNICEF, 2003). Approximate ages and stages for the introduction of foods and fluids and the skills a child may require to achieve these have been described by a number of authors, and can provide a potentially useful reference guide as required (see for example, Arvedson & Delaney, 2011).

Children continue to develop their chewing skills from around six months of age, and gradually improve in their efficiency to chew their food (Gisel, 1991). There is some debate as to when a child should have developed adequate oral-motor skills to cope with the average family diet. Some state that this should be at 12 months (Arvedson, 2008; World Health Organization, UNICEF, 2003), others at around 24 months (Gisel, 1991; Morris & Klein, 1987). Gisel assessed the efficiency of children's chewing skills on specific textures between the ages of 6 and 24 months and found that children continued to develop their skills up to approximately 24 months of age (Gisel, 1991). Given this discrepancy in the literature it can be assumed that a typically developing child should be able to manage a normal family diet by the time they reach 24 months of age. Some children may struggle to progress from one texture to another and may become stuck on their "safe foods", refusing more textured or harder foods. It is not uncommon to see a child with marked delay in progression, such as still bottle-feeding at three or four years old, or children who are thriving on a diet of purees and supplements. Children may refuse a variety of foods and textures despite having well developed oral-motor skills (Gisel, 1991). The movement patterns involved in chewing are texture dependent, and do not emerge unless a child begins to accept the foods that require these skills (Reilly et al., 1995).

Early literature on chewing skills discusses the possibility of a "critical window" for chewing development; if a child does not practice chewing this can then disrupt the sequence of motor learning, and the development of oral sensory tolerances (Edwards et al., 2015). This delay in a child's acceptance of texture progression can delay their oral-motor development and create dysfunctional oral-motor patterns. It has further been argued that this critical window is linked to a period of increased brain plasticity that optimises a child's progression onto chewing (Edwards et al., 2015). This idea of a critical window does not necessarily fit with clinical experience of oral-motor or oral-sensory development. There are certainly some children who start eating much later than 2–3 years of age, for example, who progress from full tube feeds to family foods with few problems. There are also many children who find the sensory experience of harder foods difficult to manage and continue to only eat smooth or liquid textures despite extensive oral-motor input. The idea of a critical window is a view often held by parents and other health professionals, and can contribute to anxiety when a child does not meet the above milestones in line with their peers.

Failure to progress to age-appropriate textures is a key presentation in many children with ARFID co-occurring with complex medical diagnoses. Rather than being caused by any oral-motor difficulty it is often more likely that these children have oral sensitivity (see further Chapter 10). There are also some children who have marked oral sensitivity in isolation. Such children are unable to tolerate the sensation of harder foods on their teeth, tongue, or when swallowing, in their hypopharynx (Dodrill et al., 2004). As a consequence, these children are unable to progress through to textured food because of an inability to tolerate the sensation of food in some parts of their mouth. It is important when assessing oral skills and function for the speech and language therapist to be guided by an occupational therapist or other colleague trained in assessing a child's level of oral sensitivity to ascertain if any sensitivity identified is in line with a child's wider sensory processing difficulty or is isolated to their mouth and face.

Ian initially presented in clinic aged 4 years old, on a full oral diet of milk. This was drunk via an open cup with small mouthfuls taken into the mouth and held under the tongue. Ian would then tip his head back and swallow the liquid. He was unable to lick food and any food on his tongue resulted in a gag. An oral-motor assessment showed that he was able to complete a range of non-eating tasks with adequate strength and control. Ian presented with extreme oral sensitivity, he gagged when food touched his tongue and was unable to tolerate the sensation of biting down on food with either his front or back teeth. Ian had an extensive programme of desensitisation, involving gradual texture progression, increasing bolus size or bolus viscosity, and licking and biting both food and non-food items. Progress has been slow for Ian; some of his difficulties are judged to be associated with his neurodevelopmental delay. He remains on a liquid diet, the texture is gradually increasing and he has managed to maintain gains made. His sensitivity has continued to affect only the oral cavity and has so far prevented any progression to chewing or thicker textures.

The development of oral difficulties

Much of the literature on children with feeding disorders and difficulties does not differentiate between children with neurological oral-motor impairment (the "can't" group) and children who have delayed oral-motor progression due to refusal and lack of experience (the "won't" group) (Arvedson, 1997; Mason, Harris & Blissett, 2005). Rommel and colleagues attempted to classify children's eating difficulties into medical, oral and behavioural problems. They found that 86% of children presenting at their centre had "medically explained feeding difficulties", 61% had oral difficulties (including dysphagia), and 18% had behavioural difficulties. Of the children presenting with oral difficulties, 10% had oral-motor difficulties, whereas 20% had oral-sensory impairment, with 7% showing oral-motor delay as a result of lack of experience (Rommel et al., 2003).

In a comparison of full-term babies with low risk pre-term infants (32–37 weeks gestation), the pre-term infants were found to present with higher levels of oral sensitivity and reduced oral-motor skills; increased oral-facial sensitivity and reduced oral-motor skills correlated with an increased period of nasogastric tube feeding in early infancy (Dodrill et al., 2004). These authors propose that the placement of a nasogastric tube seems to disrupt a child's oral skill and sensory development. These findings fit with clinical experience that children may develop increased sensitivity in early infancy and this may impact on their ability to develop mature chewing skills at the expected time.

Assessment of eating ability

When assessing a child with ARFID, the speech and language therapist will need to watch the child eat or drink their familiar foods in the most natural environment possible. They will assess the following key questions:

- does the child have the sufficient oral structures and musculature control to be able to functionally chew and swallow?
- does this child's medical history indicate any likely oral-pharyngeal dysphagia?

There are a range of oral-motor assessments available to clinicians who may wish to standardise this process (Barton, Bickell, & Fucile, 2018). An observation of a child eating and drinking and a good case history should be sufficient to be able to assess whether dysphagia or "can't eat" should form part of the formulation of a child's eating difficulties. For most children with ARFID, presenting difficulties are most likely to fall in the "won't eat" category. Once a child's oral skills and musculature have been observed and determined to be as both safe and functionally typical, the child should, in theory, be capable of progression to an age-appropriate diet.

Myths and misunderstandings about oral-motor skills and development

When children present with feeding and eating difficulties, chewing development is an area that appears to be particularly focussed on by both parents and professionals. There is a widely held belief that in order to speak clearly, a child needs to be able to chew. A quick internet search will reveal many websites perpetuating this myth that children who cannot chew do not develop the muscles for speech. In the literature, children who do not chew are sometimes described as having oral-motor delay. Whilst it can be true that these children may not have reached the developmental milestone of chewing, in many cases this is not due to any muscle deficit, and certainly should not affect their speech skills. Furthermore, children can thrive on a totally liquid diet and the need to chew is socially driven rather than by any nutritional need.

Summary points

- Nutritional and feeding assessment should cover what the child eats and how they eat it, two aspects of eating that are best considered together
- The dietetic assessment is multi-layered and needs to assess intake against energy requirements and nutritional requirements, including macro- and micro-nutrient requirements
- Observation of the child eating enables clinicians to consider if there are any functional or developmental issues impacting on the child's ability to eat
- Nutritional and feeding assessment is an important part of a multi-disciplinary approach to assessment, contributing information to allow a comprehensive formulation and appropriate prioritisation of interventions for children with ARFID.

References

Ali, S.R., Hamilton, R., Callaghan, M., Brown, A., & Gibson, L. (2014) A 13 year old with fussy-eating induced blindness. *Archives of Diseases in Childhood* 99, 179–80.

Allen, L.H. (2008) Causes of vitamin B12 and folate deficiency. *Food and Nutrition Bulletin* 29(2), 20–34.

Arvedson, J.C. (1997) Behavioral issues and implications with pediatric feeding disorders. *Seminars in Speech and Language* 18(1), 51–70.

Arvedson, J.C. (2008) Assessment of pediatric dysphagia and feeding disorders: clinical and instrumental approaches. *Developmental Disabilities Research Reviews* 14, 118–27.

Arvedson, J.C. & Brodsky, L. (2019) *Pediatric feeding and swallowing disorders*. Third Albany NY: Singular Publishing Group.

Arvedson, J.C. & Delaney, A.L. (2011) Development of oromotor functions for feeding. In Roig-Quilis, M. & Pennington, L. *Oromotor disorders in childhood*. Barcelona, Spain: Viguera Editores, SL, 36.

Baird, J.S. & Ravindranath, T.M. (2015) Vitamin B deficiencies in a critically ill autistic child with a restricted diet. *Nutrition and Clinical Practice* 30(1), 100–03.

Barton, C., Bickell, M., & Fucile, S. (2018) Pediatric oral motor feeding assessments: a systematic review. *Physical and Occupational Therapy in Pediatrics* 38(2), 190–209.

British Dietetic Association. (2016) *Model and process for nutrition and dietetic practice*. London, UK: British Dietetic Association. 10. ttps://www.bda.uk.com/publications/professional/model_and_process_for_nutrition_and_dietetic_practice_accessed 11 July 2019.

Dao, M.C., Subar, A.F., Warthon-Medina, M., Cade, J., Burrows, T., Golley, R.K., Forouhi, N.G., Pearce, M., & Holmes, B.A. (2019) Dietary assessment toolkits: An overview. *Public Health Nutrition* 22(3), 404–18.

Department of Health. (1991) Dietary reference values for food and energy and nutrients for the United Kingdom. *Report on health and social subjects No. 41* London, UK: HMSO.

Department of Health (2009) *UK-WHO Growth Charts* www.rcpch.ac.uk/resources/uk-who-growth-charts-2-18-years accessed 11 July 2019.

DiBaise, M. & Tarleton, S.M. (2019) Hair, nails, and skin: differentiating cutaneous manifestations of micronutrient deficiency. *Nutrition in Clinical Practice* 10.1002/ncp.10321 accessed 11 July 2019.

Dodrill, P., McMahon, S., Ward, E., Weir, K., Donovan, T., & Riddle, B. (2004) Long-term oral sensitivity and feeding skills of low-risk pre-term infants. *Early Human Development* 76, 23–37.

Edwards, S., Davis, A. McGrath, Ernst, L., Sitzman, B., Bruce, A., Keeler, D., Almadhoun, O., Mouse, H., & Hyman, P. (2015) Interdisciplinary strategies for treating oral aversions in children. *Journal of Parenteral and Enteral Nutrition* 39(8), 899–909.

Gandy, J. (2016) *Manual of dietetic practice* (5th ed.). Chichester, UK: Wiley Blackwell.

Gibson, R.S. (2005) *Principles of nutritional assessment.* Second Oxford, UK: Oxford University Press.

Gisel, E.G. (1991) Effect of food texture on the development of chewing of children between six months and two years of age. *Developmental Medicine and Child Neurology* 33, 69–79.

Hahn, T., Adams, W., & Williams, K. (2019) Is vitamin C enough? A case report of scurvy in a five-year-old girl and review of the literature. *BMC Pediatrics* 19(74), 1–6.

Keown, K., Bothwell, J., & Jain, S. (2014) Nutritional implications of selective eating in a child with autism spectrum disorder. *British Medical Journal* 10.1136/bcr-2013-202581 accessed 11 July 2019.

Kohn, J.B. (2016) What is ARFID?. *Journal of the Academy of Nutrition and Dietetics* 116(11), 1872.

Ma, N.S., Thompson, C., & Weston, S. (2016) Brief report: scurvy as a manifestation of food selectivity in children with autism. *Journal of Autism and Developmental Disorder* 46(4), 1464–70.

Magee, P.J. & McCann, M.T. (2019) Micronutrient deficiencies: current issues. *Proceedings of the Nutrition Society* 78(2), 147–49.

Mason, S.J., Harris, G., & Blissett, J. (2005) Tube feeding in infancy: implications for the development of normal eating and drinking skills. *Dysphagia* 20(1), 46–61.

McAlbee, G.N., Prieto, D.M., Kirby, J., Santilli, A.M., & Setty, R. (2009) Permanent visual loss due to dietary vitamin A deficiency in an autistic adolescent. *Journal of Child Neurology* 24(10), 1288–89.

Morris, S.E. & Klein, M.D. (1987) *Pre-feeding skills: a comprehensive resource for feeding development.* Tuscon AZ, USA: Therapy Skills Builders.

Reilly, S., Skuse, D., Mathieson, B., & Wolke, D. (1995) The objective rating of oral - motor functions during feeding. *Dysphagia* 10, 177–91.

Rommel, N., De Meyer, A.M., Feenstra, L., & Veereman-Wauters, G. (2003) The complexity of feeding problems in 700 infants and young children presenting to a tertiary care institution. *Journal of Paediatric Gastroenterology and Nutrition* 37, 75–84.

Royal College of Paediatrics and Child Health (2009a) *Using the new UK – World Health Organization 0–4 years growth charts* www.rcpch.ac.uk/sites/default/files/Using_the_growth_charts.pdf accessed 11 July 2019.

Royal College of Paediatrics and Child Health. (2009b) *Growth charts.*

Scientific Advisory Committee on Nutrition (2011) *Dietary reference values for energy.* London, UK: Scientific Advisory Committee on Nutrition.

Sharp, W.G., Berry, R.C., McCracken, C., Nuhu, N.N., Marvel, E., Saulnier, C.A., Klin, A., Jones, W., & Jaquess, D.L. (2013) Feeding problems and nutrient intake in children with autism spectrum disorders: a meta-analysis and comprehensive review of the literature. *Journal of Autism Developmental Disorders* 43(9), 2159–73.

Sharp, W.G., Postorino, V., McCracken, C.E., Berry, R.C., Criado, K.K., Burrell, T.L., & Scahill L. (2018) Dietary intake, nutrient status, and growth parameters in children with autism spectrum disorder and severe food selectivity: an electronic medical record review. *Journal of the Academy of Nutrition and Dietetics* 118(10), 1943–50.

Sharp, W.G. & Stubbs, K.H. (2018) Avoidant/restrictive food intake disorder: a diagnosis at the intersection of feeding and eating disorders necessitating subtype differentiation. *International Journal of Eating Disorders* 52, 398–401.

Shaw, V. (2015) *Clinical Paediatric Dietetics* (4th ed.). Chichester, UK: Wiley Blackwell.

Silverman, A.H. (2010) Interdisciplinary care for feeding problems in children. *Nutrition in Clinical Practice* 25(2), 160–65.

Stewart, C. & Latif, A. (2008) Symptomatic nutritional rickets in a teenager with autistic spectrum disorder. *Child Care Health and Development* 34(2), 276–78.

Taylor, C.M. & Emmett, P. (2019) Picky eating in children: Causes and consequences. *Proceedings of the Nutrition Society* 78, 161–69.

World Health Organization. (1985) *Energy and protein requirements. Report of a Joint FAO/WHO/UNU Meeting, WHO Technical Report Series.* Geneva, Switzerland: World Health Organization. 724.

World Health Organization, UNICEF. (2003) *Global strategy for infant and young child feeding.* Geneva, Switzerland: World Health Organization.

Chapter 9

Physical assessment

Lee Hudson and Emma Parish

Introduction

This chapter concerns important aspects of presentation warranting consideration as part of the medical assessment of children and young people with avoidant restrictive food intake disorder (ARFID). The assessing clinician will need to be alert to the potential for both acute medical risk and the possible presence of longer-term, chronic issues. Management of specific physical complications, and how these should ideally fit into the comprehensive treatment approach provided by other members of the multi-disciplinary team, are discussed in more detail in Chapter 13. As is reiterated in that chapter, as a relatively new diagnosis there is a paucity of research into physical aspects of care in ARFID, to include recommended components of evidence-based assessment protocols. Where relevant, parallels with malnutrition in other related conditions, in particular, anorexia nervosa, is used to guide discussion and recommendations.

As discussed in Chapter 4, ARFID can present in a variety of age groups from childhood, through adolescence and in adulthood. Individuals with ARFID can initially present to a range of healthcare professionals, and as such needs to be recognised by representatives of many disciplines, including general practitioners, school nurses, community medical and nursing teams, dieticians, health visitors, paediatricians, emergency departments, and mental health teams. Assessment and treatment for multi-facetted disorders such as ARFID is generally most effective when professionals are aligned and work in multi-disciplinary forums, with shared goals and understanding. Medical practitioners and teams can contribute skill in the assessment of physical risk and the consideration of differential diagnoses in terms of medical conditions that may account for the avoidance and restriction of food intake characteristic of ARFID (Hudson & Court, 2012; Hudson & O'Connor, 2015).

For any child or young person with ARFID, a physical assessment is essential to check for signs of failure to meet nutritional requirements and assessment of growth, as well as to aid diagnosis, and to establish and exclude alternative diagnoses. Each of these aspects of assessment is outlined individually below. In this chapter, acute and chronic concerns are discussed separately. A suggested checklist for physical assessment is presented in Table 9.1.

Table 9.1 Suggested checklist for the physical assessment of a child with ARFID

Important aspects of the history

- Duration and characteristics of weight change (e.g. amount and speed of weight loss/gain)
- Symptoms of gastrointestinal disturbance suggesting possible gastroenterological diagnosis – in particular abdominal pain, diarrhoea, vomiting
- Specifically ask about constipation and associated pain and discomfort
- Symptoms of central nervous system disease (e.g. headaches, vomiting, acute personality changes)
- Types of dietary restrictions and overall content of diet, to include any nutritional supplements (preferably alongside a dietician)
- Past medical history – this should include pre-existing diagnoses, birth history, prematurity, developmental milestones and a review of growth as a baby, infant and child. Evidence of previous, recurrent infections as in indicator of possible underlying immunodeficiency as a cause of underweight; or recurrent respiratory infections as a consequence of difficulties with swallowing.
- Medications (past and present) – particularly antidepressants or laxatives as well as over-the-counter or herbal remedies
- Social history and support of additional services such as social care
- Previous history of fractures, or family history of fractures indicating potential family history of low bone mineral density

In pubertal and near pubertal children also ask about:

- Puberty (growth spurts, any signs of puberty)
- In girls an important additional question is about menarche, and if amenorrhoea is present then it is key to establish whether primary or secondary

Important aspects of the physical examination

- Cardiovascular signs of underweight/weight loss: postural drops in blood pressure, pulse rate (refer to guidelines for reference ranges – see main text). Note that children can still be overweight with medical instability due to weight loss.
- Skin changes – anaemia, zinc deficiency, nail changes including pitting or breakage
- Full neurological assessment, including fundoscopy
- Pubertal assessment performed sensitively. In girls the first sign is breast development, parents may be able to help with this; in boys, increase in testicular volume. Where direct examination is not possible, use of charts can be used for Tanner Staging to self-report.
- Plot longitudinal growth on appropriate growth chart and calculate %median BMI (body mass index).

Important investigations to consider

- Urea and electrolytes – assessing for electrolyte disturbance or underlying renal conditions
- Coeliac screen (anti-TTG for screening, including IgA)
- Thyroid function tests
- Full blood count and ferritin – looking for anaemia (may be acute iron deficiency and warrant further iron studies, or anaemia of chronic disease). Note that ferritin may be raised in acute underweight.

(Continued)

Table 9.1 (Cont.)

- If loose stool or variable bowel habit is a key feature also consider faecal calprotectin as a screen for inflammatory bowel disease as a cause of weight loss.
- If slowing of growth or short for parental height consider a bone age X-ray, karyotype in girls for Turner's
- In delayed puberty/primary amenorrhoea, consider: Luteinising hormone (LH)/Follicle stimulating hormone (FSH), pelvic ultrasound scan and karyotype.
- For long-standing underweight 6–12 months consider a DEXA scan for low bone mineral density.

Assessment of acute medical risk

In many individuals, ARFID tends to have a prolonged and chronic course leading to longstanding malnutrition (Lucarelli et al., 2018); however, some children and young people with ARFID can still lose weight quickly and demonstrate key features of acute weight loss and risk. At present, there is no specific risk assessment tool for underweight in ARFID and the use of established tools, of which there are several, is recommended, for example Junior MARSIPAN from the UK (Royal College of Psychiatrists, 2012) or the Academy of Eating Disorders' Guide to Medical Care (Academy of Eating Disorders, 2016; Mehler & Andersen, 2017). It is important to highlight that none of these tools are validated to quantify risk; however, they are established, consensus guidelines. Key clinical features representing risk are outlined below:

BMI and weight for height

It is a common convention in clinical practice to assess underweight in children using body mass index, or BMI, and specifically standardised scores of BMI relative to the population (Hudson & Court, 2012). Percentage median BMI is a way of expressing an individual's BMI as a percentage of the 50th centile, or median BMI for the same age and biological sex. For example, consider a 10-year-old boy with a BMI of 13.2 kg/m^2. On UK charts, the 50th centile BMI for a male child aged 10 is 16.4 Kg/m^2 and thus his % median BMI is 13.2/16.4 = 80%. In research, z-score or standard deviation from the mean is used, with 80% median BMI roughly equivalent to –2 z-score. The World Health Organization defines thinness as –2 z-scores (approximately equivalent to 80% median BMI) below the mean and severe thinness as –3 z-scores below the mean, (approximately equivalent to 70% median BMI) (Cole et al., 2007). Whilst grading BMI in children with ARFID is helpful to quantify degree of underweight and for tracking change over time, it has been shown to be poorly sensitive to acute medical instability in children and young people with eating disorders (Hudson et al., 2012). In other words, some patients with ARFID might, at perceived higher %median BMI, still have acutely worrying clinical findings, so clinical assessments should always include a full evaluation around acute risk irrespective of BMI. This likely represents the importance of weight loss rate rather than absolute value at presentation, similar to the situation in anorexia nervosa. It should also be noted here that a number of children with ARFID may be overweight because the restriction in variety of foods may mean exclusively eating high-calorie foods. Overweight children losing weight rapidly, in particular, may be at reassuring %median BMI but still have medical instability due to rapidity of weight loss. Children and young people with obesity should be managed in accordance with national guidelines, for example the OSCA guidelines in the UK (Viner et al., 2012).

Cardiovascular clinical findings

The most commonly identified clinical findings with low weight, and in particular sudden weight loss, relate the cardiovascular system (Sachs et al., 2016); specifically, bradycardia and hypotension. Whilst it is not possible to quantify an individual's risk on the basis of heart rate, a slowed heart rate is a proxy for significant weight loss, or underweight. Guidelines already cited above provide specific cut-offs of concern. Children and young people with significant weight loss and cardiovascular findings should also have an ECG (electrocardiogram) performed to assess for prolonged QTc (Hudson & Court, 2012; Hudson & O'Connor, 2015)

Other acute issues

Patients with ARFID can have such a restricted diet that they excessively consume one type of food, or food group, at the exclusion of all others. They may present with findings related to nutritional imbalance; anecdotally, for example, in excessive sodium intake in the form of salty foods (for example, table salt, soy sauce, or flavoured crisps), which can lead to hypernatraemia, which in severe cases can result in seizures. In the case of excessive consumption of beta-carotene from carrots or sweet potatoes, children may be mistakenly investigated for jaundice due to skin colour changes from carotenaemia (Karthik, Campbell-Davidson, & Isherwood, 2006). Thus careful attention in the assessment must be made to content and types of food.

Chronic issues for physical assessment in ARFID

Constipation

Constipation is common in ARFID, and stool frequency and volume should be assessed at presentation. The implications of constipation for children with ARFID, and its assessment and treatment, is discussed in more detail in Chapter 13.

Evidence of micro-nutrient deficiency

As well as a dietary history, clinicians should examine for clinical signs of nutrient deficiencies. These are commonly taught in undergraduate medical teaching, and are, in practice, not always reliable (Bates, 1999). They ought to be sought in patients with ARFID however, as blood testing can be challenging (see Chapter 13) and may be prompts to point for the need for further testing. Important signs to look for are shown in Table 9.1. The topic of micronutrient deficiencies is dealt with in more detail in Chapter 13.

Growth delay, growth arrest, and pubertal delay

Whilst one of the key physical characteristics of both childhood and adolescence is growth, rate of growth (growth velocity) is not linear, with the most rapid phases being from birth up to the second year (by which time half of height is usually attained) and also during puberty. It stands to reason then, that during those periods with more rapid growth, poor nutrition is likely to have more of an effect. Younger children and those in early or mid-puberty are therefore at greatest risk of disordered growth secondary to inadequate nutrition. This may present in some children with a slowing, or even arrest of growth. All children with ARFID should therefore have their growth (weight, height, and BMI) tracked and monitored. Where there is evidence of growth delay, a bone age can be performed to look for evidence of potential for catch-up. Children with growth delay should also, where appropriate and possible, have a blood screen for other medical causes of growth delay (see Table 9.2 and differential diagnosis section below). Chapter 13 deals with the concept of growth delay, risks of stunting and management further.

Pubertal delay may occur when a child or adolescent approaches puberty and has insufficient body mass for initiation of puberty. This appears to vary between children, and so needs to be monitored. It can also be difficult to distinguish between a delay in puberty and constitutional growth delay – especially in boys where this is tends to be more common (Stanhope & Preece, 1988). However, the general principle of encouraging healthy weight and eating alongside the efforts of other members of the multi-disciplinary team is the first strategy for ARFID. It is beyond the scope of this chapter to review the topic of delayed puberty, and readers are signposted to useful reviews here (Palmert & Dunkel, 2012; Wei & Crowne, 2016). Where there is a possibility of other pathologies causing pubertal or growth delay other than feeding and underweight, consideration should be given to investigating further, potentially with the input of an endocrinologist.

Bone mineral density

At the time of writing, to our knowledge, there is only one published study on low bone mineral density in ARFID; a cross-sectional study in adult males,

Table 9.2 Differential diagnoses in a child or young person with weight loss

Gastrointestinal	• Coeliac disease • Inflammatory bowel disease • Gastroenteritis • *Helicobacter pylori* infection
Endocrine/ metabolic	• Hyperthyroidism • Diabetes • Glucocorticoid insufficiency • Addison's disease
Neurological	• CNS malignancy • Bulbar palsy • Neuromuscular conditions
Safeguarding	• Neglect • Non-accidental injury • Factitious induced illness
Other	• Structural problems that inhibit feeding (e.g. cleft lip and/or palate). • Iatrogenic/medication-related: e.g. anti-epilepsy medications. • Oral aversion (e.g. secondary to prolonged nasogastic or peripheral nutritional supplementation) • Malignancy • Chronic infection (e.g. tuberculosis)

which showed that patients with ARFID had low bone mineral density comparable to those with anorexia nervosa (Schorr et al., 2019). There are no published data on future fracture risk. In practice, anecdotally, children and young people with longstanding ARFID frequently have low bone mineral density. Until specific guidelines exist for ARFID, following local protocols for the measurement of bone mineral density as for anorexia nervosa is recommended, and in particular use of the National Institute of Clinical Excellence Guidelines for Eating Disorders, which specifically recommends considering measuring bone mineral density when underweight has been present for a year or more (NICE, 2017, recommendation 1.10.15).

There are a number of important considerations prior to measurement of bone density. Firstly, the clinician requesting and interpreting the results should be suitably qualified so that they can appropriately decide on indication and also explain findings, and implications to patients and families. Bone mineral density in children and young people should be measured in adherence with international standards (Bianchi et al., 2014; Bishop et al., 2008; Kalkwarf et al., 2014), in particular: (1) measuring in children only over five years of age because of insufficient reference data for ages younger than this; (2) raw bone mineral density measures should be converted to z-scores (standard deviations) for biological sex and age for reporting and interpreting bone mineral density; (3) use of methods for corrected for size, i.e. apparent bone mineral density (BMAD) for reporting and interpreting bone mineral density. The use of the term osteoporosis should also not be used in children and young people, but rather low bone mineral density (Bishop et al., 2008). It is important to understand and explain what the z-score of bone density actually means in the context of measurement in children. By convention, in children and young people a z-score less than –2 (so in other words less than 2 standard deviations below the mean for age and biological sex) is regarded as low. However, given that bone density is normally distributed in the healthy population, a spot measure of bone mineral density at one point in time does not give any information as to where a child or young person's pre-morbid position on the normal curve was, and importantly how far they have shifted away from normal. This may account for a finding in one study of children with anorexia nervosa that although the presence of the disorder was associated with greater contemporary fracture risk compared to controls, actual BMAD z-score was not associated with fracture risk (Faje et al., 2014). It is important to be honest with patients and families, that although it is possible that a low bone mineral density will be captured on testing for children and young people with ARFID, it will not give an accurate prediction of fracture risk. Moreover, a child with a normal z-score (above –2) may still have low bone mineral density for them relative to where they would have been pre-morbidly on the normal distribution. There is a small amount of evidence that knowledge about low bone mineral density is not particularly helpful in motivating patients with anorexia nervosa to change their eating (Stoffman et al., 2005). Further research into how best to provide this information for patients and families and how it might be used in a helpful, motivating way is needed. Management of low bone mineral density in ARFID is discussed further in Chapter 13.

Key differential diagnoses

There are a number of alternative diagnoses to consider in any child with difficulties eating and, in particular, loss of weight. A non-exhaustive list is presented in Table 9.2.

Summary and conclusions

This chapter has outlined important medical considerations for assessing a child or young person with difficulties eating, in particular the key acute concerns around medical instability due to underweight, here secondary to ARFID. It should not be forgotten however, that key to assessment is the work of the multi-disciplinary team, linking in with other team members' findings and being consistent and united in how these findings are fed back to patients and families. The management of medical complications, again alongside a multi-disciplinary team, is discussed in more detail in Chapter 13.

Summary points

- Children and young people presenting with ARFID may have weight loss as a feature, but may be at normal or high weight and still have clinical evidence of medical instability such as changes in blood pressure and pulse
- It is important that a paediatric physical assessment is done thoroughly alongside other members of the multidisciplinary team to look for other potential causes for poor eating or weight loss
- Physical assessment should include a thorough history, examination and consideration of tailored investigation as appropriate.

References

Academy for Eating Disorders (2016) *Eating disorders: a guide to medical care* (3rd ed.). Reston, VA: Academy for Eating Disorders.

Bates, C.J. (1999) Diagnosis and detection of vitamin deficiencies. *British Medical Bulletin* 55, 643–57.

Bianchi, M.L., Leonard, M.B., Bechtold, S., Hogler, W., Mughal, M.Z., Schonau, E., Sylvester, F.A., Vogiatzi, M., Van Den Heuvel-Eibrink, M.M., & Ward, L. (2014) Bone health in children and adolescents with chronic diseases that may affect the skeleton: the 2013 ISCD Pediatric Official Positions. *Journal of Clinical Densitometry* 17, 281–94.

Bishop, N., Braillon, P., Burnham, J., Cimaz, R., Davies, J., Fewtrell, M., Hogler, W., Kennedy, K., Makitie, O., Mughal, Z., Shaw, N., Vogiatzi, M., Ward, K., & Bianchi, M. L. (2008) Dual-energy x-ray aborptiometry assessment in children and adolescents with diseases that may affect the skeleton: the 2007 ISCD Pediatric Official Positions. *Journal of Clinical Densitometry* 11, 29–42.

Cole, T.J., Flegal, K.M., Nicholls, D., & Jackson, A.A. (2007) Body mass index cut offs to define thinness in children and adolescents: international survey. *British Medical Journal* 335(194), https://doi.org/10.1136/bmj.39238.399444.55 accessed 12 July 2019.

Faje, A.T., Fazeli, P.K., Miller, K.K., Katzman, D.K., Ebrahimi, S., Lee, H., Mendes, N., Snelgrove, D., Meenaghan, E., Misra, M., & Klibanski, A. (2014) Fracture risk and areal bone mineral density in adolescent females with anorexia nervosa. *International Journal of Eating Disorders* 47, 458–66.

Hudson L. & O'Connor G. (2015) The role of the paediatric team in the management of young people with severe AN. In Robinson P. & Nicholls D. (eds) *Critical care for anorexia nervosa* 41–66. Cham: Springer.

Hudson, L.D. & Court, A.J. (2012) What paediatricians should know about eating disorders in children and young people. *Journal of Paediatric Child Health* 48, 869–75.

Hudson, L.D., Nicholls, D.E., Lynn, R.M. & Viner, R.M. (2012) Medical instability and growth of children and adolescents with early onset eating disorders. *Archive of Disorders of Childhood* 97, 779–84.

Kalkwarf, H.J., Abrams, S.A., Dimeglio, L.A., Koo, W.W., Specker, B.L., & Weiler, H. (2014) Bone densitometry in infants and young children: the 2013 ISCD Pediatric Official Positions. *Journal of Clinical Densitometry* 17, 243–57.

Karthik, S.V., Campbell-Davidson, D., & Isherwood, D. (2006) Carotenemia in infancy and its association with prevalent feeding practices. *Pediatric Dermatology* 23, 571–73.

Lucarelli, L., Sechi, C., Cimino, S., & Chatoor, I. (2018) Avoidant/restrictive food intake disorder: a longitudinal study of malnutrition and psychopathological risk factors from 2 to 11 years of age. *Frontiers in Psychology* 9(1608), 1–12. https://doi.org/10.3389/fpsyg.2018.01608 accessed 12 July 2019.

Mehler, P.S. & Andersen, A.E. (eds) (2017) *Eating disorders: a guide to medical care and complications* (3rd ed.). Virginia, USA: John Hopkins University Press.

NICE Guidelines (2017) *Eating disorders: recognition and treatment.* www.nice.org.uk/guidance/ng69 recommendation 1. 10.15, accessed 12 July 2019.

Palmert, M.R. & Dunkel, L. (2012) Clinical practice. Delayed puberty. *New England Journal of Medicine* 366, 443–53.

Royal College of Psychiatrists (2012) *Junior MARSIPAN: Management of really sick patients under 18 with anorexia nervosa* [Online]. London, UK: Royal College of Psychiatrists Available:www.rcpsych.ac.uk/usefulresources/publications/collegereports/cr/cr168.asp Accessed 12 July 2019.

Sachs, K.V., Harnke, B., Mehler, P.S., & Krantz, M.J. (2016) Cardiovascular complications of anorexia nervosa: a systematic review. *International Journal of Eating Disorders* 49, 238–48.

Schorr, M., Drabkin, A., Rothman, M.S., Meenaghan, E., Lashen, G.T., Mascolo, M., Watters, A., Holmes, T.M., Santoso, K., Yu, E.W., Misra, M., Eddy, K.T., Klibanski, A., Mehler, P., & Miller, K.K. (2019) Bone mineral density and estimated hip strength in men with anorexia nervosa, atypical anorexia nervosa and avoidant/restrictive food intake disorder. *Clinical Endocrinology* 90(6), 789–97.

Stanhope, R. & Preece, M.A. (1988) Management of constitutional delay of growth and puberty. *Archives of Disorders of Childhood* 63, 1104–10.

Stoffman, N., Schwartz, B., Austin, S.B., Grace, E. & Gordon, C.M. (2005) Influence of bone density results on adolescents with anorexia nervosa. *International Journal of Eating Disorders* 37, 250–55.

Viner, R.M., White, B., Barrett, T., Candy, D.C., Gibson, P., Gregory, J.W., Matyka, K., Ong, K., Roche, E., Rudolf, M.C., Shaikh, G., Shield, J.P., & Wales, J.K. (2012) Assessment of childhood obesity in secondary care: OSCA consensus statement. *Archives of Disorders of Childhood Education & Practice* 97, 98–105.

Wei, C. & Crowne, E.C. (2016) Recent advances in the understanding and management of delayed puberty. *Archives of Disorders of Childhood* 101, 481–88.

Chapter 10

Assessment of sensory processing

Heather Scott and Karen Ray

Introduction

Eating is a complex developmental activity requiring a wide range of skills, which develop over several years in typically developing children, including motor, coordination, oral motor, cognitive, social communication, and sensory development. Eating and mealtimes happen within the context of particular social, physical, cultural, and sensory environments, and features of the environment will impact on the ability of the child to participate. Understanding the interface of the environment, the nature and demands of the relevant activity, and the child's skills, can lead to a better understanding of what is supporting or impeding participation (Law et al., 1996). To achieve successful participation in mealtimes and feeding there needs to be a good match between the child's abilities, the demands of the environment, and the activity (Law et al., 1996). For example, a child who is refusing to eat school dinner may be avoiding trying new foods, struggling with the smells and textures of the foods available, having difficulty coping with the noise and social demands of the environment, or experience a combination of these.

As avoidant restrictive food intake disorder (ARFID) is a relatively new diagnosis, there has so far been relatively little research regarding sensory sensitivities and ARFID. The majority of research into sensory processing difficulties that relates most closely to ARFID involves children who have been identified as "selective eaters" rather than those with a diagnosis of ARFID. Therefore, this terminology may be seen below in relation to specific research findings reported.

Development of sensory skills in the context of feeding and eating

Early feeding experiences are crucial in promoting exploration and acceptance of a variety of foods in terms of taste, texture, and appearance. Whilst we are born with the working mechanisms for taste and smell, it has been proposed that there are sensitive periods for exposure and therefore acceptance of new foods (Harris & Mason, 2017). Acceptance of new textures may be affected by refusal or reluctance to try unfamiliar foods, which is a common aspect of normal develop-ment in many young children. Acceptance of new textures may also be affected by the child's ability to manage chewing, with delayed oral motor skills likely to hamper this process. Those with hyper-sensitivity to sensory input are reported to have a stronger negative response to new foods with a greater disgust response and therefore less likely to accept a novel food (Harris & Mason, 2017).

Overview of sensory processing

Sensory processing is a term used to denote the ability to perceive, register, modu-late, integrate, and respond to sensory stimuli (Eeles et al., 2012; Schaaf & Lane, 2014). People have eight sensory systems: tactile (touch), gustatory (taste), olfac-tory (smell), vision (sight), auditory (hearing), vestibular (sense of movement and balance), proprioception (sense of body position in space), and interoception (the sense from inside our body including hunger and thirst). Sensory processing is part of typical development; we learn about the world and other people through sensory experiences. There is extensive evidence of the possible impact of sensory processing difficulties on every day activities including feeding (Nadon et al., 2011; Schaaf et al., 2011). Eating and mealtimes present a wide variety of sensory experiences, which vary depending on the activity and environmental demands (Little et al., 2016). Research involving children who are selective in relation to what they eat, primarily relates to difficulties with sensory modulation, which is one area of sensory processing difficulty and is discussed below.

Sensory modulation

Sensory modulation is the process by which the brain regulates and organises the sensory input that is constantly being received and produces an appropriate behav-ioural response. Difficulties with sensory modulation result from altered sensory thresholds in one or more sensory systems; what is seen is the behavioural response or self-regulation strategies, for example a child covering their ears in a noisy environment (Jorquera-Cabrera et al., 2017; Little et al., 2016). Low sen-sory thresholds lead to over- or hyper-sensitivity, so the child is constantly responding to a sensory input that typically would not be noticed. This activates the sympathetic nervous system, i.e. the "fight or flight" response (Schaaf & Lane, 2014). Over-sensitivity has been found to be associated with the presence of "picky" eating, difficulty managing oral hygiene, and increased parental stress (Cermak, Curtin & Bandini 2010). High sensory thresholds lead to under- or hypo-sensitivity, low registration of sensory input, and a delayed response. Chil-dren can be over- or under-sensitive to one or more sensory inputs, for example a child may be over-sensitive to noise and smell and be seen to avoid the school dinner hall, or a child who is over-sensitive to textures may avoid finger-feeding as their hands may get messy (tactile defensiveness).

Compensatory behaviours may be seen in a child who is attempting to self-regulate their arousal level, which may involve avoiding or seeking sensory input. For example, a child may refuse to sit next to other people who are eating to avoid smells from their food, or a child may fidget in their seat in an effort to gain more vestibular input.

Assessment of sensory modulation difficulties

Setting meaningful goals with the child or young person and their family is an important part of the assessment process and discussed further in Chapters 7 and 11. Goal setting helps to identify areas to assess, for example, the environments that the child is engaging in and who to gather additional information from, as well as allowing clear outcomes to be determined; see Chapter 3 for further information. Given the wide impact of sensory issues on everyday life it is likely that other areas of difficulty may arise; if they are outside the remit of the relevant service the child may need a referral or signposting onwards.

Approaches to assessment of sensory modulation difficulties

There is a wide range of views regarding the most effective way to assess sensory difficulties. Although there is no single tool, there is general agreement that a combined approach using a variety of methods is most helpful (Schaaf & Lane, 2014). Ideally this includes using information from parent and/or child interview, standardised questionnaires, direct observation, and gathering background information (Dugas et al., 2018; Eeles et al., 2012; Jorquera-Cabrera et al., 2017). In clinical practice, assessment of sensory modulation is usually based on observation or report of behavioural responses. These are then interpreted as being due to a high or low neurological threshold rather than this being confirmed through objective measures of the sympathetic nervous system, such as measuring cortisol levels (Burns et al., 2017). Interpreting and understanding reasons for, and what is maintaining, behaviours is essential as there can be a variety of causes, which is likely to impact on which interventions might be most effective (Burns et al., 2017). For example, a child may seek out movement due to a high-level threshold for vestibular and proprioceptive input, the behaviour may be maintained for a sensory reason, and/or because it leads to them getting removed from a situation. In general, it is recommended that sensory assessment is included as part of a wider multi-disciplinary approach to assessment, to ensure any issues identified are viewed in the context of other difficulties and factors. Different components of suggested sensory assessment are set out below.

Case history/information gathering

Chapter 7 includes discussion about information gathering during assessment for ARFID. Ensuring that there are prompts to highlight if further assessment around sensory difficulties is needed is an important aspect of this process. Obtaining information from the parent, child, and others involved, such as school staff, can provide much useful information and highlight potential sensory difficulties, in the context of the child and families' routines and environments (Eeles et al., 2012; Schaaf et al., 2011). Children often present differently in different settings, with a variety of possible reasons for this, including different sensory demands, variation in routines and any supports that may be in place (Fernández-Andrés et al., 2018).

Identification of clusters of behaviours relating to sensory thresholds can help to build a picture of the child's "sensory profile". For example, if a child dislikes touching certain foods, then it can be useful to explore if tactile over-sensitivity is also impacting on other activities, such as avoiding painting or struggling with hair washing.

When possible, it is useful to speak to the child or young person about their experiences of feeding and eating and the impact of any sensory difficulties they may have noticed. Use of visual aids, or other media such as videos, may support the child in talking about their daily activities and understanding their senses. Children and parents may find the use of an analogy, such as a "cup" (the cup being too small if someone is over-sensitive and too big if they are under-sensitive) helpful when thinking about sensory thresholds and how these impact on daily life.

Observation

Chapter 7 outlines the importance of observing a mealtime from an interactional perspective; it can also be important for observing and assessing sensory difficulties (Nadon et al., 2011). Observation in the child's everyday context can be particularly helpful (Zobel-Lachiusa et al., 2015) and allows observation of the activity and environment to understand issues arising. For example, a child may be unable to cope with the level of noise in a canteen, which may be exacerbated by them sitting next to where the trays are emptied. Table 10.1 provides some examples of behaviours that may be seen, which reflect possible sensory modulation difficulties. Behaviours should be interpreted and understood alongside other information, as different modulation difficulties may lead to the same behaviour, and there may be other reasons for behaviour not related to a sensory difficulty. For example, rocking behaviour could be the child seeking out sensory input for self-stimulation or it could be a self-soothing strategy due to the child being over-stimulated from too much noise (Burns et al., 2017).

Observation through use of video can also be helpful as it removes the impact of an observer, can reduce time needed and can allow observation across time and environments (Twachtman-Reily, Amaral & Zebrowski, 2008). Video can also be useful to observe more subtle signs and enable viewing and discussion together with clinical colleagues or parents. Some issues may be

Table 10.1 Examples of behaviours that reflect possible sensory modulation difficulties

Sense	Under-sensitive	Over-sensitive
Auditory	Unaware of noise, not responding to requests. Makes or seeks out noises	Putting hands over ears to block out noise, distracted by noises around them, including background noise. Fidgets or struggles to focus in, or leaves/avoids noisy environments. Makes noise, e.g. hums to drown out noises in the environment
Visual	Unaware of important cues in the environment. May seek out visual stimulus, e.g. make foods or utensils spin	Squinting/covering eyes in response to light. Distracted by moving objects or people, e.g. light coming in through blinds. May lead to higher levels of rigidity, e.g. prefer foods to be bland colours, get upset if food has a slight visual change
Gustatory	Prefers strong flavours, wants more seasoning/sauces, licks or tastes non-edible objects	Prefers bland foods, avoids trying new foods, may notice the taste of other foods that have touched the food they eat, e.g. if prepare food with a utensil used for something else
Olfactory	Smells foods, prefers foods with strong smells and may smells other things in the environment including people. Or may not notice smells, e.g. may not notice strong smells that others are bothered by	Smells foods and may refuse to eat food after smelling them. May gag or vomit at strong smells or leave environment. May notice smells that others are unaware of, e.g. smell that from a food that was on a utensil even after it has been washed
Tactile	Touches, fiddles and plays with objects, food and or saliva. May over stuff mouth or mouth non-food objects. Unaware of food around mouth/hands or touch from other people	Avoids touching food or certain textures of foods, may avoid feeding themselves to avoid getting hands and or face messy. May avoid or dislike engaging with meal preparation and other self-care activities, e.g. tooth brushing
Vestibular	Moves and fidgets a lot, struggles to stay seated for the mealtime or lean onto other people and the table. May seek out movement, e.g. prefer sitting on a chair that swivels	May be fearful when not well supported when sitting especially with feet not on the floor, e.g. dislike sitting on a stool or may prefer to be held. May struggle when lifted and moved and avoid playground equipment like swings

(Continued)

Table 10.1 (Cont.)

Sense	Under-sensitive	Over-sensitive
Proprioception	Poor coordination, may move head towards the food rather than bringing the food to their mouth. May lean onto or bump into other people or push against the table. May over stuff mouth, prefer crunchy foods or mouth non-food objects	Poor coordination, lack of grading with movements, dislike of crowds or sitting too close to people
Interoception	May not notice if they are hungry or thirsty or may keep eating and not notice they are full	May be overly aware of feeling from inside, may find this confusing and not know whether they are feeling, hungry or thirsty or anxious

difficult to see, for example smells, or what is happening outside the view of the video such as other children playing and distracting the child being assessed.

Proxy and self-questionnaires

There are various questionnaires available that can be used to assess sensory modulation difficulties, with several papers comparing the various sensory assessment tools (Burns et al., 2017; Dugas et al., 2018; Eeles et al., 2012; Jorquera-Cabrera et al., 2017). It is recommended that assessment questionnaires are used as part of the assessment process, alongside other information gathered and observations made (Dugas et al., 2018). Questionnaires can provide an overview of behaviours across time and contexts, presenting a wider view than an observation alone. They also allow information to be gathered from parents, caregivers, and school staff relatively easily (Schaaf & Lane, 2014). Self-report questionnaires can be helpful to use with young people, but may not be feasible, for example due to cognitive and communication difficulties. Interpretation of questionnaire scores requires a clinician with understanding of sensory processing and the impact on participation, and an ability to consider other factors that may be contributing to the presenting behaviours (Farrow & Coulthard, 2012).

Table 10.2 sets out information on a number of self- or proxy sensory questionnaires. The Sensory Profile-2 (Dunn, 2014) and Sensory Processing Measure (Parkham, 2007) are two of the most commonly used assessments. The Sensory Processing Measure has more questions on oral sensitivities, but neither this nor the Sensory Profile provides detailed information around oral

Table 10.2 Summary of self/proxy sensory questionnaires

Assessment name	Age range	Overview
Child Sensory Profile	3–14 years	The Sensory Profile (version 2) assesses areas of auditory, visuals, tactile, vestibular, and oral-sensory processing. Quadrant scores (sensory seeking, sensory sensitive, sensation avoiding, or low registration) are also identified. These quadrants are based on neurological thresholds (oversensitivity or lack of responsivity) and behavioural responses (passive or active self- regulation behaviours) (Dunn, 2014).
Short Sensory Profile	3–14 years	38 item caregiver questionnaire
Infant Sensory Profile	0–6 months	
Toddler Sensory profile	7–35 months	
Adolescent Sensory Profile	11 years +	Can be completed by self-proxy
Sensory Profile School Comparisons	3–14	
Sensory Processing Measure (SPM)	5–12 years	The SPM assesses social participation, vision, hearing, touch, body awareness, balance and motion, planning and ideas as well as providing a total sensory system score, which also includes scores from taste and smell. Scores are classified into typical, some problems or definite dysfunction. Includes home, school, classroom forms (Parkham, 2007).
SPM pre-school	2-5years	Care giver and school questionnaire
Sensory Rating Scale (SRS)	0–36 months	SRS identifies sensory responsivity across touch, movement, hearing, vision, smell, tactile as well as questions on general temperament (Provost & Oetter, 1994). The questions are available in the referenced article.
Sensory Eating Problems Scale (SEPS)	Children in the study were 24 months +	SEPS identifies sensory issues related to feeding: food touch aversion, gagging, single food focus, temperature sensitivity, expulsion and overstuffing (Seiverling et al., 2019). The questions are in the referenced article.

sensory issues or interoception. The Sensory Eating Problems Scale was developed to gain more specific information around sensory issues relating to feeding and the questions can be accessed in the article referenced (Seiverling et al., 2019). This scale might be a useful way to screen for sensory difficulties, but it does not include questions about sensory issues in the environment that may be impacting on mealtimes. The Sensory Rating Scale has had less rigorous evaluation than The Sensory Profile and Sensory Processing Measure but a version can be accessed in the article referenced (Provost & Oetter, 1994).

Food diaries

Some of the benefits of using food diaries have been highlighted in Chapter 8 in relation to nutrition. Food diaries can be structured to provide additional information about eating environments, whether the child is being fed or is self-feeding, and help to explore sensory preferences including those related to texture, consistency, taste, smell, and temperature. For example, a child who is over-sensitive to a certain texture may avoid mixed textures or a child who is over-sensitive to noise may eat less when in a noisy environment.

Children at risk of developing sensory processing difficulties

Research has identified that children with some conditions are more likely to have difficulties with sensory modulation which impact on feeding; understanding which groups are at elevated risk can support early assessment and intervention.

Children presenting with autism spectrum disorder

Up to 90% of children with autism spectrum disorder have been found to have sensory difficulties, with under-sensitivity being most common (Cermak, Curtin, & Bandini, 2010; Schaaf et al., 2011). Other estimates include between 46 to 89% of children with autism presenting with feeding difficulties (Johnson et al., 2014). Definite differences on the Sensory Profile in the areas of taste/smell sensitivity, auditory filtering, and visual/auditory sensitivity can indicate a high risk of developing feeding difficulties in children with autism (Nadon et al., 2011). Food texture is noted by several authors investigating children with autism, to be one of the main factors affecting food selectivity along with appearance, brand, taste, smell, and temperature (Cermak, Curtin, & Bandini, 2010; Nadon et al., 2011).

Children with autism often struggle with many aspects of feeding and mealtimes, so it is important to understand sensory issues alongside any other issues present, for example, understanding appropriate social behaviour so that appropriate interventions are identified (Johnson et al., 2014).

Children with intellectual disability

Children with intellectual disability are more likely than typically developing children to have problems with sensory processing (Engel-Yeger, Hardal-Nasser, & Gal, 2016). Although children with more severe levels of intellectual disability tend to present with greater sensory processing problems overall, children with milder levels have been found to be more likely to present with over-sensitivity in taste and smell, which in one study significantly predicted food selectivity and food refusal (Engel-Yeger, Hardal-Nasser, & Gal, 2016).

When considering sensory difficulties in children with Down syndrome, research has identified higher levels of difficulties with low energy and weakness (likely due to low muscle tone), auditory processing, under-sensitivity and sensory seeking (Bruni et al., 2010; Will et al., 2019). Interestingly, Bruni and colleagues found that over half the children included in their study scored within the typical range for tactile, taste, and smell sensitivity (Bruni et al., 2010). This lends support to the importance of assessing oral motor skills, whether children have enough postural support when sitting, and whether there is sufficient sensory feedback to enable effective feeding, for example, whether foods are giving enough flavour and proprioceptive feedback for the child to register them in their mouth.

Children born prematurely

Children who are born prematurely and have spent time within neonatal intensive care units have been found to be at greater risk of developing sensory sensitivities, particularly tactile sensitivity (Crozier et al., 2016) and are more likely to experience difficulties transitioning to solid foods (Sanchez et al., 2016). Proposed reasons for higher risks of sensory difficulties in these children relate to the impact of brain damage and altered sensory experiences from the hospital environment, for example, bright lighting and increased tactile and oral stimulation from use of ventilation equipment.

Children with long-term medical conditions

It is useful to consider for any child who has a condition that has required lengthy hospital stays, surgery, or periods where they are not fed by mouth, how this interrupted period of development may have affected progression of feeding, particularly thinking about altered sensory experiences and social opportunities for feeding (Borowitz & Borowitz, 2018). For example, children with cardiorespiratory issues have been found to have definite differences in taste and smell on the Short Sensory Profile, which may contribute to limited food preferences (Davis et al., 2013). It has been found that children hospital-ised and introduced to textures later than usual are less likely to accept textures later in childhood. If weaning occurs after the first year children may be more prone to oral defensiveness, may refuse anything other than smooth textures, and may be more likely to gag and vomit (Greville-Harris & Coulthard, 2016).

From assessment to intervention planning

A number of interventions for children presenting with ARFID are covered in chapters 14–17. Although there is extensive evidence of the potential impact of sensory modulation difficulties, evidence supporting the use of sensory interven-tions for children who are selective with what they will eat is limited. There is some evidence for the use of sensory interventions (including those involving alterations to the child's environment) supporting improvements in behaviour or attention more generally, which maybe applicable to mealtimes (Watling & Hauer, 2015). Despite sensory strategies having only a limited evidence base they are often used in practice; for example, one study has highlighted that par-ents often use sensory-based interventions such as use of calming sensory input, and identifying quieter environments, to support participation in daily activities, including mealtimes, alongside other strategies (Schaaf et al., 2011).

The Sequential Oral Sensory approach is a transdisciplinary approach based on systematic desensitisation, to promote engagement with food from visual tolerance to eating (Toomey & Ross, 2011). Sensory components of foods are considered and grading can be used within "steps to eating" and "food chain-ing", for example to facilitate moving from a dry to wetter texture.

Several authors recommend multi-disciplinary approaches, which include addressing sensory issues through parent training, use of coaching, sensory strategies, social and sensory stories (Cermak, Curtin, & Bandini, 2010; Zobel-Lachiusa et al., 2015). Given the correlations between sensory over- and under-sensitivity, anxiety, intolerance of uncertainly with restrictive repetitive behaviours and selective eating (Schaaf & Lane, 2014; Wigham et al., 2014), it can be useful to consider interventions that address both anxiety and difficul-ties with sensory processing. For example, supporting children and young people to develop their ability to understand and develop their own strategies to facilitate improved sensory and emotional regulation (Edgington, Hill, & Pellicano, 2016; Zucker et al., 2019).

It may be helpful to consider service provision models that have the poten-tial to reach a wider number of children (see also Chapter 17). For example, a tiered approach to service delivery, involving interventions at a universal level (open to all, for example training to school staff), targeted interventions (open to those at risk or with some difficulties, for example parent workshops), and specialist interventions (for example, one-to-one support). The "sensory snack time", introduced in a special school, is an example of a whole class approach utilising principles from a Sequential Oral Sensory approach, including play, sensory strategies and systematic desensitisation, involving training to support implementation by school staff (Galpin, Osman, & Paramore, 2018). The introduction of "sensory snack time" was found to be associated with a reduction in mealtime behaviour problems and an increase in variety of food eaten (Galpin, Osman, & Paramore, 2018).

Further research is needed in terms of specific treatment approaches, including sensory interventions, which may support children with sensory difficulties leading to avoidance and restriction of food intake.

Summary points

* Feeding is a complex developmental skill; assessment of sensory difficulties is best included as part of a wider multi-disciplinary assessment and understood in the context of other aspects of the child's presentation
* Sensory modulation difficulties have been found to often correlate with selectivity with eating
* A wide range of children, including children with and without other concurrent diagnoses, are at risk of having sensory processing difficulties which may affect feeding and eating
* A range of methods, including observation, should be utilised to assess difficulties with sensory modulation
* Sensory assessment questionnaires can be useful but scores should be interpreted using other sources of information and not used in isolation
* The child's behaviour may be impacted on by the demands of different environments and this needs to be considered when assessing and identifying appropriate intervention
* There is some evidence supporting the use of sensory based intervention approaches alongside behavioural strategies, but there is limited evidence for sensory interventions in children with ARFID

References

Borowitz, K.C. & Borowitz, S.M. (2018) Feeding problems in infants and children: Assessment and etiology. *Pediatric Clinics of North America* 65 59–72.

Bruni, M., Cameron, D., Dua, S., & Noy, S. (2010) Reported sensory processing of children with Down syndrome. *Physical and Occupational Therapy in Paediatrics* 30 (4) 280–93.

Burns, C., Dixon, D., Novack, M., & Granpeesheh, D. (2017) A systematic review of assessments for sensory processing abnormalities in autism spectrum disorder. *Review Journal of Autism and Developmental Disorders* 4 (3) 209–24.

Cermak, S.A., Curtin, C., & Bandini, L.G. (2010) Food selectivity and sensory sensitivity in children with autism spectrum disorders. *Journal of the American Dietetic Association* 110 (20) 238–46.

Crozier, S.C., Goodson, J.Z., Mackay, M.L., Synnes, A.R., Grunau, R.E., Miller, S.P., & Zwicker, J.G. (2016) Sensory processing patterns in children born very preterm. *American Journal of Occupational Therapy* 70 (1) 1–7.

Davis, A., Bruce, A., Khasawneh, R., Schulz, T., Fox, C., & Dunn, W. (2013) Sensory processing issues in young children presenting to an outpatient feeding clinic: A retrospective chart review. *Journal of Pediatric Gastroenterology and Nutrition* 56 (2) 156–60.

Dugas, C., Simard, M., Fombonne, E. & Couture, M. (2018) Comparison of two tools to assess sensory features in children with autism spectrum disorder. *American Journal of Occupational Therapy* 72 (1) 1–9.

Dunn, W. (2014). *Sensory profile 2.* Bloomington, MN: Psych Corp.

Edgington, L., Hill, V., & Pellicano, E. (2016) The design and implementation of a CBT-based intervention for sensory processing difficulties in adolescents on the autism spectrum. *Research in Developmental Disabilities* 59 221–33.

Eeles, A., Spittle, A., Anderson, P., Brown, N., Lee, K., Boyd, R., & Doyle, L. (2012) Assessments of sensory processing in infants: A systematic review. *Developmental Medicine & Child Neurology* 55 (4) 314–26.

Engel-Yeger, B., Hardal-Nasser, R., & Gal, E. (2016) The relationship between sensory processing disorders and eating problems among children with intellectual developmental deficits. *British Journal of Occupational Therapy* 79 (1) 17–25.

Farrow C. & Coulthard H. (2012) Relationship between sensory sensitivity, anxiety and selective eating in children. *Appetite* 58 (3) 842–46.

Fernández-Andrés, M., Sanz-Cerverza, P., Salgado-Burgos, C., Tárraga-Mínguez, R., & Pastor-Cerezuela, G. (2018) Comparative study of sensory modulation vulnerabilities in children with and without ASD in family and school contexts. *Journal of Occupational Therapy, Schools, & Early Intervention* 11 (3) 318–28.

Galpin, J., Osman, L., & Paramore, C. (2018) Sensory snack time: A school-based intervention addressing food selectivity in autistic children. *Frontiers in Education* 3 (77) doi:10.3389/feduc.2018.00077 accessed 14 July 2019.

Greville-Harris, G., & Coulthard, H. (2016) Early eating behaviours and food acceptance revisited: Breastfeeding and introduction of complementary foods as predictive of food acceptance. *Current Obesity Reports* 5 (1) 113–20.

Harris, G. & Mason, S. (2017) Are there sensitive periods for food acceptance in infancy?. *Current Nutrition Reports* 6 (2) 190–96.

Johnson, C. Turner, K., Stewart, P., Schmidt, B., Shui, A., Macklin, E., Reynolds, A., James, J., Johnson, S., Courtney, P., & Hayman, S. (2014) Relationships between feeding problems, behavioral characteristics and nutritional quality in children with ASD. *Journal of Autism and Developmental Disorders* 44 2175–84.

Jorquera-Cabrera, S., Romero-Ayuso, D., Rodriguez-Gil, G. & Triviño-Juárez, J. (2017) Assessment of sensory processing characteristics in children between 3 and 11 years old: A systematic review. *Frontiers in Pediatrics* 5 (57) doi:10.3389/fped.2017.00057 accessed 14 July 2019.

Law, M., Cooper, B., Strong, S., Stewart, D., Rigby, P., & Letts, L. (1996) The person-environment-occupation model: A transactive approach to occupational performance. *Canadian Journal of Occupational Therapy* 63 (1) 9–23.

Little L., Dean, F., Tomchek, S., & Dunn, W. (2016) Classifying sensory profiles of children in the general population. *Child Care Health and Development* 43 (1) 81–88.

Nadon G., Feldman, D., Dunn, W., & Gisel, E. (2011) Association of sensory processing and eating problems in children with autism spectrum disorders. *Autism Research and Treatment* 1–8. doi:10.1155/2011/541926 accessed 14 July 2019.

Parkham, L. (2007). *SPM Sensory Processing Measure.* Los Angeles, Calif.: Western Psychological Services.

Provost, B. & Oetter, P. (1994) The sensory rating scale for infants and young children. *Physical & Occupational Therapy in Pediatrics* 13 (4) 15–35.

Sanchez, K., Spittle, A., Slattery, J., & Morgan, A. (2016) Oromotor feeding in children born before 30 weeks gestation and term-born peers at 12 months corrected age. *Journal of Pediatrics* 178 113–18.

Schaaf, R. & Lane, A. (2014) Toward a best-practice protocol for assessment of sensory features in ASD. *Journal of Autism and Developmental Disorders* 45 (5) 1380–95.

Schaaf, R., Toth-Cohen, S., Johnson, S., Outten, G., & Benevides, T. (2011) The everyday routines of families of children with autism. *Autism* 15 (3) 373–89.

Seiverling, L., Williams, K., Hendy, H., Adams, W., Yusupova, S. & Kaczor, A. (2019) Sensory Eating Problems Scale (SEPS) for children: psychometrics and associations with mealtime problems behaviors. *Appetite* 133 223–30.

Toomey, K. & Ross, E. (2011) SOS approach to feeding. *Perspectives on swallowing and swallowing disorders (Dysphagia)* 20 (3) 82.

Twachtman-Reily, J., Amaral, S., & Zebrowski, P. (2008) Addressing feeding disorders in children on the autism spectrum in school based settings: Physiological and behavioural issues. *American Speech-Language-hearing Association* 39 261–72.

Watling, R. & Hauer, S. (2015) Effectiveness of Ayres sensory integration and sensory-based interventions for people with autism spectrum disorder: A systematic review. *American Journal of Occupational Therapy* 69 (5) 1–8.

Wigham, S., Rodgers, J., South, M., McConachie, H. & Freeston, M. (2014) The interplay between sensory processing abnormalities, intolerance of uncertainty, anxiety and restricted and repetitive behaviours in autism spectrum disorder. *Journal of Autism and Developmental Disorders* 45 (4) 943–52.

Will, E., Daunhauer, L., Fidler, D., Raitano Lee, N., Rosenberg, C., & Hepburn, S. (2019) Sensory processing and maladaptive behavior: Profiles within the Down syndrome phenotype. *Physical & Occupational Therapy In Pediatrics* 1–16. doi:10.1080/01942638.2019.1575320 accessed 14 July 2019.

Zobel-Lachiusa J., Andrianopoulos M., Mailloux Z. & Cermak S. (2015) Sensory differences and mealtime behavior in children with autism. *American Journal of Occupational Therapy* 69 (5) 1–8. doi:10.5014/ajot.2016.70S1-RP401C accessed 14 July 2019.

Zucker, N., LaVia, M., Craske, M., Foukal, M., Harris, A., Datta, N., Savereide, E. & Maslow, G. (2019) Feeling and body investigators (FBI): ARFID division—an acceptance based interoceptive exposure treatment for children with ARFID. *International Journal of Eating Disorders* 52 (4) 466–72.

Part IV

Management

Chapter 11

Overview of treatment and management

Rachel Bryant-Waugh

Introduction

As avoidant restrictive food intake disorder (ARFID) is a relatively new diagnostic category, there is still a long way to go in determining the most effective treatments. It has been suggested that, at present, it is not possible to reliably recommend specific treatments for ARFID, as the required treatment trials that would usually guide evidence-based practice have not yet taken place (Hay et al., 2014). A number of psychological interventions for ARFID are currently under development, which include modifications of family based approaches as well as cognitive behavioural interventions (see Chapters 14 and 15). These "new" interventions are predominantly based on existing therapies for other eating disorders, and to some extent on those for other psychiatric disorders (Mammel & Ornstein, 2017). In due course, these ARFID interventions will require rigorous testing, ideally in the form of randomised controlled trials, to be able to determine their effectiveness.

Whilst the development of novel, ARFID-specific interventions is undoubtedly an important focus of attention, there are two important things to bear in mind when considering optimal approaches to management. First, research evidence from treatment trials represents only one aspect of evidence-based practice; the other two components, patient values and clinical expertise, have been recommended to be given equal weight in decision-making about treatment for any one individual (Sackett et al., 2002). Second, although the term ARFID may be relatively new, the difficulties included in this diagnostic category, are not new. Much can be learned, perhaps in particular from the fields that overlap with ARFID, such as paediatric feeding problems, anxiety disorders, and neurodevelopmental disorders. It seems important to encourage both clinicians and researchers to be open to existing knowledge and expertise, and to formally test well-established approaches with people now diagnosed as having ARFID. This might apply particularly to those for whom ARFID may be a new and somewhat unfamiliar presentation, as is the case for many clinicians working in the eating disorders field. As has been pointed out, we should not forget that we previously had a range of treatment approaches that worked well with children with feeding and eating difficulties when their problems were called something else (Waller, 2019). The debate whether ARFID is a "feeding disorder" or an "eating disorder" seems particularly unhelpful in this respect. Kennedy and colleagues rightly comment that until now, ARFID has primarily been studied within the context of eating disorders, despite its roots being in feeding disorders (Kennedy, Wick, & Keel, 2018; see also Chapter 4). It would seem most helpful to view ARFID as one of the feeding and eating disorders, all of which share a disturbance in eating behaviour with related negative consequences for health, development and general functioning. Compartmentalising into disorder specific "territories" and adopting a silo-like approach, with associated limited horizons, do not appear likely to be in patients' bests interests overall.

This aim of this chapter is to offer an overview of recommended treatment and management approaches for children with ARFID. It starts out by setting down a few basic principles that can be helpful to consider as the starting points for treatment or as the basic building blocks of a comprehensive approach to management. This is followed by a description of the different components of treatment that might be indicated. Given the heterogeneity of ARFID presentations, a modular approach is often recommended. This means that an individualised approach to determining an appropriate treatment package is required, which is ideally based on levels of risk and individual circumstances. The subsequent sections set out how this decision-making process might be achieved, providing guidance on useful steps to take and the rationale for these. The chapter closes with thoughts and suggestions about possible areas to develop in the future, to facilitate collective attempts to improve treatment efforts for all children and families affected by ARFID.

Basic principles of treatment and management

As reflected in the range of chapters included in this book, ARFID is generally considered to require a multi-disciplinary approach to assessment, and, in children, in the majority of cases also to treatment (Herpertz-Dahlmann, 2017). As ARFID straddles physical and psychological spheres of functioning and wellbeing, the input of clinicians trained in physical health care, as well as those trained in mental health care is required. The majority of children should be able to be successfully managed on an out-patient basis, with appropriate attention and support in relation to addressing the avoidant or restrictive eating behaviour, nutritional intake, and any medical consequences of an inadequate diet. However, some children may present with high levels of risk, or require extra support for a range of reasons; this can raise the possibility that more intensive treatment may be required. Depending on the nature and level of risk, such children may be treated as day-patients or as in-patients, in medical or in mental health settings (Miller & Bravender, 2018). Irrespective of the professional disciplines of the treating team and the intensity of service delivery, any intervention for ARFID in children should be family-focussed and developmentally appropriate (Mairs & Nicholls,

2016). In addition, a number of key features are recommended to be included in any treatment approach. These are discussed below.

Attending to motivation

It seems obvious to state that the child's own experience of their situation is important to assess and understand, yet this may often not take place, or, if it does, the child's perspective may be ignored or overridden. The same applies to ensuring that parents' and carers' experience is assessed and understood, and subsequently considered in the early stages of treatment planning. The main reason for this is that most psychological interventions require the active engagement and participation of those involved. If behaviour is to be changed (which in ARFID might include, eating behaviour, choice of foods, mealtime interactions, parenting behaviour, and much more), the presence of some level of wish to work on effecting change is very important.

Human behaviour is, to a large extent, functional; we do things that make sense to us and to try to steer what we consider to be a manageable way through life. We are hard-wired in terms of self-preservation and most people's behaviour serves to limit threat, discomfort, distress and danger. When our experience is intensely negative, we tend to respond with classic "fight or flight" responses, typically manifested as refusal or avoidance behaviours. These responses, which mirror what can happen in ARFID in terms of active refusal to eat certain foods or steadfast avoidance of others, make sense to the individual, even though they may be considered "dysfunctional". Attempts to change such responses without addressing the factors fuelling this need to fight or flee, typically lead to increased refusal or avoidance, as the individual strives to protect themselves from harm.

In this way, it is very important to establish the presence of a degree of motivation to work on effecting change at the start of treatment. In children with ARFID, this will require the clinician to consider this, both from the child's perspective as well as the perspectives of parents and other carers closely involved with the child. In very young children, parental motivation is key, but as children develop their own thoughts, beliefs and emotional experience and expression, their level of wish or willingness to try to change things is equally as important to establish. Clinical experience suggests that when motivation seems absent in children between the ages of around three to seven years, it can be particularly challenging to effect change. This is likely to be the result of younger children's behaviour being more malleable through parental intervention, and older children becoming more self- and socially aware. This can open chinks of possibility for enhancing motivation to work on their eating. Zucker and colleagues have described a novel intervention for ARFID, which explicitly sets out to make the process fun in order to motivate and engage children in this age-range (Zucker et al., 2019).

The questions below represent useful areas to explore individually with the child and the parents to determine motivation, and to highlight areas that might need some attention:

- Do you want to make changes and if so what do you want to change?
- Are you ready to make changes (is this the right time)?
- Do you think you are able to make the changes needed?
- What do you think the main barriers to making changes will be?
- What do you think the main advantages of making changes will be?
- What do you think the main disadvantages of making changes will be?

Establishing expectations and agreeing goals

Equally important to establish at the outset, are the nature of everyone's expectations, the proposed purpose of the treatment, and how and when everyone will know whether this has been achieved. Thwarted expectations and lack of focus are likely to result in dissatisfaction, disengagement and ultimately act against the best interests of the child. The most successful treatment for ARFID occurs when there is active participation, so that if there is an expectation that clinicians will somehow remove difficulties or "'cure" problems, outcomes may be compromised. Spending time establishing what everyone's expectations are at the start of treatment is usually time well spent. Discovering that there may be very different levels of expectation early on, allows this to be discussed so that as far as possible everyone is clear about the aims and objectives of the treatment. Parents will typically have longer-term aspirations about management; some will be hoping to "fix" their child, whereas others may be hoping to achieve a relatively small step forward that nevertheless reduces the burden of ARFID on the child and family. Some parents may hold a belief that over time the child will make improvements, whereas others may be feeling resigned and hopeless. Emphasising the importance of each individual's personal role in achieving the changes that are agreed is important. These roles may differ, depending on individual circumstances, between different members of one family, as well as across different families. With clearly defined roles, to include the roles of any clinicians involved, expectations become clearer.

Early goal setting is an important part of this process of starting out on the most helpful foot. This may require some discussion, as initially, not everyone may agree about the priorities. For example, a parent may be keen to work on increasing their child's willingness to try new foods, whereas the clinician may be more concerned about their weight and growth, considering the nutritional value of the diet adequate for the time being. In this example, the child may not be expressing any clear wish to be able to try new foods or to gain weight or grow, but may be beginning to notice that other children are commenting on them having "baby food" in their school lunchbox. Each party has a perfectly valid priority and understandable concern, and the clinician will need to work out how best to combine these to arrive at a focus that everyone feels ready to work on. Here, it might be that instead of taking in a pouch of pureed fruit marketed as an infant food, which the child has had at lunchtime since infancy, they work at altering their routine by taking in another more age-appropriate food of higher energy value that they already accept. The pouch could still be enjoyed when at home, whilst the new lunchtime food represents additional calories to the diet. The parents' wish to address willingness to try something different has been started with making a change to the routine in the first instance. This might then be built upon by increasing the child's confidence in being able to do things differently, eventually moving to trying new foods. This is a small example, and there are many other possible scenarios; the most important messages here being that the clinician should anticipate that initial goals are likely to differ and be willing to take all into account in agreeing specific goals to work on. Goals need to make sense to people in order to maintain motivation to work on them.

The other key component of clarity of purpose is being able to have a discussion about when everyone will know whether goals have been met, and if they have not, what will be done about it. Many clinicians are familiar with the concept of SMART goals; goals that should be Specific, Measureable, Attainable, Relevant, and Time-limited. This framework can be very useful when approaching treatment for ARFID. Some parents may come with a wish that treatment will result in their child "eating normally", however long that takes. Clinical experience suggests that an initial focus on risk reduction and achieving even small changes, followed by a period of consolidation and confidence development, can be beneficial. Sometimes the time is not right, or prolonged treatment results in waning enthusiasm and increasing resistance. Sometimes expectations are set too high, or aims are too general, such as aiming "to enjoy food". Treatment course and outcome is likely to be compromised under such circumstances. Of course at times, even with well-defined, agreed upon SMART goals, the outcome of an intervention does not produce the desired result. If risk is not high, it may be most appropriate to have a break in treatment. If risk is high, more intensive treatment may be indicated.

Collaboration and teamwork

When working with children and families affected by ARFID, it is suggested that clinicians adopt a collaborative stance, preferably positioning themselves as part of a team together with the child and family. In this context, a collaborative stance involves taking time to listen, understand, and talk things through when potentially problematic differences of perspective and opinion are apparent. It can be helpful to overtly frame tackling the eating difficulties as a collective task. As long as expectations and goals have been worked through as suggested above, and individual roles of all those involved in treatment clearly identified, this emphasis on treatment as a collaborative, collective endeavour seems entirely logical.

As mentioned earlier, in the case of children, there will most likely be more than one clinician involved in the management of ARFID. Teamwork therefore frequently involves extending this collaborative stance to other colleagues directly involved in the child's care as well as working collaboratively with the family. Most clinicians will be familiar with situations involving differences of professional opinion, and in relation to ARFID, these may certainly arise. To some extent, this is unsurprising, given the relatively limited body of evidence relating to virtually all aspects of ARFID as well as often limited clinical experience in this field. As with differences of perspective and opinion that are potentially problematic encountered in discussion with family members, such differences are most helpfully addressed in the same way with colleagues. Taking time to listen, trying to understand, and talking things through, are usually more constructive ways of arriving at decisions in the best interests of the child than becoming exasperated with colleagues and ending up giving mixed messages to the family.

Beyond the treatment team, there will be others involved in the child's care and in their day-to-day life. This is addressed further in Chapter 17, where more detailed discussion is set out about working with staff in educational settings and other agencies or bodies that may be involved with the child. In the same way that collaboration and teamwork can help efforts to manage and treat the child with ARFID to progress more smoothly, taking the trouble to apply these aspects of care more broadly, is usually most helpful for the child. For example, it may be considered that a particular child should be allowed to take chocolate into school to eat during the day as this is one of the few foods they will eat, and maintaining school attendance has been agreed as important. Staff at the school may refuse to allow this as it contravenes their healthy eating policy. It is not difficult to imagine that such a situation can easily result in stalemate. Talking with a responsible staff member at the school, acknowledging the importance of school policies as well as the child's continued attendance, exploring opportunities to facilitate different arrangements on a temporary basis whilst the child's difficulties are being worked on in outpatient treatment, and being clear about the rationale for every decision in relation to the best interests of the child, could assist greatly. Here again, clarity around expectations, goals, and roles, combined with respectful communication and a willingness to take all aspects of a situation into account, are recommended as important components of any management approach. This applies when working with the family, when working with colleagues, and when working with others involved in the child's everyday life.

Optimising effectiveness and efficiency

Lastly, in relation to basic principles of treatment and management, the responsibility of clinicians to work as effectively and efficiently as possible warrants some discussion. Working effectively means that the treatment approaches being offered are actually making a positive difference, whereas working efficiently means that effort is not duplicated, placing undue burden on children and families, or carrying on longer than is needed, in some cases unintentionally perpetuating difficulties. Perhaps one of the best ways to keep track of these aspects of care is to engage in regular monitoring of progress and outcomes.

The UK-based Child Outcomes Research Consortium (CORC) has produced some helpful guidance on recommended approaches to tracking experience and outcomes (Law & Wolpert, 2014). Six main questions are proposed as follows: What is the problem?; What do you want to change?; How are we getting on together?; How are things going?; Have we done as much as we can or need to do?; How has this experience been for you? (ibid. p. 22). The first two questions form part of the process of assessment and deciding what to address in treatment. Measures that can be helpful in capturing specific features of ARFID at presentation have been discussed in Chapter 6, and the importance of making clear decisions about what to address in treatment has been discussed above. The next two questions relate to checking the progress of treatment once it has started and include monitoring whether those involved feel that the sessions are useful and going according to plan, as well as whether there are any changes in the areas that are being worked on through treatment. The final two questions represent important considerations to inform decisions to finish treatment and to obtain useful feedback for future service improvements.

In an ideal world, such questions can, and arguably should, become an integral part of treatment approaches through the regular use of standardised measures. However, in reality many clinicians struggle to fit everything in and some may express concern about overloading children and families with forms and questionnaires. Nevertheless, it is extremely important to keep such questions in mind as treatment progresses, as without regular checks it is not possible to know if everyone's time and effort – first and foremost the child's and their family's – are being optimally utilised.

Interventions toolkit

Having discussed some basic principles of treatment, consideration needs to be given to what is in the clinician's intervention and management toolkit. Part IV of this book includes a number of chapters exploring a comprehensive range of treatment components in more detail. Broadly, the key types of intervention fall into the following categories:

1. Psychological interventions (see Chapters 14, 15 and 16)

    a. Individual interventions, including behavioural and cognitive behavioural approaches and techniques such as exposure hierarchies, systematic desensitisation, food chaining

   b.   Parent interventions, including focussed skills training, anxiety management
   c.   Family interventions, including mealtime management, addressing interaction
   d.   Group interventions, including skills and support as well as educational groups

2.   Nutritional interventions, including tube and supplement weaning (see Chapter 12)
3.   Medical interventions, including weight and growth monitoring and the management of any physical consequences of avoidance and restriction of food intake (see Chapter 13)
4.   Sensory management, including the use of sensory modulation strategies where indicated (see Chapters 10 and 14).

As discussed, the treatment approach for any one individual ideally flows from the assessment process and is characterised by a collaborative stance with attention to motivation, expectations, goals, teamwork and effective, efficient working. In most cases treatment will be multi-modal, due to the inherent nature of ARFID, which covers both psychological and physical parameters. Concurrent interventions addressing weight, nutrition, behaviour and emotional functioning are often indicated (Spettigue et al., 2018).

Treatment planning and selecting appropriate interventions

In most situations, treatment will therefore be informed by two key aspects of the child's presentation: the main areas identified as contributing to and main-taining the eating difficulty and the nature and level of risk. It can be helpful in ensuring that treatment attempts are optimally targeted, to follow the five simple steps outlined below (see Table 11.1). These can be used to structure and assist the decision-making process about what to include and what to prioritise.

The main task in the first step is to ascertain the nature and severity of the problem. This can usually be achieved through comprehensive assessment, including clinical interview, assessment of nutritional adequacy, basic physical evaluation, observation, and obtaining information from other sources (e.g. the child's school), as well as standardised measures (as described in Chapters 6, 7, 8, 9, and 10). This enables a diagnosis to be established where appropriate and an assessment of risk to be made.

The second step involves identifying factors that may have contributed to the current clinical presentation, which includes identifying predisposing and precipitating factors, both individual and interactional. This information plays an important part in constructing a formulation, or a means of arriving at an understanding of why the current difficulties might exist. Being able to "make

Table 11.1 Stepwise approach to management

Step	Task	Function
1	ascertain nature and severity of the presenting problem	current risk assessment and diagnosis where appropriate
2	identify potential predisposing and precipitating factors	with step 1, enables formulation to be constructed
3	identify potential maintaining factors	indication of areas to target in intervention
4	evaluate effects/impact of problem	allows clinical prioritisation of intervention
5	ascertain views of family about experience, aims and priorities	combine with steps 1–4 to arrive at an agreed treatment plan

sense" of difficulties is important, as plans for treatment can then be understood and made in a meaningful context.

This is followed by the third step, which involves identifying maintaining or perpetuating factors. These are the aspects of the presentation which are serving to keep the difficulties going. Maintaining factors that are amenable to change might include behaviours, beliefs, interactions, emotional responses, or a combination of these; their identification allows planned interventions to be appropriately targeted.

The fourth step involves evaluating the effects and the impact of the problem on all concerned. Combined with the risk assessment, this allows prioritisation of intervention from a clinical perspective.

The fifth step involves combining all the above information with the views and priorities of the child and the family, to arrive at an agreed way forward, whilst ensuring at all times that the child's best interests are maintained. As part of agreeing how to proceed, clarity about aims, as discussed above, is required, as well as an "end point" for treatment.

It should be evident from the discussion above that an essential aspect of the process of management planning is to identify if risk is present, and if so where it is located. The four most common areas of risk in relation to ARFID in children are:

- risk to growth and development
- risk related to nutritional inadequacy
- risk related to impairment of the child's social and emotional development
- risk to family relationships and functioning.

All are discussed further in the chapters addressing treatment in this fourth part of this book, but will clearly be important in deciding whether to work on overall amount, the range of foods eaten, eliminating or reducing tube or supplement dependence, or working on socially useful foods.

What is needed in the future?

It is certainly the case that there remains a need for more treatment research, utilising robust evaluation methodologies, including formal randomised controlled trials. At present, there may be something of an over-reliance on very small case series data, pilot studies, and single case study examples to guide practice (Kelly et al., 2014). Whilst these sources of information are valid and useful, they should not be understood as delivering definitive findings; by definition they will be unlikely to be representative given the small numbers of participants typically involved in these types of studies. The current limited number of papers reporting treatment trials means that it is not possible to make confident research evidence based treatment recommendations at present.

Given the variability in presentation inherent in the current definition of ARFID, it seems extremely unlikely that a "one size fits all" approach to treatment will emerge as clearly superior. If a modular approach is indeed to prove the best way forward, more detailed work on reliable characterisation of presenting features, and matching these with standardised treatment interventions that can be consistently delivered, will need to take place. Similarly, effective preventative efforts require reliable early identification of markers of risk, which again calls for more work on characterisation, exploration of the boundaries between normal variation in eating behaviour and clinically significant difficulties, as well as longitudinal studies exploring course.

Calls for a greater focus on measurement, characterisation of presentation, development of standardised or manualised treatment interventions, and identification of optimal treatment settings, have been clearly made (Sharp et al., 2016, 2017).

Finally, in terms of furthering our knowledge about recommended treatment approaches, there is currently a significant gap in qualitative research. There is a great need to investigate what people of all ages, affected by ARFID, find helpful and unhelpful in treatment, and how they would prefer treatment to be delivered.

Summary points

- There is currently a limited evidence base in relation to interventions specifically tested with children with ARFID
- Treatment is generally informed by main areas identified as contributing to and maintaining the difficulty
- Current psychological intervention approaches include individual behavioural and cognitive behavioural interventions as well as family based work, to include parent training

- Typically, treatment of ARFID requires a multi-disciplinary approach
- Select from existing evidence based approaches, anxiety based interventions in particular
- It is helpful to be clear about specific areas of risk and to work through planning steps before commencing treatment

References

Hay, P., Chinn, D., Forbes, D., Madden, S., Newton, R., Sugenor, L., Touyz, S., & Ward, W; Royal Australian and New Zealand College of Psychiatrists. (2014) Royal Australian and New Zealand College of Psychiatrists clinical practice guidelines for the treatment of eating disorders. *Australian and New Zealand Journal of Psychiatry*, 48(11), 977–1008.

Herpertz-Dahlmann, B. (2017) Treatment of eating disorders in child and adolescent psychiatry. *Current Opinion in Psychiatry*, 30(6), 438–45.

Kelly, N.R., Shank, L.M., Bakalar, J.L., & Tanofsky-Kraff, M. (2014) Pediatric feeding and eating disorders: current state of diagnosis and treatment. *Current Psychiatry Reports*, 16(5), 446.

Kennedy, G.A., Wick M.R., & Keel, P.K. (2018) Eating disorders in children: is avoidant-restrictive food intake disorder a feeding disorder or an eating disorder and what are the implications for treatment? *F1000Research* 7, 88. doi: 10.12688/f1000research. 13110.1 accessed 15 July 2019.

Law, D. & Wolpert, M. (2014) Guide to using outcomes and feedback tools with children young people and families, p. 22 www.corc.uk.net/media/1950/201404guide_to_using_outcomes_measures_and_feedback_tools-updated.pdf, accessed 15 July 2019.

Mairs, R. & Nicholls, D. (2016) Assessment and treatment of eating disorders in children and adolescents. *Archives of Disease in Childhood*, 101(12), 1168–75.

Mammel, K.A. & Ornstein, R.M. (2017) Avoidant/restrictive food intake disorder: a new eating disorder diagnosis in the diagnostic and statistical manual 5. *Current Opinion in Pediatrics*, 29(4), 407–13.

Miller, C. & Bravender, T. (2018) Mental disorders and learning disabilities in children and adolescents: eating disorders. *FP Essentials*, 475, 23–29.

Sackett, D.L., Strauss, S.E., Richardson, W.S., Rosenberg, W., & Haynes, R.B. (2002) *Evidence-based Medicine: How to Practise and Teach EBM* (2nd ed.). London: Churchill Livingstone.

Sharp, W.G., Stubbs, K.H., Adams, H., Wells, B.M., Lesack, R.S., Criado, K.K., Simon, E.L., McCracken, C.E., West, L.L., & Scahill, L.D. (2016) Intensive, manual-based intervention for pediatric feeding disorders: results from a randomized pilot trial. *Journal of Pediatric Gastroenterology and Nutrition*, 62(4), 658–63.

Sharp, W.G., Volkert, V.M., Scahill, L., McCracken, C.E., & McElhanon, B. (2017) A systematic review and meta-analysis of intensive multidisciplinary intervention for pediatric feeding disorders: how standard is the standard of care? *Journal of Pediatrics*, 181, 116–24.

Spettigue, W., Norris, M.L., Santos, A., & Obeid, N. (2018) Treatment of children and adolescents with avoidant/restrictive food intake disorder: a case series examining the feasibility of family therapy and adjunctive treatments. *Journal of Eating Disorders*, 6, 20.

Waller, G. (2019) ARFID: old wine in a new bottle? *British Journal of Psychiatry Advances*, 25(2), 99–100.

Zucker, N.L., LaVia, M.C., Craske, M.G., Foukal, M., Harris, A.A., Datta, N., Savereide, E., & Maslow, G.R. (2019) Feeling and body investigators (FBI): ARFID division – an acceptance-based interoceptive exposure treatment for children with ARFID. *International Journal of Eating Disorders*, 52(4), 466–72.

Chapter 12

Nutritional management and tube weaning

Sarah Cawtherley, Claire Higgins, and Úna McCrann

Introduction

This chapter addresses nutritional management in children presenting with avoidant restrictive food intake disorder (ARFID), an area that has thus far received relatively little research attention. Reference is made to the limited research base specifically relating to approaches to enhance nutritional and energy adequacy of a child with ARFID's diet, and possible ways to address any deficiencies that might develop through inadequate food intake are proposed. Clinical examples are used to illustrate how specific foods and supplements can be successfully introduced to improve a child's nutritional profile. When physical risk is high and a child is not able to make the required improvements in terms of their intake through oral eating, supplemental feeding may need to be considered. Some of the issues that may arise as a consequence are outlined, in particular the possibility of developing dependence on supplement feeding. The recommendation that tube weaning should be considered and planned for at the outset of a period of tube feeding is discussed, with an overview of some of the approaches to tube weaning described in the literature. As with so many aspects of the management of ARFID, the need to tailor approaches to nutritional management to the particular needs of the child and family is highlighted.

Realistic goals and joined-up approach

When managing the expectations of the family, and at times those of the network around the child, in relation to nutritional management, it is important to be realistic in setting goals and timeframes. Some children take a long time to accept or achieve changes in their intake, which may be fine as long as physical risk is not high, and can indeed be preferable in terms of keeping the child engaged. Where physical risk is high, more immediate intervention may be required. In the same way as with other aspects of management, close liaison with others involved in the child's care and day-to-day life is recommended. This might include staff at school as there may be times when a child will be able to introduce a food or make a change to their intake in one setting, such as school, but not at home (see also Chapter 17). Child temperament, developmental stage, motivation to change, and the child's clinical presentation, all need to be considered as part of nutritional management planning. Discussion with multi-disciplinary colleagues is important to allow comprehensive consideration of the child's nutritional status and to allow appropriate prioritisation and focus of interventions.

Some children may be on less than optimal diets but may be meeting their nutritional requirements with over-the-counter oral supplements. In such instances nutritional interventions may not be the highest priority, but another aspect of the child's presentation, such as social isolation, might be. Conversations with the family about what would be helpful to change and how this might be achieved might need to be regularly revisited as a child builds their confidence with expanding their diet or accepting more age-appropriate supplementation. Families may want their child to eat family foods and they may be disappointed in the food that a child prefers. Planning any nutritional intervention therefore needs to include consideration of the adequacy of the preferred foods and any differences between parental hopes and expectations and the child's eating behaviour and food preferences. Nutritional assessment and intervention can also help families to move towards accepting limited diets that are "good enough".

Nutritional management

There is a limited evidence base to guide how best to support and treat children with ARFID regarding their dietary intake and nutritional management. Following on from the dietary assessment (see further Chapter 8) there are a number of questions that can be helpful to take into account when deciding the best approach for these children:

1. Is the child's diet nutritionally adequate? Does it meet their macro-nutrient and micro-nutrient requirements?
2. Is their diet meeting their energy requirements? Is the child underweight, a healthy weight or overweight?
3. Is their range of food limited?

It is important to recognise that a child can be at normal weight or even overweight and still suffer from nutritional inadequacies. In such instances they may be able to consume enough food and consequently sufficient calories, but from a limited range of foods, which may result in micro-nutrient deficiencies. On the other hand, some children could have micro-nutrient deficiencies and in addition be underweight. If the child is underweight then an important early priority for intervention is management aimed at increasing weight, which can be followed by addressing any micro-nutrient deficiencies and/or limited food intake.

Micro-nutrient deficiencies

There have been many studies that have surveyed national intake to assess population patterns in terms of diet, nutrient intake and nutritional status. The most recent UK report, the National Diet and Nutrition Survey Rolling Programme, is a continuous cross-sectional survey of the general population aged 1.5 years and over, living in private households in the UK (NDNS RP, 2019). This reveals that over the past nine years, fruit and vegetable consumption has been below the recommended five portions per day, total fat consumption continues to exceed recommendations, and there has been a downward trend in intake of most vitamins and minerals (NDNS RP, 2019). This survey indicates that the UK general population as a whole does not meet all its daily micro-nutrient requirements. The UK is not unique in this respect and fortification of certain commonly consumed foodstuffs is used in many countries, to offset the risk of some deficiencies. Due to the avoidance and restriction of food intake in children presenting with ARFID, micro-nutrient deficiencies are relatively common in this population. Future research would be beneficial to determine which deficiencies occur most frequently in children with ARFID and how these may be similar or different to the deficiencies noted in the general population. The use of fortified foods, especially ones that are associated with a child's preferred food can be useful to address micro-nutrient deficiencies.

Fortified foods

Fortification of food has been a strategy to prevent micro-nutrient deficiencies in high-income countries for more than a century. This involves the addition of essential micro-nutrients to widely consumed staple foods during the production process (Keats et al., 2019). Commonly fortified foods include: breakfast cereals, bread, biscuits, margarines, milk, oils. These products can be helpful for children with ARFID as well as the general population. If the child's diet is limited in some micro-nutrients it may be possible to alter some of their foods to similar foods that have been fortified, which can contribute important micro-nutrients that they would otherwise be lacking. It is important to be mindful that some of these fortified foods may contain other ingredients that, if consumed in excess, could cause them to exceed their requirements in other nutrients. This may particularly be the case in relation to sodium or salt.

Micro-nutrient supplementation

When it is not possible to enhance the diet with fortified foods or new foods, consideration needs to be given to over-the-counter supplements or prescription-based supplements. There is a wide range of possible supplements available and a child's preference for taste and texture needs to be considered before the introduction of any of these. Parents generally have a good idea of what may be acceptable to try. If the child is unable to manage a tablet format, then a liquid or powder version may be required, which may be possible to incorporate into cold food or drink. However, this may need to be done with caution and in a gradual manner as it may alter the taste of the food or drink, which could cause the child to refuse it. From experience, some children with ARFID are extremely sensitive to change in taste and may be able to detect even tiny amounts of added supplement, therefore a slow titration process can sometimes be required.

Some children may not just need a micro-nutrient supplement; some may need additional calories and an oral nutritional supplement may be of benefit. If this is the case, some of these also contain vitamins and minerals, therefore a child may not require both the vitamin and mineral supplement and the oral nutritional supplement together. Some families may enquire about the use of transdermal delivery of vitamin and mineral supplements; this is in the early stages of research, with only a limited number of studies having been conducted (Rejinold et al., 2019). This is an interesting area of research that could prove to be beneficial for individuals unable to take oral micro-nutrient supplements; however, at this stage it is not possible to make clear recommendations for children with ARFID.

Management of weight restoration

If the child is underweight, or their weight has plateaued, in some cases leading to falling growth centiles, this is likely to be a result of not consuming sufficient calories to meet their nutritional requirements for energy. It is important that this is corrected and this can be addressed in a number of different ways:

- use of their preferred foods
- fortification of food (i.e. adding extra calories)
- the use of oral nutritional supplements
- enteral nutrition in the form of nasogastric feeding, or gastrostomy feeding where appropriate.

The use of preferred foods

If a child presenting with ARFID is assessed as having faltering growth or being underweight then it is important to look at ways to aid weight restoration. An increase of a child's preferred or safe foods can help to increase the calorie content of their diet, which will help them to meet their energy requirements. Once they are meeting their energy requirements then they should start to gain weight. As preferred foods are usually ones that they will consume without hesitation, this may be the easiest way of increasing the calorie content of the diet. Some children will be able to work on expanding their range at the same time as increasing their consumption of preferred foods, for others it may be important to work on one change at a time. Increasing the variety of foods that a child will consume can be achieved through gradual exposure to new foods, for example, the use of "food chaining" (see also Chapter 14).

Where possible, if weight gain is the focus, considering more calorie dense versions of the same or similar options may be beneficial. For example, if a child likes strawberry yoghurt, another brand containing more calories may be accepted. It is important that any foods chosen to work on are commonly available ones that are used within the family environment and are culturally appropriate. Some families, perhaps particularly those who espouse "healthy eating" principles, may find buying high-calorie products a challenge. Reassurance may be needed regarding the health benefits for the child in question. Where possible the child should be involved in the decision-making process about what foods to try to introduce, as this will often improve the likelihood of success. Liaison with schools and nurseries to discuss the rationale for such children's needs for high calorie foods may be important (see further Chapter 17).

Food fortification

The use of food fortification in terms of calories, for example by adding additional butter, cream, cheese, or oil to foods to maximise the calorie density, is commonly used with children who have problems with low weight within the general population. This method can also be used in children with ARFID but caution needs to be exercised for those who are sensitive to differences in taste and texture, particularly if additional calories are being incorporated into their preferred foods. The resulting change in taste or texture could lead them to refuse the food entirely. This is not always the case and some children are able to cope with additional calories being added into their preferred foods if this is done gradually.

Oral nutritional supplements

If a child's weight is low and they have not been able to increase the amount of their preferred foods or use food fortification to help with weight gain as outlined above, then an oral nutritional supplement may be required to provide the additional calories to help meet their energy requirements. It is recommended that this is prescribed and monitored by a dietitian.

Oral nutritional supplements contain macro- and micro-nutrients in varying concentrations and not all are nutritionally complete. When deciding upon which is the most appropriate, individual dietetic assessment should allow individually tailored advice to be given. This should be monitored regularly to make sure that the supplement remains appropriate. Oral nutritional supplements come in a variety of different formats, including milk or juice based supplements, high energy powders to mix with water or milk, yoghurt/pudding style supplements, and low-volume, high-concentration shots, which are usually fat and or protein-based products. It is important that religious observances, cultural preferences, or any allergies or medical exclusions are taken into account when selecting the appropriate supplement for a child.

Enteral nutrition

Enteral nutrition includes nasogastric feeding, percutaneous endoscopic gastrostomy feeding (PEG), nasojejunal, and percutaneous endoscopic gastrostomy–jejunal (PEG-J) feeding. Enteral feeding may have been instigated in children with significant medical histories, in children unable to meet their nutritional requirements orally, or in children who may have developed an aversion to eating and develop dependence on tube feeding.

There is currently a limited amount of research into the use of enteral nutrition in children with ARFID. One survey found that many physicians working on inpatient units in the US would use the same management protocol for ARFID patients as they do for patients with anorexia nervosa, with only 22.7% (n = 5/22) having a specific ARFID protocol (Guss, Richmond, & Forman, 2018). The most common form of nutrition used was "regular food", with 50% of participating physicians commonly using nasogastric tubes as part of initial management, and 45% using oral nutritional supplements. It has been suggested that patients with ARFID are more likely to require nasogastric tube feeds in comparison to patients with other eating disorder diagnoses, but further research is required to confirm whether this is indeed the case across different settings. Guss and colleagues discuss the view that children presenting with ARFID should be treated differently to those with anorexia nervosa as they are more likely to need exposure-based work on expanding their food preferences (Guss, Richmond, & Forman, 2018). It may therefore be the case that they identified higher rates of nasogastric tube feeding in children with ARFID because these patients were initially being treated, presumably unsuccessfully, in the same way as those with anorexia nervosa.

If the decision for enteral feeding is recommended, it ideally needs to be considered within a multi-disciplinary framework, taking into consideration medical risk, sensory sensitivities, and emotional impact on the child and family. Factors such as the child's ability, temperament, sensory processing, levels of food avoidance, and aversion need to be considered when determining whether short-term nasogastric or longer-term PEG feeding is indicated. Once the decision for enteral feeding is made, it is recommended that at the time of tube insertion consideration is given regarding the plan to subsequently remove it once agreed goals have been reached (see, for example, NICE Guidance on Faltering Growth, 2017, recommendation 1.2.26).

It has been suggested that the use of nasogastric feeding in ARFID may be contraindicated in some children who are particularly sensitive and may not tolerate the tube (Katzman, Norris & Zucker, 2019). Inserting a tube is not without complications and requires careful consideration and risk assessment.

Therefore the use of nasogastric feeding should be thought about carefully to prevent further complications, with food fortification, increasing preferred foods, use of calorie dense foods, and supplementation all attempted as far as possible alongside considering nasogastric feeds. There are of course times when nasogastric feeding is required to aid with medical stabilisation, as severe malnutrition, micro-nutrient deficiencies, and low body weight can lead to severe morbidity and mortality.

John (13 years old) had a significant fear of swallowing following a choking incident. This led to him reducing his already limited diet to liquid and food he could dissolve in his mouth. Over a period of time supplements were trialled and he was unable to take them. Significant weight loss and poor nutrition were beginning to have a negative impact on him medically, cognitively and on his daily level of functioning. Following a multi-disciplinary team assessment, and discussions with the family, the treating team, and his local team, it was concluded that a period of nasogastric tube feeding should be recommended prior to an intensive treatment programme to address John's fear of swallowing. Following psychoeducation regarding swallowing, nutritional intervention, and anxiety management, John slowly began to accept the supplements orally, the nasogastric tube was removed and he was gradually able to expand his oral diet.

Malcolm was two years old with a history of selectivity around food within the family; both his father and his brother were highly selective. Malcolm was finding the transition from breast feeding to oral intake difficult. He began to lose weight and was not managing any fluids. Professionals were concerned about his growth and the strain on the family. Malcom's mother presented as highly anxious, which was considered to be a factor in Malcolm's difficulties. After careful consideration and discussion with his parents, the multi-disciplinary team, and his local medical team, the decision was taken to insert a gastrostomy tube rather than commence nasogastric feeding, as the history indicted that Malcolm was extremely sensory sensitive and had high oral aversion. Post PEG insertion and the commencement of feeds, the family relaxed, and baseline nutrition via the PEG restored Malcolm's nutritional status. This allowed Malcolm time and opportunity to explore food. The initial plan was to use the PEG for a period of six months. However, Malcolm advanced well with exploring foods and enjoyed baby-led weaning. He rapidly increased his oral intake and after two months, breast feeding stopped entirely, tube feeding reduced, and he was managing an age appropriate diet orally. The PEG was removed after only three months.

Management of re-feeding syndrome

In some cases, although rare, children with ARFID may be at risk of re-feeding syndrome if they have lost a significant amount of weight over a short period of time or they are consuming significantly less calories than their needs based upon their energy requirements (see Chapters 8 and 9 for further assessment information). Managing any child at risk of re-feeding syndrome, regardless of diagnosis, should be done as part of a multidisciplinary team with careful monitoring of electrolytes to avoid the child developing re-feeding syndrome (see further Chapter 13).

Management on enteral feeds

Guidance for the management of enteral feeds tends to follow three basic principles:

1. Establish enteral feeds, ensuring the child is on the optimal feed for them
2. Stabilise weight and gain enough weight to consider reduction of feeds
3. Consider and plan the process of feed reduction and tube removal

Management of feeds is generally overseen by dietitians and paediatricians. The right feed needs to be established, along with finding a suitable rate and pattern of feeding that fits in with the family routine and any medical considerations; for example, feeds could be timed to coincide with mealtimes, or administered in the form of overnight feeding. Although most tube feeding involves the use of proprietary supplement products, some children are fed with a blended diet. This needs monitoring by a dietitian to make sure that it is nutritionally adequate. Blended diets often follow specific recipes and are becoming more popular; however, consideration needs to be given to their use in terms of safety, nutrition, appropriateness, and effectiveness (Breaks et al., 2018). Bobo (2016) has written about some of the benefits of administering blended diets via a gastrostomy tube, and some families report that this can help reduce reflux symptoms allowing their children to thrive physically.

When considering tube feed reduction, it is important that enough time is scheduled between feeds to provide a window of appetite to allow the child to become hungry. It may take a few days for this to happen. In some cases, in particular, where other factors are contributing to food avoidance, such as anxiety, hunger in itself may be insufficient to promote eating behaviour. In some instances, tube weaning may fail as feed is reduced, due to insufficient management of expectations; some children's weight will drop initially and both parents and professionals can become concerned and react too quickly by re-instating feeds. Family and professional anxiety often needs careful containment as weight loss can often be an issue with tube weaning. As long as weight is monitored and the child's needs carefully considered at all times, weight gain will usually pick up after an initial drop.

Tube weaning

Different approaches to tube weaning are described in the literature, ranging from a rapid reduction of tube feeds, to a slow and steady approach. The main approaches include:

1.   Inpatient intensive/rapid reduction approach
2.   Intensive out-patient approach e.g. day programme
3.   Slow and steady approach
4.   Occasional nights off, building up in number
5.   Intensive start and then steady approach

Each child and family is different and the assessment of the type and timing of tube weaning ideally considers which approach might be best suited to the child's needs, skills and abilities as well as family circumstances. A rapid approach (such as that described by Wilken et al., 2017) may be appealing to some families but other families may find this difficult, with resulting heightened stress and anxiety. Most professionals recognise that children ideally need an individually tailored approach (Dovey et al., 2016).

In a comparison of tube weaning in treatment centres across five different countries (Switzerland, Austria, USA, UK, and Australia), centres adopted different approaches, including a psychodynamic approach (promoting child autonomy and a positive feeding relationship with the caregiver), a psychosocial approach focussed on attachment, an operant conditioning approach, and a controlled starvation approach. Sensori-motor and psychological approaches were important elements of all programmes. The authors concluded that tube weaning can successfully be achieved rapidly or gradually with no one approach clearly superior in terms of effectiveness (Gardiner, Vuillermin, & Fuller, 2017).

A number of centres develop in-house protocols for tube weaning. Typically, these will include indicators for when a child may be ready to wean from tube feeds, including medical stability, swallow safety, appropriate time for the child and family, growth centiles and the child's ability to consume food and drink orally. Psychological support for the child and family may be required throughout the process. It is recommended that weight, growth and ability to eat are regularly monitored as the stages of tube weaning are followed. Consideration of sensory issues and food exposures or food play may also be helpful to support oral intake during tube weaning. Most tube weaning approaches have in common that a child and family need to be "ready", the child needs to be able to swallow small amounts, and reduction in tube feeds need to happen in order to allow a child to experience hunger.

It is common for children who are tube fed to have the majority of their nutritional and energy requirements met with the feed, leaving little opportunity for hunger or eating. The basic premise of tube weaning is that if the enteral feed is reduced this potentially creates a window of opportunity for the child to eat. Participation at mealtimes is important, and children can be given food to explore, preferably encouraging them to start with food that they may have success with (Wigg, 2017). Depending on a child's age and how long they have been tube fed, they may have missed out on the weaning stage, so soft foods may be easier.

Maham (3 years old) attended for an intensive treatment week to start the process of tube weaning. He received at least half of his calorie and nutrition requirements via his tube. He was weighed on day one and his feed was cut by 20%. Maham was involved in food picnics, a painting with food session, and in exploring non-food textured play items. He and his family participated in three meal times and three snack times per day, using rewards (stickers and praise) as a motivator. On day two Maham's feed was reduced again by another 20% as he was managing small portions of food orally, and he had good levels of energy. By the end of day two he was managing toddler appropriate size of meal and snacks. Maham received his water via the PEG and on day three his tube feeds were stopped. Days four and five were an opportunity for consolidation and Maham continued to manage without his tube feeds. Maham had been weighed on days one, three and five, and observations were made of his portion sizes and of his energy levels throughout. Managing parental anxiety was a key element of the intensive support as this is often identified as a block to progress.

An in-patient tube weaning protocol has been described by Brown and colleagues as involving a multidisciplinary approach over a three-week intensive programme. These authors discuss multiple factors that can contribute to a child becoming reliant on enteral feeds. They also outline some of the difficulties that parents and carers face when trying to tube wean at home and acknowledge the significant strain that this can put on relationships (Brown et al., 2014).

Silverman and colleagues also outline a programme for intensive inpatient tube weaning for children who present with long-term tube feeding. They use a behavioural approach over a two-week intensive period. Follow up of the children after 12 months showed good results overall (Silverman et al., 2013). As an inpatient programme this approach can be intense and is not suitable for all families, as it requires significant time and emotional commitment. A more gradual approach is outlined by Wright and colleagues (Wright, Smith, & Morrison, 2011), who identify factors associated with success and failure on transitioning from long-term enteral feeds. Their protocol begins with a reduction of feeds equal to 10–15% of the child's current energy intake with the aim of maximising the energy content of accepted solid foods. Children are followed up every 1–2 months and advice given to caregivers to avoid weighing the child in between clinics. If a gain of weight is achieved, a further reduction is recommended by the same or larger amount. If weight is static, then a similar or smaller reduction is recommended. If weight loss has occurred, then the feed remains unchanged and a review is arranged in a further month. This is also a multi-disciplinary approach with telephone contact between clinics with a psychologist to support the parents. Parental anxiety was again identified as a major potential block to progress in this study. The authors advise that it is essential to have a cohesive team approach and support for parents during tube weaning. The age of the child was also identified as a factor that influenced success of tube weaning, with greater success for those aged five years and under (Wright, Smith, & Morrison, 2011).

> Aaron (9 years old) had been PEG tube fed for many years. He and his family had attempted rapid tube weaning twice but Aaron had become unwell. The following year he and his family engaged in a more gradual approach, reducing his feed by 100mls monthly. As the family lived some distance from the clinic, they had fortnightly telephone calls and monthly visits to the clinic. Aaron initially lost some weight, as expected. He was assessed as meeting his nutritional requirements and with support he and his parents were reassured that he was managing well with the addition of an over-the-counter vitamin and mineral supplement. They reflected that Aaron's father had also been a slender child and felt reassured by this. The slow and steady approach worked well for the family and within six months Aaron no longer needed his tube for nutrition or fluids. Aaron began tube weaning on pureed foods and gradually built up his ability and confidence to chew foods; he is now managing family foods.

Despite the debate around the variety of approaches and methods used for tube weaning, a consensus appears to be emerging about the importance of individualising the approach for each child and family. Consideration needs to be given to the best method for each child including what will suit their temperament, the extent of family anxiety and whether this needs containing, and the ability to transfer eating skills to home and other environments if tube weaning is achieved on an inpatient basis. Consideration also needs to be given to the continued support the family may require in the community, both medically and socially, to sustain and build on changes achieved. Successful tube weaning therefore relies to some extent on professionals adapting approaches according to each child and family.

Summary points

*   Management of nutritional adequacy rests on considering two main components of a child's diet:
    *   Energy requirements and adequacy of intake (children presenting with ARFID can be meeting their energy requirements with calorie dense preferred foods but still be nutritionally inadequate)
    *   Nutritional requirements and adequacy of intake

*   When considering supplementary feeding, clinicians will need to give careful consideration to select the most appropriate supplement and its suitability for the child in question

- Nutrition, weight and growth need to be considered and monitored
- Tube weaning may follow different approaches; outcomes depend on multiple factors and there is no one size fits all approach for children with ARFID

References

Bobo, E. (2016) Re-emergence of blenderized tube feedings: exploring the evidence. *Nutrition in Clinical Practice* 31 (6), 730–35.

Breaks, A., Smith, C., Bloch, S., & Morgan, S. (2018) Blended diets for gastrostomy fed children and young people: a scoping review. *Journal of Human Nutrition and Dietetics* doi: 10.1111/jhn.12563.

Brown, J., Kim, C. Lim, A., Brown, S., Desai, H., Volker, L., & Katz, M. (2014) Successful gastrostomy tube weaning program using an intensive multidisciplinary team approach. *Journal of Pediatric Gastroenterol Nutrition* 58 (6), 743–49.

Dovey, T.M., Wilken, M., Martin, C.I., & Meyer, C. (2016) Definitions and clinical guidance on the enteral dependence component of the avoidant/restrictive food intake disorder diagnostic criteria in children. *Journal of Parenteral and Enteral Nutrition* 42 (3), 499–507.

Gardiner, A.Y., Vuillermin, P.J., & Fuller, D.G. (2017) A descriptive comparison of approaches to paediatric tube weaning across five countries. *International Journal of Speech-Language Pathology* 19, 121–27.

Guss, C.E., Richmond, T.R., & Forman, S. (2018) A survey of physician practices on the inpatient medical stabilization of patients with avoidant/restrictive food intake disorder. *Journal of Eating Disorders* 6 (22). doi:10.1186/s40337-018-0212-4

Katzman, D.K., Norris, M.L., & Zucker, N. (2019) Avoidant restrictive food intake disorder: first do no harm. *International Journal of Eating Disorders*, 1–3 doi: org/10.1002/eat.23021.

Keats, E.C., Neufeld, L.M., Garrett, G.S., Mbuya, M.N.M., & Bhutta, Z.A. (2019) Improved micro-nutrient status and health outcomes in low- and middle-income countries following large-scale fortification: evidence from a systematic review and meta-analysis. *American Journal of Clinical Nutrition* 109, 1696–708.

National Diet and Nutrition Survey assesses the diet, nutrient intake and nutritional status of the general population of the UK Published 9 September 2016 Last updated 23 January (2019) www.gov.uk/government/statistics/ndns-time-trend-and-income-analyses-for-years-1-to-9

NICE Guidance on Faltering Growth. (2017) Recommendation 1. 2.26 www.nice.org.uk/guidance/ng75/chapter/Recommendations#organisation-of-care

Rejinold, N.S., Kim, H.K., Isakovic, A.F., Gater, D.L., & Kim, Y. (2019) Therapeutic vitamin delivery: chemical and physical methods with future directions. *Journal of Controlled Release* 298, 83–98.

Silverman, A.H. Kirby, M. Clifford, L.M. Ficher, E. Berlin, K.S. Rudolph, C.D., & Noel, R.J. (2013) Nutritional and psychosocial outcomes of gastrostomy tube-dependent children completing an intensive inpatient behavioral program. *Journal of Pediatric Gastroenterology and Nutrition* 57 (5) 668–72.

Wigg, V. (2017) A practical guide to tube weaning (personal communication).

Wilken, M., Bartmann, P., Dovey, T.M., & Bagci, S. (2017) Characteristics of feeding tube dependency with respect to food aversive behaviour and growth. *Appetite* 123, 1–6.

Wright, C.M., Smith, K.H., & Morrison, J. (2011) Withdrawing feeds from children on long term enteral feeding: factors associated with success and failure. *Archive of Diseases in Childhood* 96, 433–39.

Chapter 13

Medical management

Lee Hudson

Introduction

Chapter 9 has addressed the assessment of important medical considerations in avoidant restrictive food intake disorder (ARFID). This chapter discusses key medical aspects of care relating to treatment of ARFID, including medical complications. Being a relatively new diagnosis, there is a paucity of research into the specific management of medical complications in ARFID. Much of the research and principles applied here, come from the field of general child health, where children have had poor nutrition in other settings, and the literature relating to anorexia nervosa.

Before outlining specific and more common medical issues, there are two important core principles that must be borne in mind for anyone supporting the medical care of patients and families of patients with a diagnosis of ARFID. First, central to effective medical management is co-working with the multidisciplinary team around the child, in particular through shared understanding of the importance of issues identified and through good communication. Preferably this will happen before, if possible whilst, and certainly after, seeing a patient and their family. Achieving effective changes through intervention requires the confidence of patients and families, and this can be diminished if plans are not consistent or appear conflicting with those of others. Patient and family members' views are also key in any plans made about what to target in management. This is of particular and paramount importance when ARFID co-exists with complex medical conditions, for example cystic fibrosis or diabetes mellitus. In such instances, medical treatment can be very specific and priorities in the management of one condition may differ from the treatments for ARFID itself. Challenges to this first concept of the importance of co-working include geographical splits between specialities, differences in opinions over priorities between individuals and teams, misunderstandings of the important context of ARFID by medical teams, and the importance of the medical team's role in comprehensive management being overlooked or misunderstood. Added to this is, of course, the age-old and common barrier of available time. Anecdotal experience suggests that preparatory conversations and meetings between teams outside of the acute business of seeing patients are the best opportunities to engender co-working and education. The identification of local medical professionals with an interest and understanding of the condition is also helpful, who, as well as providing direct clinical input, may also act as local leaders and champions for patients with ARFID.

The second over-arching principle is that of the importance of pragmatism, in particular over priorities for investigation and interventions. Medical teams working with children are usually adept at pragmatism, in the form of making careful choices about choosing battles and priorities in the interests of a child's holistic wellbeing. Indeed, pragmatism is an essential core component for all those providing health care to children. There are many occasions in the management of ARFID where a pragmatic approach, joined up with the whole team, will need to be applied in order to act in the best interests of the child and meet the overall goals of the team and family – a good example being balancing the decision to implement nasogastric feeding for nutrition over psychological impact on the child and their overall feeding (Katzman, Norris, & Zucker, 2019). The essence of medical management in ARFID is about carefully assessing, and balancing, physical risk alongside the issues and priorities identified by other team members providing psychological care for a child and their family, and being able to appropriately guide when the medical, and physical risk needs to be prioritised (for example, where acute medical risk is present, as outlined in Chapter 9). Throughout, the importance of clearly explaining risk and recommendations to patients and families is, of course, paramount.

Constipation

Constipation is common in many children with difficulties with feeding and eating whether this is due to ARFID or not (Torres & Gonzalez, 2015). This can be due to types of food eaten, associated dehydration, or in children at low weight, due to the changes associated with underweight itself. A number of studies have shown that gut transit time can be reduced in underweight individuals, particularly in those with eating disturbances (Hirakawa et al., 1990; Holt et al., 1981; Kamal et al., 1991). Constipation itself can also have an impact on appetite and amount eaten (Chao et al., 2008). All of this can make for potentially medically confusing presentations from a diagnostic perspective, especially if the underlying feeding or eating problems have not been recognised. This calls for careful history taking about nutritional intake and growth parameters in medical assessment. If there is perplexity around causation, a useful strategy is to observe for improvement in constipation with weight gain once eating difficulties are identified and treated, alongside rational medical testing (for example, thyroid function). It is also important that constipation and associated symptoms (such as abdominal pain and/or bloating) are recognised and taken seriously as part of the presentation and treatment of

ARFID. Allocating such symptoms into separate physical or psychological camps (for example, as "anxiety") is generally unhelpful, especially as it is often impossible to disentangle the differences between abdominal pain caused by anxiety, and those caused by constipation (Sato & Fukudo, 2015). Such distractions can lead to delay in progress for the child and family, and sometimes loss of confidence. Thus, identification and treatment of constipation should be implemented promptly and follow existing consensus guidelines, for example, the guidelines for the diagnosis and management of childhood constipation from the National Institute for Clinical Excellence (Bardisa-Ezcurra, Ullman, & Gordon, 2010), alongside any psychological and nutritional interventions required. Pro-kinetic medications to increase gastric emptying in the context of underweight, such as domperidone, have been trialled in patients with anorexia nervosa (Stacher et al., 1993); however, all of these medications have potential side effects and their use in ARFID and related feeding and eating disorders has not been studied sufficiently to make recommendations at this time, especially in younger children.

Associated growth and bone density issues

There are currently no published studies on the management of either low bone mineral density or disordered growth specific to ARFID. This means that in order to inform practice with this patient group, parallels must be drawn from other related areas of research and practice. For example, the fields of starvation and malnutrition in children in low income countries, and anorexia nervosa in higher income countries, offer useful insights and evidence. Such comparisons, however, are not without problem. Starvation in low-income countries is usually accompanied by more severe socio-economic burden and higher rates of infectious disease (Mcallister et al., 2019). In anorexia nervosa there are commonly other factors present, such as excessive exercising and the presence of a clear drive to lose weight. Moreover, those with anorexia nervosa will tend to present more acutely, with more sudden loss of weight (Hudson & Court, 2012). As highlighted in Chapter 9, the course of ARFID for many children appears to be longstanding, leading to long periods of malnutrition (Lucarelli et al., 2018). Over time, reduced access to nutrition and associated endocrine responses (Singhal, Misra, & Klibanski, 2014) will lead to low bone mineral density and growth or pubertal delay for many, and growth arrest for some. The key concern associated with growth delay or arrest in any child or adolescent is potential permanence, and failure to reach an appropriate adult, final height – so-called "stunting". Stunting is associated with a range of potential deleterious health and socio-economic outcomes in later life; the greatest risk for stunting being in the first two years of life (when growth rates are highest) and a time where, in contrast to anorexia nervosa, ARFID can be present (Branca & Ferrari, 2002; De Onis & Branca, 2016). Literature on growth delay in older children and adolescents with anorexia nervosa is currently unclear whether growth delay remains permanent or there is ultimate catch-up growth (Modan-Moses et al., 2012). From existing research and from clinical observation, it would appear that some children and young people experiencing growth delay may not catch up, with resultant stunting. At any age therefore, careful attention to growth in ARFID is paramount, and where growth and/or puberty appear to be affected, a range of nutritional interventions, in particular alternative routes of feeding, must be considered by teams, with the primary guiding principle being restoration of weight to stimulate growth. The same is the case for children and young people with features of acute medical risk as discussed in Chapter 9. Education around risk for growth and development associated with underweight is important for patients and families in discussing plans and strategies to support ARFID with them. However, further research is needed as to how best to deliver this information, especially to children and adolescents, and how it may potentially be used as an educational intervention to improve feeding and eating in this age group.

Similarly, weight restoration has been shown to be the best method to improve low bone density, although, in the case of anorexia nervosa, it is not clear whether weight restoration will improve bone density entirely to pre-morbid levels (Robinson, Micali & Misra., 2017b). To what degree recovery of bone density will be complete is difficult to ascertain at both a research and individual level as unlike measures of growth and weight, the majority of children will not have had a pre-morbid measurement of their bone mineral density. A diet supplemented with vitamin D and calcium is recommended; however, this alone, without weight gain, is likely to be of limited impact (Nicholls, Hudson, & Mahomed, 2011). For female patients where weight gain is longstanding, improvement in weight has not been achieved despite interventions, and, where bone mineral density continues to fall, the potential intervention of oestrogen patch supplementation may be considered; one randomised controlled trial reports a very modest increase in bone mineral density in those with patch therapy versus controls (Misra et al., 2013). Yet again, however, this hormonal intervention is likely to be inferior to weight restoration. Bisphosphonates are known to increase bone mineral density in adults, and have been used as therapy in adults with anorexia nervosa (Robinson et al., 2017a). However, the long-term effects of bisphosphonates in children and young people are not clear, and are potentially teratogenic for future pregnancies. They should therefore be used with caution in children and young people, limited to cases where there are multiple fractures due to low bone mineral density or bone pain in this patient group, and only prescribed by those with expertise (Baroncelli & Bertelloni, 2014; Srivastava & Alon, 2003).

Micro-nutrient deficiencies

Alongside the macro-nutritional assessments relating to height and weight and impact on growth, children and young people frequently have insufficient intake of recommended micro-nutrients in ARFID. An assessment of intake and possible deficiency is best done jointly between a dietitian and a physician. The dietitian can assess the dietary intake over time, and paediatrician performs a clinical examination to identify any clinical evidence of nutritional deficiencies (see also Chapter 8). It may be decided that ultimately blood testing is required to assess for deficiencies, for which particular consideration must be given to the potential findings and effect on the child. A significant proportion of children will exhibit anxiety around procedures in health care settings, especially venepuncture (sometimes called "needle phobia") (Mclenon & Rogers, 2019). This may be more pronounced in children with ARFID who have co-existing anxiety and neurodevelopmental disorders (Davit et al., 2011). Pragmatic consideration must be given to the medical need for testing and likelihood of significant findings on testing, versus the potential psychological impact on the child and family. Where blood tests are felt necessary, preferably they should be performed in locations separate to the place of psychological therapy for the eating difficulties, to limit impact on the child's feelings about that place and thus potentially the efficacy of therapy. For pragmatic reasons, if blood testing is not possible, it may be more effective to empirically commence a multi-vitamin and minerals. That said, compliance and concordance with multi-vitamin therapy might also be challenging for children and young people. It is important that teams work together on this, with knowledge of a range of formulations and strategies that can be employed to encourage intake of vitamin and mineral supplements for children who find this difficult. Importantly, for older children and adolescents, the ethical concepts of hiding supplements in food must be discussed with families. In addition, the potential, more general consequences that might emerge when a child or adolescent feels "tricked" or loses trust in carers and treating teams when discovering supplementation have been hidden and given to them without their knowledge, must be openly acknowledged.

Medication as adjunctive support for ARFID

Appetite stimulating medications have received attention in the literature in a range of conditions where appetite is suppressed and leads to a reduction of feeding and eating, such as cancer (Coularis et al., 2008) and cystic fibrosis (Nasr & Drury, 2008). As low interest in eating and low appetite have been identified as key features in some patients with ARFID (American Psychiatric Association, 2013), medications that may increase appetite are therefore of potential interest for this group of patients. The drug perhaps receiving the most recent interest in children and adolescents as a means for increasing appetite is cyproheptadine. Cyproheptadine is an older-generation antihistamine, which causes hunger as a side effect. It is favoured amongst the range of appetite stimulating drugs, as anti-histamines are commonly prescribed and generally safe medications for the general child and adolescent population. Cyproheptadine, and its effect on both appetite and weight gain, have recently been systematically reviewed (Harrison et al., 2019). The authors report the drug to be safe, have few side effects, and found to be effective for appetite and weight gain in a number of different health conditions. Cyproheptadine has also been subject to randomised controlled trials in both children and adults. There is also evidence that cyproheptadine may be effective for certain sub-groups of children with primary difficulties in feeding, for example those with Russell-Silver syndrome (Lemoine et al., 2018). That said, amongst this literature, the only studies published on the role of cyproheptadine in primary feeding disorders are retrospective or case series, and whilst the medication has been around for a long time and appears to be safe apart from in over-dose, there is a clear need for more research, including randomised controlled trials for its use in ARFID. Indeed, the author's experience of cyproheptadine with ARFID has been mixed; although safe and generally well tolerated, for some children it has had a positive effect, in others no effect (data not published). At present, it seems appropriate to suggest that cyproheptadine could be used alongside a multi-disciplinary team where psychological assessment has identified lack of appetite as a key feature, in particular in those where psychological interventions may not have worked or where children and young people are dependent on tube-feeds (including feeding via a gastrostomy tube).

The use of a number of other, psychotropic medications has been reported for patients with ARFID (Spettigue et al., 2018) with the use of some of these medications having recently been investigated individually, with separate publications reporting on small number studies. In a feasibility, double-blinded, randomised controlled study comparing D-cycloserine (DCS) as an adjunctive therapy to behavioural intervention, to behavioural intervention alone, in children with feeding disorders, the combined treatment was reported to increase observed measures of eating at meal time (bites and swallow), although there were no reported data on effect on weight (Sharp et al., 2017). In one retrospective case note review from a single centre, the anti-depressant mirtazapine was used in a small number of child and adolescent patients with ARFID (Gray et al., 2018). The authors reported greater rate of weight gain after, compared to before, initiating mirtazapine. They also reported problems with drowsiness in around half of cases, and, in some cases, increased anxiety. A further, retrospective case note review of children and adolescents in an outpatient programme for ARFID, compared weight gain in a small number of individuals before and after using the anti-psychotic medication, olanzapine, as adjunctive therapy, with greater weight gain after commencing compared to prior (Brewerton & D'Agostino, 2017). All of these studies are small in numbers of participants included, and either feasibility studies or retrospective in design; consequently, these medications require further validation and research before being considered effective medications or recommended treatment interventions for ARFID.

For example, olanzapine is a mainstream, commonly used drug internationally and is known to have a role in reducing anxiety, especially in the context of eating disorders (Crow, 2019). However, it is also known to carry with it a number of cardio-metabolic side-effects. Nevertheless, it will likely continue to be considered and used on a case-by-case basis by professionals with expertise in its usage, as will, no doubt, serotonin reuptake inhibitors commonly used for anxiety disorders in children and adolescence (Wang et al., 2017). It is unclear to what extent any of these medications treat ARFID itself, components of ARFID or other co-morbidities such as anxiety, and further research is needed to understand this better.

The re-feeding syndrome and ARFID

The re-feeding syndrome is an important consideration for any child or young person with starvation who is supported with increased calorific nutrition. It is a potential complication of commencing increased calories in individuals who have had a recent starvation, characterised by both electrolyte (for example, phosphate) and clinical complications (cardiovascular and neurological). It is beyond the scope of this chapter to fully review the re-feeding syndrome literature, but readers are directed here to a number of reviews which they may find useful (Hudson & Court, 2012; Hudson & O'Connor., 2015; O'Connor & Nicholls, 2013). The context of re-feeding syndrome and ARFID merits discussion here. Once again, there is a lack of published evidence base on specific issues for re-feeding syndrome in ARFID, though there is evidence that patients are being admitted to hospital with ARFID because of concerns about nutrition (Katzman, Norris & Zucker, 2019; Makhzoumi et al., 2019; Strandjord et al., 2015). It is important to highlight that re-feeding syndrome is a potential consequence of re-introducing calories, and if monitored in high-risk cases, harm is rare (O'connor et al., 2016). Underfeeding syndrome, sometimes because of a concern about the re-feeding syndrome, especially in hospital settings is a much more common phenomenon (Nicholls, Hudson, & Mahomed, 2011). As has been discussed before, many children and young people with ARFID tend to run a chronic course of underweight (Lucarelli et al., 2018) and are theoretically at less risk; however, attention should be paid to those where calories are being re-introduced at very low body mass index (<70% of median BMI), where neutropenia is present before re-feeding (a proxy for degree of underweight), and those who have been observed to have had recent, more sudden reductions in intake or weight loss (O'Connor & Nicholls, 2013; O'connor et al., 2016). For such patients, brief inpatient admissions should be considered for monitoring during the first week of re-feeding. Local protocols should be put in place to guide safe monitoring and interventions for the re-feeding syndrome, especially as many clinicians treating children and young people may not have the knowledge base to recognise and manage it (Hudson et al., 2013).

Summary points

- Central to effective medical management is co-working with the multi-disciplinary team around the child, in particular through mutual understanding of the importance of issues and priorities
- Pragmatism over priorities for medical investigation and interventions must be applied, balancing the effects on psychological factors for children and young people with ARFID
- Where acute medical risk, or chronic risk impacting on growth and development, is present, weight restoration should be the team priority
- The most effective intervention for the growth and bone mineral density complications in ARFID is weight gain
- Whilst there is evidence for the safe use of cyproheptadine as an appetite stimulant in ARFID, better-quality research is needed as well as for other medication use in ARFID, for example anti-psychotic medications
- Patients with ARFID may be at risk, especially when weight loss has increased and intake decreased, but more research is needed around interventions for re-feeding children and young people

References

American Psychiatric Association. (2013) *Diagnostic and statistical manual of mental disorders.* (5th ed.) Arlington, VA: Author.

Bardisa-Ezcurra, L., Ullman, R., & Gordon, J. (2010) Diagnosis and management of idiopathic childhood constipation: summary of NICE guidance. *British Medical Journal* 340, c2585.

Baroncelli, G. I. & Bertelloni, S. (2014) The use of bisphosphonates in pediatrics. *Hormone Research in Paediatrics* 82, 290–302.

Branca, F. & Ferrari, M. (2002) Impact of micronutrient deficiencies on growth: the stunting syndrome. *Annals of Nutrition Metabolism* 46(1), 8–17.

Brewerton, T.D. & D'Agostino, M. (2017) Adjunctive use of olanzapine in the treatment of Avoidant Restrictive Food Intake Disorder in children and adolescents in an eating disorders program. *Journal of Child & Adolescent Psychopharmacology* 27, 920–22.

Chao, H.C., Chen, S.Y., Chen, C.C., Chang, K.W., Kong, M.S., Lai, M.W., & Chiu, C.H. (2008) The impact of constipation on growth in children. *Pediatric Research* 64, 308–11.

Couluris, M., Mayer, J.L., Freyer, D.R., Sandler, E., Xu, P., & Krischer, J.P. (2008) The effect of cyproheptadine hydrochloride (periactin) and megestrol acetate (megace) on weight in children with cancer/treatment-related cachexia. *Journal of Pediatric Hematology/Oncology* 30, 791–97.

Crow, S.J. (2019) Pharmacologic treatment of eating disorders. *Psychiatric Clinics of North America* 42, 253–62.

Davit, C.J., Hundley, R.J., Bacic, J.D., & Hanson, E.M. (2011) A pilot study to improve venipuncture compliance in children and adolescents with autism spectrum disorders. *Journal of Developmental Behavioral Pediatrics* 32, 521–25.

De Onis, M. & Branca, F. (2016) Childhood stunting: a global perspective. *Maternal & Child Nutrition* 12(1), 12–26.

Gray, E., Chen, T., Menzel, J., Schwartz, T., & Kaye, W.H. (2018) Mirtazapine and weight gain in Avoidant and Restrictive Food Intake Disorder. *Journal of the American Academy of Child & Adolescent Psychiatry* 57, 288–89.

Harrison, M.E., Norris, M.L., Robinson, A., Spettigue, W., Morrissey, M., & Isserlin, L. (2019) Use of cyproheptadine to stimulate appetite and body weight gain: A systematic review. *Appetite* 137, 62–72.

Hirakawa, M., Okada, T., Iida, M., Tamai, H., Kobayashi, N., Nakagawa, T., & Fujishima, M. (1990) Small bowel transit time measured by hydrogen breath test in patients with anorexia nervosa. *Digestive Diseases & Sciences* 35, 733–36.

Holt, S., Ford, M.J., Grant, S., & Heading, R.C. (1981) Abnormal gastric emptying in primary anorexia nervosa. *British Journal of Psychiatry* 139, 550–52.

Hudson, L. & O'Connor., G. (2015) The role of the paediatric team in the management of young people with severe AN. In Robinson, PH. & Nicholls, D. (ed.) *Critical care for anorexia nervosa* 41–66. London: Springer.

Hudson, L.D. & Court, A.J. (2012) What paediatricians should know about eating disorders in children and young people. *Journal of Paediatric Child Health* 48, 869–75.

Hudson, L.D., Cumby, C., Klaber, R.E., Nicholls, D.E., Winyard, P.J., & Viner, R.M. (2013) Low levels of knowledge on the assessment of underweight in children and adolescents among middle-grade doctors in England and Wales. *Archives of Diseases in Childhood* 98(4), 309–11.

Kamal, N., Chami, T., Andersen, A., Rosell, F.A., Schuster, M.M., & Whitehead, W.E. (1991) Delayed gastrointestinal transit times in anorexia nervosa and bulimia nervosa. *Gastroenterology* 101, 1320–24.

Katzman, D.K., Norris, M.L., & Zucker, N. (2019) Avoidant restrictive food intake disorder: first do no harm. *International Journal of Eating Disorders* 52, 459–61.

Lemoine, A., Harbison, M.D., Salem, J., Tounian, P., Netchine, I., & Dubern, B. (2018) Effect of cyproheptadine on weight and growth velocity in children with Silver-Russell syndrome. *Journal of Pediatric Gastroenterology & Nutrition* 66, 306–11.

Lucarelli, L., Sechi, C., Cimino, S., & Chatoor, I. (2018) Avoidant/Restrictive Food Intake Disorder: a longitudinal study of malnutrition and psychopathological risk factors from 2 to 11 years of age. *Frontiers in Psychology* 9, 1608. https://doi.org/10.3389/fpsyg.2018.01608 accessed 12 July 2019.

Makhzoumi, S.H., Schreyer, C.C., Hansen, J.L., Laddaran, L.A., Redgrave, G.W., & Guarda, A.S. (2019) Hospital course of underweight youth with ARFID treated with a meal-based behavioral protocol in an inpatient-partial hospitalization program for eating disorders. *International Journal of Eating Disorders* 52, 428–34.

Mcallister, D.A., Liu, L., Shi, T., Chu, Y., Reed, C., Burrows, J., Adeloye, D., Rudan, I., Black, R.E., Campbell, H., & Nair, H. (2019) Global, regional, and national estimates of pneumonia morbidity and mortality in children younger than 5 years between 2000 and 2015: a systematic analysis. *Lancet Global Health* 7, e47-57.

Mclenon, J. & Rogers, M.A.M. (2019) The fear of needles: A systematic review and meta-analysis. *Journal of Advanced Nursing* 75, 30–42.

Misra, M., Katzman, D.K., Estella, N.M., Eddy, K.T., Weigel, T., Goldstein, M.A., Miller, K.K., & Klibanski, A. (2013) Impact of physiologic estrogen replacement on anxiety symptoms, body shape perception, and eating attitudes in adolescent girls with anorexia nervosa: data from a randomized controlled trial. *Journal of Clinical Psychiatry* 74, e765-71.

Modan-Moses, D., Yaroslavsky, A., Kochavi, B., Toledano, A., Segev, S., Balawi, F., Mitrany, E., & Stein, D. (2012) Linear growth and final height characteristics in adolescent females with anorexia nervosa. *PLoS One* 7, e45504. 10.1371/journal.pone.0045504 accessed on 12 July 2019.

Nasr, S.Z. & Drury, D. (2008) Appetite stimulants use in cystic fibrosis. *Pediatric Pulmonology* 43, 209–19.

Nicholls, D., Hudson, L., & Mahomed, F. (2011) Managing anorexia nervosa. *Archive of Diseases of Childhood* 96, 977–82.

O'Connor, G. & Nicholls, D. (2013) Refeeding hypophosphatemia in adolescents with anorexia nervosa: a systematic review. *Nutrition in Clinical Practice* 28, 358–364.

O'connor, G., Nicholls, D., Hudson, L., & Singhal, A. (2016) Refeeding low weight hospitalized adolescents with anorexia nervosa: a multicenter randomized controlled trial. *Nutrition in Clinical Practice* 31, 681–89.

Robinson, L., Aldridge, V., Clark, E.M., Misra, M., & Micali, N. (2017a) Pharmacological treatment options for low bone mineral density and secondary osteoporosis in anorexia nervosa: a systematic review of the literature. *Journal of Psychosomatic Research* 98, 87–97.

Robinson, L., Micali, N., & Misra, M. (2017b) Eating disorders and bone metabolism in women. *Current Opinion in Pediatrics* 29, 488–96.

Sato, Y. & Fukudo, S. (2015) Gastrointestinal symptoms and disorders in patients with eating disorders. *Clinical Journal of Gastroenterology* 8, 255–63.

Sharp, W.G., Allen, A.G., Stubbs, K.H., Criado, K.K., Sanders, R., McCracken, C.E., Parsons, R.G., Scahill, L., & Gourley, S.L. (2017) Successful pharmacotherapy for the treatment of severe feeding aversion with mechanistic insights from cross-species neuronal remodeling. *Translational Psychiatry* 7, e1157. 10.1038/tp.2017.126 accessed 12 July 2019.

Singhal, V., Misra, M., & Klibanski, A. (2014) Endocrinology of anorexia nervosa in young people: recent insights. *Current Opinion in Endocrinology, Diabetes and Obesity* 21, 64–70.

Spettigue, W., Norris, M.L., Santos, A., & Obeid, N. (2018) Treatment of children and adolescents with avoidant/restrictive food intake disorder: a case series examining the feasibility of family therapy and adjunctive treatments. *Journal of Eating Disorders* 6, 20.

Srivastava, T. & Alon, U.S. (2003) The role of bisphosphonates in diseases of childhood. *European Journal of Pediatrics* 162, 735–51.

Stacher, G., Abatzi-Wenzel, T.A., Wiesnagrotzki, S., Bergmann, H., Schneider, C., & Gaupmann, G. (1993) Gastric emptying, body weight and symptoms in primary anorexia nervosa. Long-term effects of cisapride. *British Journal of Psychiatry* 162, 398–402.

Strandjord, S.E., Sieke, E.H., Richmond, M. & Rome, E.S. (2015) Avoidant/Restrictive Food Intake Disorder: illness and hospital course in patients hospitalized for nutritional insufficiency. *Journal of Adolescent Health* 57, 673–78.

Torres, A. & Gonzalez, M. (2015) Chronic constipation. *Revista Chilena De Pediatria* 86(4), 299–304.

Wang, Z., Whiteside, S.P.H., Sim, L., Farah, W., Morrow, A.S., Alsawas, M., Barrionuevo, P., Tello, M., Asi, N., Beuschel, B., Daraz, L., Almasri, J., Zaiem, F., Larrea-Mantilla, L., Ponce, O.J., Leblanc, A., Prokop, L.J., & Murad, M.H. (2017) Comparative effectiveness and safety of cognitive behavioral therapy and pharmacotherapy for childhood anxiety disorders: a systematic review and meta-analysis. *JAMA Pediatrics* 171, 1049–56S.

Chapter 14

Individual interventions

Amy Siddall, Louise Bradbury and Sara Milne

Introduction

Avoidant restrictive food intake disorder (ARFID) is diverse in its clinical presentation; the factors which may have contributed to, and may be maintaining the difficulties vary between individuals. For this reason there is variation in the treatment approaches that may be most appropriate to offer. Thomas and colleagues have conceptualised ARFID within a basic three-dimensional neurobiological model, which they propose can inform aetiology and treatment (Thomas et al., 2017b). Their model references the three example features, mentioned in the diagnostic criteria for ARFID, which may underlie the avoidant and restrictive eating behaviour: sensory-based food avoidance; lack of interest in food and eating; and concern about aversive consequences of eating. However, clinical experience suggests that other factors may additionally influence eating behaviour. The factors contributing to, and maintaining an individual's difficulty with food can vary in nature and severity, and are not necessarily mutually exclusive. For example, one individual may present with both sensory-based avoidance and concern about the aversive consequences of eating. Understanding the components of any one individual's presentation is a useful first step to determine how best to prioritise and to target treatment.

Three broad types of intervention are emerging as promising approaches in the individual treatment of ARFID: behavioural, cognitive behavioural, and sensory approaches. As these interventions are not specific to the treatment of ARFID, this chapter considers these approaches more generally, as well as how they might be adapted and applied to the treatment of ARFID. Whilst treatment is often informed by the aspects of the presentation considered most responsible for contributing to or maintaining the avoidance or restriction of food intake (Bryant-Waugh, 2013; Thomas, Wons, & Eddy, 2018; Dumont et al., 2019), other factors may play a role in selecting which approach is indicated. For example, an individual's age and developmental level might determine whether a behavioural or cognitive behavioural approach is more appropriate.

Review of evidence obtained from research and clinical experience

There are currently no specific research-based recommendations for the treatment of children presenting with ARFID (Herpertz-Dahlmann, 2017). Whilst there is limited published treatment research specifically relating to ARFID, there is a significant body of literature from other, related areas, such as paediatric feeding disorders, anxiety, and autism. This includes potentially useful pointers to inform and guide treatment of specific shared aspects of presentation. At present any guidance for the treatment of ARFID is therefore derived from three main sources: the limited literature on preliminary findings relating specifically to ARFID; from treatment research carried out with clinical populations with similarities and overlaps with ARFID; and from practice-based evidence.

Behavioural interventions

Behavioural interventions are based on the premise that behaviours are learned and can be modified. This has clear relevance for a presentation such as ARFID, which is characterised by behaviours that result in difficulties for the individual. In terms of theoretical underpinnings of behavioural work, Mowrer (1939) suggested that a disproportionate fear "is a learned response, occurring to signals ('conditioned stimuli') that are premonitory of (for example, have in the past been followed by) conditions of injury or pain ('conditioned response')". The main proposal is that fears are acquired through this process of "conditioning". The strength of the fear is held to be likely to be determined by the number of repetitions of this association process and the intensity of the pain or fear experienced in the presence of the relevant stimulus (Rachman, 1977). It is suggested that once objects or situations acquire fear-provoking qualities, they also acquire motivating qualities to avoid the feared experience (Rachman, 1977). Such behavioural analyses suggest that a child may develop avoidant behaviour in relation to food as a result of an aversive experience and that these behaviours are further maintained by the decrease in negative experience achieved through avoidance.

From a practical point of view such ideas underpin behavioural interventions such as exposure interventions, which are intended to break the link between fear and avoidance behaviour. Exposure treatment aims to encourage individuals to come into contact with the feared stimuli (either in their imagination or *in vivo*) and to maintain this contact until the fear associated with the contact is successfully managed or subsides. Such interventions are often offered in a stepped manner, commencing with exposures, or contacts, that are unlikely to be experienced as too overwhelming for the individual. Exposure has been described as the most effective way to treat specific phobias (Marks, 1979) and can be delivered in a number of different formats. Research indicates that the efficacy of exposure is optimal when it is graduated, repeated and prolonged, with practice tasks clearly specified in order to allow the individual to acquire new non-threatening experiences of the stimuli (Marks, 1979). Behavioural interventions such as exposure therapy have been described as effective in the treatment of ARFID (Kreipe & Palomaki, 2012; Kenney & Walsh, 2013).

Behavioural interventions, such as those based on operant conditioning theory (Skinner, 1938, 1958) can also be useful to consider when the primary objective is to change avoidant behaviour, or as in ARFID where children may be seeking to avoid aversive stimuli in the form of food. In operant conditioning, positive reinforcement involves the addition of a reinforcing stimulus following a desired behaviour, to link this with reward and to increase the likelihood that the behaviour will occur again in the future. In theory, when a favourable outcome, event, or reward occurs after an action, that particular response or behaviour will be strengthened. In a small case series of patients with ARFID, Pitt and Middleman (2018) highlighted the need to address additional behavioural components contributing to unusual eating habits through the process of positive reinforcement. This study suggested that positive reinforcers can be used in the treatment of ARFID to modify the range of foods an individual will eat, increase the number of bites of a food that are accepted, or decrease the time taken for meals.

Typically, behavioural strategies and approaches are implemented alongside input from a wider multi-disciplinary team and commonly include modifications to mealtime structure, behaviour management, and carer training. Silverman (2015) outlines how positive reinforcement and having a contingency to reinforce the target behaviour, such as using reward charts, can assist with decreasing maladaptive behaviours that may have developed in response to anxiety and disgust related to food, promoting desired eating behaviours in their place. Evidence for behavioural approaches in children who meet the criteria for ARFID rests largely on single case studies, or small samples of very young children. Murphy and Zlomke (2016) described a behavioural feeding intervention with a six-year-old girl with ARFID. Treatment was parent mediated and included parent coaching, differential reinforcement, and graded exposure to new foods with contingency strategies. Their findings demonstrated an increase in accepted foods, with less problematic feeding behaviours, and a greater quantity of food consumed following intervention. Whilst these results are positive, it remains difficult to attribute the demonstrated improvements to any one element of the intervention, suggesting that behavioural strategies and parent training combined may have led to the success.

In order to maintain gains from behavioural interventions, a number of treatment approaches with children with avoidant and restrictive eating difficulties include a parental coaching component (Lukens & Silverman, 2014; Ornstein, Essayli, & Nicely, 2017). Parents are trained to act as effective coaches for daily, in-home exposures to non-preferred foods, and given advice on managing mealtime behaviours. Whilst these elements of the intervention appear to be important in maintaining gains at follow up, it is difficult to identify which factor may be having a significant impact on the outcome of treatment, that is, whether this is due to the parent component or specific to the direct behavioural work with the child in clinic. Importantly, a child may not be able to effect behavioural change independently, highlighting the crucial role of the parent in helping to maintain change. The role of parents in individual interventions is discussed further at the end of this chapter.

Interventions focussed on improving parental mealtime management represent another approach which may help to address parental behaviours inadvertently reinforcing food avoidance. Linscheid (2006) noted factors that may be helpful to consider when using behavioural strategies in the context of family mealtimes to promote better appetite and increased food intake. Interventions are recommended to focus on implementing mealtime schedules and limiting their duration, in order to capitalise on the child's hunger and satiety cycle. A further suggestion is to control how long food is offered for, rather than food being readily available, to promote an internal drive to feed. An additional strategy is to ensure that there are predictable meal and snack times as well as periods where no food is offered, to optimise positive sensations in anticipation of food. Such considerations may be particularly helpful for parents of children with ARFID in whom limited intake or low interest in food is a feature. Any such treatment decisions need to take into account other issues which may be impacting on an individual's hunger drive, such as medical issues (for example, constipation) or emotional issues (for example, internal negative sensations associated with negative emotions) before proceeding to implement such behavioural strategies as the main intervention.

Cognitive-behavioural therapy (CBT)

When emotional factors, such as anxiety, are associated with eating and are a primary maintaining factor, CBT may be considered a useful intervention method. In practice, CBT incorporates both behavioural and cognitive approaches. With children, the nature and content of the cognitive component of this treatment approach, depends on their developmental stage, level of cognitive functioning, and extent to which they can assimilate information and learn with the support of an attentive adult. Whilst there is no set age at which CBT can be used with children, typically it would not be considered appropriate to offer direct cognitive behavioural treatment to children who are below primary school age (Fuggle, Dunsmuir, & Curry, 2013).

CBT and exposure-based therapy continue to be the best established psychological treatments for children with anxiety (Higa-McMillan et al., 2016). In published papers describing CBT as a treatment method for ARFID, the eating difficulty has mostly been conceptualised as involving a phobic element and an anxiety model of CBT utilised (Singer et al., 1992; Marcontell, Laster, & Johnson, 2002; Bryant-Waugh, 2013; King, Urbach & Stewart, 2015; Thomas et al., 2017a; Dumont et al., 2019). King and colleagues (2015) apply a two-factor model of anxiety to ARFID (Mowrer, 1960), proposing that a fear of eating is shaped by classical conditioning (here, repeated pairings of eating with gastrointestinal sensations interpreted as highly threatening and/or associated with previous traumatic outcomes) and maintained by operant conditioning (here, refusal to eat reducing anxiety experienced when encountering eating cues, thus negatively reinforcing food avoidance), with additional psychosocial factors shaping and maintaining eating-related anxiety.

Reviewing the literature regarding the use of CBT for the treatment of ARFID, common elements occur, including regular eating, self-monitoring of food intake, cognitive restructuring, exposure and response prevention, relaxation training and behavioural experiments (Szalai & Cserép, 2017; Aloi, Sinopoli, & Segura-Garcia, 2018; Thomas, Wons, & Eddy, 2018; Dumont et al., 2019;). However, Dumont and colleagues propose that the implementation of exposure techniques to all ARFID presentations (as described in Thomas, Wons, & Eddy, 2018) is challenging, because not all presentations are primarily characterised by anxiety but may be driven by lack of interest in food or disgust. Instead they propose that treatment should be based on an inhibitory learning paradigm of using cognitive techniques and expectancy violation to facilitate change.

Szalai and Cserép (2017) propose that imagination, relaxation and biofeedback can be used to support patients to develop their ability to self-regulate. This could be particularly helpful for children who have experienced an aversive, uncontrolled experience of gagging upon trying new foods, perhaps due to sensory sensitivities. The use of computer-based, heart rate variability biofeedback programmes has been applied to the treatment of anxiety with good effect (Frank et al., 2010; Henrique et al., 2011), with similar approaches used in clinical settings to help children identify and manage their anxiety symptoms. This can be particularly useful when supporting children who struggle to identify with anxiety or discuss their emotional state, and can support them to take control of their physiological symptoms and see measurable effects from implementing relaxation methods. Some children are able to continue such work at home, using personal heart rate monitors, readily available via smartphones and wrist devices. The feedback from these devices can be used alongside *in vivo* exposure to indicate to the clinician and child how the presentation of novel foods impacts on their anxiety and the consequent need to learn how to manage this.

The impact of disgust might also need consideration when utilising a CBT approach. Fear and disgust are prominent emotional states that are associated with avoidance of distressing stimuli (Taboas, Ojserkis, & McKay, 2014). Disgust, an emotion believed to have evolved to protect us from ingesting potentially harmful substances (Miller, 1997), has been proposed to predispose individuals to negative interpretation bias, thus contributing to the emergence of anxiety disorders (Matchett & Davey, 1991). Disgust may also maintain anxious avoidance of specific stimuli (Klein et al., 2014). For some individuals, and certainly for some children with ARFID, disgust may arise when faced with certain food items. Harris and colleagues found that disgust partially mediated the association between anxiety and "picky eating" and fully mediated the association between anxiety and ARFID (Harris et al., 2019).

Menzel and colleagues (2019) make distinctions between the physiological responses of anxiety and disgust. They propose that given the discrepant profiles between the two, they may not respond similarly to intervention, citing that compared to fear, disgust exhibits slower rates of habituation and resistance to extinction (Smitz, Telch, & Randall, 2002; Olatunji et al., 2009). However, Taboas and colleagues (2014) examined the effect of CBT on disgust reactions in children with obsessive compulsive disorder and other anxiety disorders, finding that CBT was associated with reduction in disgust reactivity. Symptom reduction may be achieved by targeting anxiety, but the pace of change may be slower than for those who do not experience disgust.

Interventions with a sensory focus

Research findings suggest that both anxiety and sensory sensitivity may be associated with selective eating in non-clinical populations of children (Farrow & Coulthard, 2012). In turn, this suggests that sensory desensitisation may be a relevant treatment approach in working with children with ARFID, whose presentation is characterised by sensory-based food avoidance. Desensitisation may, for example, involve repeated exposures to new foods commencing with exploration and food play with no initial pressure to eat. This is likely to most beneficial when elements of the food play activities are specifically linked with the presenting difficulties. For example, for a child who experiences the smell of food as aversive, food play is only likely to be effective when specifically focussed on foods which smell. Similarly, a food play activity focussed on the smell of foods is unlikely to be beneficial in terms of desensitisation for those children who experience the visual appearance of food as aversive and restrict their diet accordingly. In developing any treatment plan it is important to carefully consider each step of the approach, usually ensuring that the intervention involves a graded hierarchy (developed collaboratively where appropriate), and that it is also age-appropriate. As discussed above, from a behavioural perspective, it is likely that pairing exposure to rewarding experiences may be beneficial. A systematic review and meta-analysis of interventions to improve feeding difficulties in children with autism has shown systematic desensitisation to be an effective approach in this population (Marshall et al., 2015). This review also highlights that sensory desensitisation alongside operant conditioning maybe helpful elements of treatment. Pairing exposure work with rewarding experiences alongside frequent practice may help widen the limited variety of foods accepted, and to move towards reducing avoidant or restrictive behaviours in fearful eaters.

When starting focused work on sensory desensitisation, it appears from clinical experience to be helpful to firstly consider introducing foods with similar sensory qualities to those already accepted. Harris and Shea (2018) have referred to this idea as "spreading the sets", with the central idea being to broaden the range of restricted foods by introducing similar foods, with gradual changes over time. This echoes the principles of "food chaining", a technique aimed at supporting children to try new foods similar to those they currently enjoy and eat consistently (Fraker et al., 2007). Food chaining focusses on identifying similarities between new foods and already accepted foods in terms of their colour, texture, shape, flavour, or smell. New foods to try are selected on the basis of changing one of these features at a time, to help build confidence. An example of this would be to try a chicken nugget of a different brand, or in a different shape, to the chicken nugget already accepted.

Gradual exposure to aversive stimuli using graded steps and hierarchies to break down large goals into smaller, achievable steps (Stallard, 2009), can be another helpful approach. Whilst graded exposure is not specifically a sensory approach, this approach can be utilised with a sensory focus where appropriate. This can be relevant in the treatment of ARFID when incorporating the technique of food chaining (Fraker et al., 2007). Sequential Oral Sensory (SOS) steps to eating is another graded approach focussing on the need to tolerate, interact with, and smell food before moving on to touching and tasting (Toomey & Ross, 2011). This stepped approach was designed with the focus on allowing children to interact with food in a playful and non-pressured way.

Another sensory approach described in a recent study by Zucker and colleagues is an intervention that aims to teach young children with ARFID to engage more positively with their own bodily sensations. The authors suggest that this intervention may help to decrease aversiveness, increase self-awareness, and increase approach behaviours. The technique employed in the study is described as an acceptance-based interoceptive exposure treatment, which uses playful cartoons and developmentally sensitive exposures to teach children how to map interoceptive sensations onto meanings, e.g. emotions and actions (Zucker et al., 2019). Whilst the findings suggest that this approach may potentially decrease ARFID symptoms and increase self-regulation skills, this was a single case design and must be considered tentatively.

Factors to consider before commencing treatment

Motivation

The child's motivation should be considered before proceeding with any intervention. Efforts to encourage, persuade, or coerce individuals into change are likely to reduce their internal motivation (Fuggle, Dunsmuir, & Curry, 2013) and for this reason the timing of when to treat ARFID must be considered, always alongside an evaluation of risk. Clinical experience of working with younger children, suggests that parental motivation levels may be high but mismatched with the child who may have little or no interest in making change. Anecdotally, increases in children's motivation to change can be seen around certain time points, such as after moving to secondary school with an associated increased desire to "fit in" with peers, or becoming increasingly bored with the limitation of the existing diet. Sometimes, the change in motivation, for the young person, is an increasing realisation of the negative impact of current eating habits on their health. As with any intervention it is important to start by collaboratively setting realistic and achievable goals with the child in order for them to experience success and thus increase their confidence and motivation to work on other, more challenging goals. Nicholls and Jaffa (2007) noted that motivational work may be needed or useful if the child is not committed to change, recommending that consideration is given to returning to treatment at a later date if motivation levels are low. Schmidt (2005) identifies two key factors influencing a child's readiness to change; firstly whether they recognise that there is a problem, and secondly the extent of their belief and confidence in their ability to change. Decision balance worksheets can also help children to consider the advantages and disadvantages of change.

Individual adaptations

When planning an intervention, the child's age, developmental level, learning ability, and any neurodevelopmental factors should be taken into consideration. Appropriate adaptations may need to be made to accommodate these factors. For example, with younger children a stronger focus may be placed on the behavioural elements of CBT-based approaches, whilst older children and adolescents may be able to engage more with cognitive change techniques. Some individuals, particularly those with high-functioning autism, might also prefer to use worksheets as part of their treatment. When working with children with more severe autism, when there might also be context specific eating, it may be important for them to have regular exposure sessions based in nursery or school. As is discussed further in Chapter 17, in such cases working with the local network of professionals, such as school staff, will be important in eliciting change.

The role of the primary caregiver

When providing treatment to children the significance of the role of the primary caregiver should be considered. Stallard (2009) suggests that caregivers can potentially take on three different roles in treatment; as facilitator, as co-clinician, or as co-client. It can be helpful to include a primary caregiver in treatment regardless of the child's age and ability, if only to feed back the work at the end of each session. This may enable caregivers to fully understand the difficulty, and potentially model and facilitate work at home between sessions. The literature advising on treatment for eating disorders also highlights including families in treatment, particularly where there may be accommodation of a child's symptoms in attempts to alleviate family conflict and stress (Whitney & Eisler, 2005; Sepulveda, Kyriacou, & Treasure, 2009).

Risk

Consideration should be given to any risk factors identified at assessment. For example, factors discussed in Chapters 8 and 9 in relation to nutrition and physical health may indicate that certain goals for treatment must be prioritised. A hierarchy of needs in terms of treatment should be developed based on these identified risks and will inform the planning of the intervention.

Conclusions

Whilst the existing literature guiding the treatment of ARFID is limited, it is important to consider that there are existing evidence-based approaches for the treatment of feeding difficulties and selective eating, widely used prior to the introduction of ARFID as a diagnosis in 2013. As discussed by Bryant-Waugh (2013) there is a need for more formal testing of existing treatments in larger cohorts as well as for more longitudinal data. When considering an individual intervention for the treatment of ARFID, it is important to consider this evidence-base, but to also be guided by the formulation of the individual's difficulties and the primary factors which are thought to be maintaining the problem with eating. There are good evidence-based treatments available for related conditions such as anxiety and sensory sensitivities which may be important to refer to and consider when planning an individual intervention for ARFID. From clinical experience, confirmed by recent research, there is often a mixed presentation (Reilly et al., 2019), which will likely require an individualised formulation and therefore an individualised approach to intervention. Further research is required to develop clear evidence-based treatments specifically for ARFID and means by which treatment might best be standardised to be most effective.

Summary points

- There is currently a limited evidence base for the treatment of ARFID, with no one treatment modality demonstrated to be the most effective
- Three broad types of individual interventions may be considered: behavioural, cognitive behavioural, and sensory approaches, all of which are likely to require appropriate primary caregiver involvement

- Treatment is usefully informed by a comprehensive formulation, taking account of the features considered to be responsible for contributing to and maintaining avoidance or restriction of food intake
- Motivation should be assessed carefully prior to treatment
- Interventions should be adapted to the individual's age, ability level and neurodevelopmental profile.

References

Aloi, M., Sinopoli, F., & Segura-Garcia, C. (2018). A case report of an adult male patient with avoidant/restrictive food intake disorder treated with CBT. *Psychiatria Danubina* 30 (3), 370–73.

Bryant-Waugh, R. (2013). Avoidant restrictive food intake disorder: an illustrative case example. *International Journal of Eating Disorders* 46 (5), 420–23.

Dumont, E., Jansen, A., Kroes, D., de Hann, E., & Mulkens, S. (2019). A new cognitive behaviour therapy for adolescents with avoidant/restrictive food intake disorder in a day treatment setting: a clinical case series. *International Journal of Eating Disorder* 52 (4), 447–58.

Farrow, C.V. & Coulthard, H. (2012). Relationships between sensory sensitivity, anxiety and selective eating in children. *Appetite* 58 (3), 842–46.

Fraker, C., Fishbein, M., Cox, S., & Walbert, L. (2007) *Food chaining: the proven 6-step plan to stop picky eating, solve feeding problems and expand your child's diet.* Boston: Da Capo Press.

Frank, D.L., Khorshid, L., Kiffer, J.F., Moravec, C.S., & McKee, M.G. (2010). Biofeedback in medicine: who, when, why and how?. *Mental Health in Family Medicine* 7 (2), 85–91.

Fuggle, P., Dunsmuir, S., & Curry, V. (2013) *CBT with children and young people and families.* London: Sage Publications Ltd.

Harris, A.A., Romer, A.L. Hanna, E.K., Keeling, L.A., LaBar, K.S., Sinnott-Armstrong, W., Strauman, T.J., Wagner, H.R., Marcus, M.D., & Zucker, N. (2019). The central role of disgust in disorders of food avoidance. *International Journal of Eating Disorders* 52 (5), 543–53.

Harris, G. & Shea, E. (2018) *Food refusal and avoidant eating in children, including those with autism spectrum conditions: a practical guide for parents and professionals.* Philadelphia: Jessica Kingsley Publishers.

Henrique, G., Keffer, S., Abrahamson, C., & Horst, S.J. (2011). Exploring the effectiveness of a computer-based heart rate variability biofeedback program in reducing anxiety in college students. *Applied Psychophysiology and Biofeedback* 36 (2), 101–12.

Herpertz-Dahlmann, B. (2017). Treatment of eating disorders in child and adolescent psychiatry. *Current Opinion in Psychiatry* 30 (6), 438–45.

Higa-McMillan, C.K., Francis, S.E., Rith-Najarian, L., & Chorpita, B.F. (2016). Evidence base update: 50 years of research on treatment for child and adolescent anxiety. *Journal of Clinical Child and Adolescent Psychology* 45 (2), 91–113.

Kenney, L. & Walsh, T. (2013). Avoidant/restrictive food intake disorder (ARFID). *Eating Disorder Review* 24 (3), 1–4.

King, L.A., Urbach, J., & Stewart, K.E. (2015). Illness anxiety and avoidant-restrictive food intake disorder: cognitive behaviour conceptualization and treatment. *Eating Behaviours* 19, 106–09.

Klein, A.M., Titulaer, G., Simons, C., Allart, E., de Gier, E., Bögels, S.M., Becker, E.S., & Rinck, M. (2014). Biased interpretation and memory in children with varying levels of spider fear. *Cognition & Emotion* 28 (1), 182–92.

Kreipe, R.E. & Palomaki, A. (2012). Beyond picky eating: avoidant/Restrictive Food Intake Disorder. *Current Psychiatry Reports* 14 (4), 421–31.

Linscheid, T.R. (2006). Behavioural treatments for paediatric feeding disorders. *Behaviour Modification* 330, 6–23.

Lukens, C.T. & Silverman, A.H. (2014). Systematic review of psychological interventions for pediatric feeding problems. *Journal of Pediatric Psychology* 39, 903–17.

Marcontell, D.K., Laster, A.E., & Johnson, J. (2002). Cognitive-behavioural treatment of food neophobia in adults. *Anxiety Disorders* 16, 341–49.

Marks I. (1979). Exposure therapy for phobias and obsessive-compulsive disorders. *Hospital Practice* 14 (2), 101–18.

Marshall, J., Ware, R., Ziviani, J., Hill, R.J., & Dodrill, P. (2015). Efficacy of interventions to improve feeding difficulties in children with autism spectrum disorders: a systematic review and meta analysis. *Child Care, Health and Development* 41 (2), 278–302.

Matchett, G. & Davey, G.C. (1991). A test of a disease-avoidance model of animal phobias. *Behaviour Research and Therapy* 29 (1), 91–94.

Menzel, J.E., Reilly, E.E., Luo, T.J., & Kaye, W.H. (2019). Conceptualising the role of disgust in avoidant/restrictive food intake disorder: implications for the etiology and treatment of selective eating. *International Journal of Eating Disorder* 52 (4) https://doi.org/10.1002/eat.23006 accessed 14 July 2019.

Miller, W.I. (1997) *The anatomy of disgust*. Cambridge, MA: Harvard University Press.

Mowrer, O.H. (1939). A stimulus response theory of anxiety. *Psychological Review* 46, 553–65.

Mowrer, O.H. (1960) *Learning theory and behavior*. New York: Wiley.

Murphy, J. & Zlomke, K.R. (2016). A behavioral parent-training intervention for a child with avoidant/restrictive food intake disorder. *Clinical Practice in Pediatric Psychology* 4 (1), 23–34.

Nicholls, D. & Jaffa, T. (2007) Selective eating and other atypical eating problems In Jaffa, T. & McDermott, B. (eds) *Eating Disorders in Children and Adolescents*. New York: Cambridge University Press. 144–57.

Olatunji, B.O., Wolitzky-Taylor, K.B., Willems, J., Lohr, M., & Armstrong, T. (2009). Differential habituation of fear and disgust during repeated exposure to threat-relevant stimnation-based OCD: an analogue study. *Journal of Anxiety Disorders* 23, 118–23.

Ornstein, R.M., Essayli, J.H., & Nicely, T.A. (2017). Treatment of avoidant/restrictive food intake disorder in a cohort of young patients in a partial hospitalization program for eating disorders. *International Journal of Eating Disorders* 50, 1067–74.

Pitt, D.P. & Middleman, A.B. (2018). A focus on behaviour management of avoidant/restrictive food intake disorder (ARFID): a case series. *Clinical Pediatrics* 57 (4), 478–80.

Rachman, S. (1977). The conditioning theory of fear-acquisition: a critical examination. *Behaviour Research Therapy* 15 (5), 375–87.

Reilly, E.E., Brown, T.A., Gray, E.K., Kaye, W.H., & Menzel, J.E. (2019). Exploring the co-occurrence of behavioural phenotypes for avoidant/restrictive food intake disorder in a partial hospitalization sample. *European Eating Disorders Review* 27 (4), 429–35.

Schmidt, U. (2005) Engagement and motivational interviewing In P. Graham (ed.) *Cognitive-behaviour therapy for children and families* (2nd ed.) 67–83. Cambridge: Cambridge University Press.

Sepulveda, A.R., Kyriacou, O., & Treasure, J. (2009). Development and validation of the accommodation and enabling scale for eating disorders (AESED) for caregivers in eating disorders. *BMC Health Services Research* 9 (171), 1–13.

Silverman, A.H. (2015). Behavioural management of feeding problems in children. *Annals of Nutrition and Metabolism* 66 (5), 33–42.

Singer, L.T., Ambuel, B., Wade, S., & Jaffe, A.C. (1992). Cognitive-behavioural treatment of health-impairing food phobias in children. *Journal of American Academy of Child and Adolescent Psychiatry* 31 (5), 847–52.

Skinner, B.F. (1938) *The behavior of organisms: an experimental analysis.* New York: Appleton-Century.

Skinner, B.F. (1958). Reinforcement today. *American Psychologist* 13 (3), 94–99.

Smitz, J.A., Telch, M.J., & Randall, P.K. (2002). An examination of the decline in fear and disgust during exposure-based treatment. *Behavior Research and Therapy* 40, 1243–53.

Stallard, P. (2009) *Anxiety: cognitive behaviour therapy with children and young people.* East Sussex: Routledge.

Szalai, T.D. & Cserép, M. (2017). Treatment methods of avoidant/restrictive food intake disorder. *Psychiatry Today* 29 (1), 5–24.

Taboas, W., Ojserkis, R., & McKay, D. (2014). Change in disgust reactions following cognitive-behavioural therapy for childhood anxiety disorders. *International Journal of Clinical and Health Psychology* 15, 1–7.

Thomas, J.J., Brigham, K.S., Sally, S.T., Hazen, E.P., & Eddy, K.T. (2017a). Case 18-2017: an 11-year-old girl with difficulty eating after a choking incident. *New England Journal of Medicine* 376 (24), 2377–86.

Thomas, J.J., Lawson, E.A., Micali, N., Misra, M., Deckersbach, T., & Eddy, K.T. (2017b). Avoidant/restrictive food intake disorder: a three-dimensional model of neurobiology with implications for etiology and treatment. *Current Psychiatry Reports* 19 (8), 54 https://doi.org/10.1007/s11920-017-0795-5 accessed 14 July 2019.

Thomas, J.J., Wons, O., & Eddy, K.T. (2018). Cognitive-behavioural treatment of avoidant/restrictive food intake disorder. *Current Opinion in Psychiatry* 31 (6), 425–30.

Toomey, K. & Ross, E. (2011). SOS approach to feeding. *Perspectives on Swallowing and Swallowing Disorders (Dysphagia)* 20, 82–87.

Whitney, J. & Eisler, I. (2005). Theoretical and empirical models around caring for someone with an eating disorder: the reorganisation of family life and inter-personal maintenance factors. *Journal of Mental Health* 14, 575–85.

Zucker, N.L., LaVia, M.C., Craske, M.G., Foukal, M., Harris, A.A., Datta, N., Savereide, E., & Maslow, G.R. (2019). Feeling and body investigators (FBI): ARFID division—an acceptance based interoceptive exposure treatment for children with ARFID. *International Journal of Eating Disorders* 52 (4), 466–72.

Chapter 15

Parent/carer and family interventions

Prabashny Pillay and Claire Higgins

Introduction

For children with avoidant restrictive food intake disorder (ARFID), interventions to target the behavioural, emotional, and interactional difficulties they face might be delivered individually, in a group setting, with a family, or through working primarily with parents. The focus of this chapter is on parent/carer and family interventions. It describes the background for family work in the context of ARFID, drawing on the evidence from family interventions with other feeding and eating disorders, as well as on the evidence for parent/carer and family interventions with children and adolescents more widely, in particular those presenting with anxiety. Recommendations and considerations for a family-based approach are outlined, including working with siblings and the extended family, along with the importance of working in culturally appropriate ways.

Evidence supporting family interventions with ARFID

A large body of evidence exists in support of the effectiveness of research-informed models of family interventions for several child and adolescent mental health presentations, including mood disorders and anorexia nervosa. The evidence base for family interventions with ARFID specifically is, by comparison, still in the early stages of development. Consensus that family work may be indicated in the treatment of ARFID is emerging, with recommendations for family focussed and developmentally appropriate interventions becoming more common (e.g. Mairs & Nicholls, 2016).

According to one review of the evidence base for family, or systemic, interventions for child-focussed problems, family-based behavioural programmes can be particularly effective in addressing severe feeding difficulties and improving weight gain in infants and children (Carr, 2014). Such programmes typically involve parents prompting, shaping, and reinforcing progressive steps towards appropriate feeding behaviour, whilst setting boundaries around mealtimes, ignoring inappropriate feeding responses, and creating a relatively pleasant mealtime environment for the child (Sharp et al., 2010). A number of papers discussing the assessment and treatment of ARFID suggest that parent and family interventions are important, particularly in relation to psycho-education and coaching parents to implement various techniques with their child, such as modification of their own behaviours during mealtimes to foster more positive interactions and enhance outcomes (Mammel & Ornstein, 2017; Thomas, Wons, & Eddy, 2018).

A number of randomised controlled trials have found family-based interventions to be an effective treatment for anorexia nervosa in children and adolescents (e.g., Eisler et al., 2000; Le Grange et al., 1992; Lock & Le Grange, 2013; Russell et al., 1987). Thomas, Wons, and Eddy (2018) refer to published case reports that describe the use of family-based treatment for children and adolescents with ARFID, similar to the models recommended for anorexia nervosa. What is perhaps different in the family-based treatment approaches to children with ARFID described so far, is that the focus at mealtimes tends to be on parents supporting their child to increase the types and variety of food consumed, with an emphasis on educating parents about the factors unique to ARFID (Rienecke, 2017).

Fitzpatrick, Forsberg, and Colborn (2015) outline principles of the Lock and Le Grange (2013) family-based treatment that they suggest can be modified to the ARFID population. They propose this may primarily be suitable for those with longstanding and clinically significant food "neophobia", highlighting the importance of psychoeducation about nutrition and a focus on eating behaviours. These authors further suggest that "externalising" the condition, that is, separating the child from the disorder, is made complicated by the fact that ARFID is often longstanding, sometimes involving lifelong challenges, in contrast to anorexia nervosa, where symptoms represent a dramatic change in functioning. For this reason, an enhanced focus on parents supporting eating behaviours that improve dietary volume as well as variety through repeated exposure to novel foods is proposed. It is important to note that there are as yet no published findings from formal treatment trials for this intervention and early indications should therefore be treated cautiously.

Manualised family interventions for adolescent anorexia nervosa typically involve 18–20 sessions over one year; reviewing the needs of the child four weeks after treatment begins and then every three months, to establish how regular sessions should be and how long treatment should last. Emphasis is placed on the role of the family in helping the child to recover and the importance of not blaming the child or their family members/carers. Such interventions also usually include psychoeducation about nutrition and the effects of malnutrition. An early phase of treatment typically involves supporting the parents or carers to take a central role in helping the person manage their eating, whilst emphasising that this is a temporary role; and aiming to establish a good therapeutic alliance with the child, their parents/carers and other family members. In the next phase, the child is supported, with help from their parents or carers, to establish a level of independence appropriate for their level of development; and in the final phase, the focus is on plans for when treatment ends, relapse prevention, and sources of support thereafter (Eisler et al., 2016; Lock & Le Grange, 2005). It is widely recognised that family-based treatment does not work for all families presenting with anorexia nervosa, and research recommendations have been made to look more closely at the families it does work best for (Rienecke, 2017).

It is important to note that one of the key aspects in any family-based approach that may be considered for children presenting with ARFID, is likely to be the empowerment of parents/carers. Parents and carers can helpfully be encouraged to develop a level of understanding and acceptance of their child's eating difficulties, with parental empowerment supporting the management of stress around mealtimes. Such a stance involves considering the possibility that initially "re-feeding" may mean working with the child's known and familiar foods rather than expanding outside their range.

Recommendations and considerations for clinical practice

As yet there is no evidence-based family intervention specifically for ARFID. It seems unlikely that a generalised approach will emerge as universally effective, given the varied presentations within the ARFID clinical population. However, it is clear from the literature, case descriptions, and clinical practice, that an interdisciplinary approach is generally required and that tailoring the team and management approach to the individual needs and values of the child and their family is most likely to produce sustainable long term outcomes.

Factors that influence the decision to take a family approach include the motivational level of the child, their age, their developmental level, and the impact of the presentation on the child's social functioning and on family relationships. If a child presents with low interest in food, then their motivation to change can often be correspondingly low. Some children report not being bothered about the type of food that they eat and that their eating behaviour has little negative impact on them socially. For such children, a parent-led intervention that incorporates incentive programs for the child, as well as support in managing parental expectations and anxiety, may be beneficial.

When deciding what approach to take it is also important to assess risk. If physical risks are high, intervention to target nutritional adequacy and energy requirements will need to be addressed as a priority. Other important starting points include ensuring a shared understanding of the difficulties as well as setting realistic goals (see Chapter 11). If parents, child, and clinician hold a similar understanding of the difficulties and agree on the approach to take to target agreed goals, then engagement in treatment is likely to be higher and potentially more effective.

Attending to collaboration and the therapeutic alliance

For many parents it is often a relief to hear that there is a diagnosis that can explain their child's eating issues. A formulation that is developed collaboratively with the family is more likely to keep potentially unhelpful professional assumptions and generalisations at bay, to be meaningful to the family, and to result in tailored interventions that produce positive outcomes for the child. A key aspect of collaborative practice in child and adolescent mental health care is putting the child and their families at the centre of service provision and addressing the goals from their perspectives through dialogue and participatory engagement.

There is value in attending to the therapeutic alliance within family interventions; in this instance alliance may be defined as the quality and strength of the collaborative relationship between the family and therapist, including aspects such as mutual trust and respect, and consensus about, and commitment to the goals of therapy, as well as how these are worked towards. In addition, the appropriate use of self-disclosure to establish a sense of trust in the relationship and direct acknowledgment of the child and family's fears and concerns related to treatment, are also thought to help build trust and provide emotional security (LoTempio et al., 2013).

Pandya and Herlihy (2009) found that there is little research exploring whether culture or ethnicity affect the quality of the alliance in either individual or family interventions; they conclude that, when working with families from black and minority ethnic groups, certain aspects of the alliance need more attention, namely safety in front of the therapist and emotional connection to the therapist. Furthermore, it was thought that working in a more alliance-focused way may override the need for culture-specific practices, for example, safety in therapy when discussing cultural issues may be more important than being ethnically matched to the therapist.

Respectful and sensitive practice – culture, values, ethnicity, religion

It is important to go beyond an awareness of difference and actively explore with families their understanding of the role of family values, ethnicity, culture, religion, experience of migration and other contextual factors in relation to the presenting issues. Often families will describe sources of strength, resilience and motivation that may not otherwise reveal themselves. This may stem from families often expecting to be told what they should do and believing that the resources are with the professionals. They may also bring forth contentious practice and self-imposed expectations that they recognise as being unhelpful to the child and family.

Each therapist and family represents multiple cultural identities (e.g., nationality, ethnicity, race, gender, sexual orientation, etc.), hence addressing the interwoven phenomena of culture, gender, and power is important to all. Therapists working cross-culturally should be aware of the risk that their cultural lens might pathologise or judge the practices of other cultures, and impose outside cultural values, however subtle or inadvertent (Keeling & Piercy, 2007). It is equally important to state that a behaviour that is embedded in a particular culture does not automatically make it appropriate; being culturally sensitive does not mean being indifferent to or condoning unjust and unsafe practices.

It is necessary to find ways of examining the preconceptions that inform our practice in an effort to be more sensitive to our own biases and recognise them as such, which is a first step towards practice that recognises the cultural specificity of the ideological assumptions we bring to our work, rather than talking of these assumptions as universal truths (Pakes & Roy-Chowdhury, 2007). Curiosity regarding family beliefs and expectations around food is particularly important and an awareness of the clinician's own family and cultural beliefs about meal times and types of food that children "should" be eating is essential in order not to impose their own cultural beliefs on another family and to help them to find ways to adapt and change within their own goals.

> Syed (a five-year-old boy) was referred for specialist help as he was currently fed by nasogastric tube due to concerns about his falling growth centiles and drop in weight. He accepted a small range of soft foods that he would eat but was not able to eat enough to sustain his energy or nutritional requirements. He showed little interest in foods outside his preferred texture range. Syed's parents were originally from Bangladesh and spoke in the assessment about the advice that they were getting from relatives still living in Bangladesh. They made reference to grandparents advising to "beat him until he eats" and described this as usual for their family. Parents were aware of the conflicting advice from elders at home and the advice from professionals to allow Syed to explore food and play with food. It is possible that this family were able to talk openly about the pressure they felt from their family because the clinician had remained curious about family expectations and had asked whether they had received any advice from other family members and had been curious about feeding practices in their country of origin. The clinician also reflected with the family about her own family beliefs of having to eat everything on the plate or the food would be re-served at breakfast time. This perhaps gave Syed's parents the idea that all families have firmly held beliefs – some good, and some not so good – about eating.

Empowering and enabling parents/carers

It is not unusual that parents who have been contending with their child's feeding and eating difficulties over the course of many weeks, months or years, may feel exhausted, frustrated, hopeless, and helpless. A key aspect of family intervention is to address the factors that may adversely affect parental confidence in their ability to facilitate change in their child's eating, which may differ between families according to their experiences. Collaboratively identifying child-centred goals around feeding and eating that are realistic and achievable, not only builds the child's confidence, but can also facilitate parental confidence-building in supportive implementation of techniques and interventions with their child.

The family dinner is a prime opportunity for change as it is usually the most reliable time of the day for families to connect with one another, hence families who do not already eat together may be encouraged to do so, with a view to exploring the family's preferences and the perceived obstacles that preclude meals together (Fishel, 2016).

Mealtime coaching – facilitating behavioural change

There are suggestions in the literature that regular family meals correlate with a child developing healthier eating habits, stronger self-esteem, parent-child connectedness, and resilience, and also present with lower levels of depression, stress, and anxiety. The elements of a family dinner that are believed to facilitate these benefits include a warm and welcoming atmosphere, and relaxed conversation at the table (Fishel, 2016). Families contending with the repeated daily challenge and impact of ARFID can often be in a state of frustration and helplessness, hence coaching parents to create an environment and interactions that are calmly supportive and reduce stress around mealtimes for the whole family is worth dedicating time to.

Mealtimes may be thought of as a place where new roles, behaviours, and ways of interacting with one another can be experimented with and enacted on a daily basis. Maladaptive mealtime interactions such as mealtime conflict, high parental control and critical comments, may be respectfully, though explicitly, challenged with families. The intention is to suggest more adaptive interactions such as positive communication between family members, a strong parental team (which may include extended family members such as grandparents), and parental recognition and reinforcement of any positive child interactions during mealtimes (Godfrey, Rhodes, & Hunt, 2013). It is, however, recognised that children presenting with ARFID may have avoided mealtimes and developed a range of coping strategies, including distraction with a tablet or other screen, or eating separately to others, that may be in contravention to how a family would "ideally" like to eat at mealtimes. For some children distraction is the only way that they are able to eat, and it is important to recognise whether distraction has becomes a habit or a necessity. Helping families decide the goals they are working on is important and reassurance that distraction, when essential, is acceptable can be helpful.

George (nine years old) had been gastrostomy fed from birth. He had been able to wean off the feeds and showed some selectivity to foods but was managing to expand his diet slowly. He remained at a low weight and parents were keen for him to maximise his eating to gain weight. George ate better in his room than he did with the family. Parents were keen for George to eat with the family and when they tried to enforce family mealtime regularly, he lost weight. They agreed to compromise, George would eat in his room Monday to Friday and at weekends he would join the rest of the family to eat at the dinner table. They accepted that over time this goal could be revised.

Managing an anxious child in the context of ARFID

Family-based cognitive behavioural therapy for child and adolescent anxiety disorders has been found to be as effective as individual cognitive behavioural therapy, and more effective than individual therapy in cases where parents also have anxiety disorders (Carr, 2014; Creswell & Cartwright-Hatton, 2007). A number of intervention programmes have been developed for parents of anxious children (see Cartwright-Hatton et al., 2011; Creswell et al., 2016). Change is effected through helping parents understand their child's anxiety and helping them to develop strategies to respond differently, thereby interrupting the perpetuating cycle of avoidance and supporting the child to manage their emotions more effectively. Others have advocated for experiential interventions, such as communication approaches that explore and address maladaptive family roles, for families of children with anxiety disorders, including the role of parental acceptance, control, and modelling in maintaining children's anxiety symptoms (Kaslow et al., 2012). Rapee and colleagues (2010) outline a programme for intervention for parents of pre-school children identified as socially inhibited. The focus over a six-week period was on the nature of anxiety and its development, parent management techniques focusing on how overprotection maintains anxiety, teaching the application of cognitive restructuring to the parents own worries, and highlighting important high-risk periods for children such as starting school. They found that at follow-up the treatment group had lower scores for being at risk of developing anxiety disorders than the control non-treatment group. Results do need to be interpreted with caution as the group were pre-school age and often anxiety disorders appear at a later stage in childhood than the time of follow-up. However, the components of the sessions seem to be logical; teaching a parent/carer how to manage their own anxiety and expectations and you will in turn be helping them to help their child manage their emotions.

Encouragement of children and parents to engage in communication and problem-solving around the anxiety surrounding food and eating has the potential to enhance the quality of parent–child interaction which can facilitate more positive anxiety management. Whilst the child may learn anxiety-management skills such as relaxation, cognitive strategies and using social support, parents can learn about the value of positive reinforcement of their child's use of these skills, of ignoring their child's avoidant or anxious behaviour, and managing their own anxiety. In this way they can act as a co-therapist supporting their child to effect change (see further Chapter 14).

Encouraging and supporting parents and families to create space for "emotion-talk" is integral to the understanding, expression and management of emotions such as anxiety in the family. This is in relation to both meal times, and general patterns of emotional regulation and expression for parents themselves and their children, separately and together.

Sensory work with parents

When a child presents with sensory issues, low motivation, and an element of fear around food, it may be best to demonstrate to parents, ways to help their child to become de-sensitised. They can then implement this at home. Chapter 10 outlines how several authors recommend approaches to address sensory issues through parent training, sensory strategies, social and sensory stories, and through changing the environment. Research into strategies implemented by parents to address sensory issues has highlighted that parents identify a range of strategies, including sensory-based interventions such as use of calming sensory input, and identifying quieter environments to support participation as helpful (Cermak, Curtin, & Bandini, 2010; Schaaf et al., 2011; Zobel-Lachiusa et al., 2015).

> Joe (12 years old) attended a specialist centre for support with expanding his range of preferred food. He presented with a lack of interest in food and a sensory issue regarding the texture of food. The agreed goals of the work were to help the family understand the sensory issues that prevented Joe from expanding his diet easily and to help them reduce tension at mealtimes. The parent work focussed on the high levels of anxiety in the parents. They explained that Joe had a difficult medical history, and described how they worry he will become unwell again. Exploring this anxiety allowed the parents to acknowledge their level of concern and how this gets activated at mealtimes even when Joe is eating an adequate diet. The sensory qualities of food were explored, as an activity with his parents, and Joe was able to explain the anxiety that he has about the texture of food. Parents were then able to adjust their expectations and begin to let go of the worry that they had. Joe was also able to try a new vegetable and accept this into his diet.

A "whole family" approach

Meeting the whole family can provide a broader understanding of the challenges and impact on individuals and relationships, and, at the very least, the clinician should acknowledge the existence and importance of family viewpoints other than those represented in the session, including significant extended family and grandparents. It has been contended that clinicians' primary focus tends to be on the parent–child relationship, whilst the sibling relationship tends to be on the periphery, sometimes taken for granted rather than explored (Young, 2013). Although it is understandable that emphasis might be placed on parents' sense of their parental authority and functioning, and the factors that influence this, it may not be the complete story if other family relationships are left unconsidered. Often the social and emotional impact on the entire family, particularly siblings (Turns, Eddy, & Smock-Jordan, 2016), can be quite significant; and maintaining a perceived consistency and fairness in their parenting approach for the child with ARFID, as well as their siblings, can be quite a challenge for parents/carers and extended family members. This can be especially true if they perceive their sibling's preferred foods to be superior to their own, for example, whilst they have to eat vegetables their sibling gets to eat exactly what they want to.

Involving the wider system – school, extended family and friends

When working to effect any change with a child and family it is important to consider who else can support the work. Chapter 17 details work with the wider system. Supporting generalisability to other settings including the family home, school, and wider family contexts that form a significant part of the child and family's life can be an essential part of treatment.

Reflections from clinical practice

Co-constructing the formulation can present a challenge when professionals and the family hold different views about how to make sense of the presenting concerns and/or ways forward – transparent conversation and multi-agency perspectives can be helpful in negotiating middle ground in this respect. Encouraging a shared sense of responsibility for change, between the child with ARFID, their family members, and relevant others in their wider network, feels crucial to clinical practice, especially in terms of exploring the relational context within which change may occur. It is imperative to consider any socio-economic factors that could affect the family; this includes asking sensitively about financial and other pressures that could influence the family's ability to attend clinic appointments and manage needs such as housing, heating and food availability. Collaborative practice optimises outcomes, hence recognising the needs of families and working with what they bring to sessions can be the key to positive outcomes (Pandya & Herlihy, 2009). Some would argue that developing relationships rather than developing motivation should be the initial focus, which then leads to greater capacity for change (Sundet et al., 2016).

Summary points

- Clinicians should develop a collaborative formulation and goals that are meaningful to the family to facilitate sustainable change
- Attention to individual family values and circumstances combined with culturally respectful practice is recommended
- A focus on empowering parents within child-focussed care is usually helpful in sustaining change and encouraging progress following treatment
- Parents and carers can benefit from being supported to move from a linear understanding of causality of their child's eating difficulties to a relational understanding and management approach
- When implementing change, it can be helpful to explicitly address the role of emotions
- Working with parents to manage their own and their child's anxiety about food and risk is important
- More research is needed on family interventions for ARFID to include parent groups, mealtime coaching, parent-led cognitive behavioural approaches, and home sensory programmes for eating.

References

Carr, A. (2014) The evidence base for family therapy and systemic interventions for child-focused problems. *Journal of Family Therapy* 36, 107–57.

Cartwright-Hatton, S., McNally, C., Field, A.P., Rust, S., Laskey, B., Dixon, C., Gallagher, B., Harrington, R., Miller, C., Pemberton, K., Symes, W., & Woodham, A. (2011) A new parenting-based group intervention for young anxious children: results of a randomized controlled trial. *Journal of the American Academy of Child and Adolescent Psychiatry* 50 (3), 242–51.

Cermak, S.A., Curtin, C., & Bandini, L.G. (2010) Food selectivity and sensory sensitivity in children with autism spectrum disorders. *Journal of the American Dietetic Association* 110 (20), 238–46.

Creswell, C. & Cartwright-Hatton, S. (2007) Family treatment of child anxiety: outcomes, limitations and future directions. *Child and Family Clinical Psychology Review* 10 (3), 232–52. doi: 10.1007/s10567-007-0019-3 Accessed 13 July 2019.

Creswell, C., Parkinson, M., Thirlwall, K., & Willets, L. (2016) *Parent-led CBT for child anxiety: helping parents help their kids.* New York: Guildford Press.

Eisler, I., Dare, C., Hodes, M., Russell, G., Dodge, E., & Le Grange, D. (2000) Family therapy for adolescent AN: the results of a controlled comparison of two family interventions. *Journal of Child Psychology and Psychiatry* 41 (6), 727–36.

Eisler, I., Simic, M., Blessitt, E., Dodge, L., & team (2016) *Maudsley service manual for child and adolescent eating disorders.* King's Health Partners, www.national.slam.nhs.uk/wp-content/uploads/2011/11/Maudsley-Service-Manual-for-Child-and-Adolescent-Eating-Disorders-July-2016.pdf Accessed 3 June 2019.

Fishel, A.K. (2016) Harnessing the power of family dinners to create change in family therapy. *Australian and New Zealand Journal of Family Therapy* 37, 514–27.

Fitzpatrick, K.K., Forsberg, S.E., & Colborn, D. (2015) Family-based therapy for avoidant restrictive food intake disorder: families facing food neophobias In Loeb, K.L., LeGrange, D.L., & Lock, J. (eds) *Family therapy for adolescent eating and weight disorders* 256–76. New York: Routledge.

Godfrey, K., Rhodes, P., & Hunt, C. (2013) The relationship between family mealtime interactions and eating disorder in childhood and adolescence: A systematic review. *Australian and New Zealand Journal of Family Therapy* 34, 54–74.

Kaslow, N.J., Robbins-Broth, M., Smith, C.O., & Collins, M.H. (2012) Family-based interventions for child and adolescent disorders. *Journal of Marital and Family Therapy* 38 (1), 82–100.

Keeling, M.L. & Piercy, F.P. (2007) A careful balance: multinational perspectives on culture, gender, and power in marriage and family therapy practice. *Journal of Marital and Family Therapy* 33 (4), 443–63.

Le Grange, D., Eisler, I., Dare, C., & Russell, G.F.M. (1992) Evaluation of family treatments in adolescent anorexia nervosa: a pilot study. *International Journal of Eating Disorders* 12, 347–57.

Lock, J. & Le Grange, D. (2005) Family-based treatment of eating disorders. *International Journal of Eating Disorders* 37, 64–67.

Lock, J. & Le Grange, D. (2013) *Treatment manual for anorexia nervosa. A family-based approach* (2nd ed.). New York: Guilford.

LoTempio, E., Forsberg, S., Bryson, S.W., Fitzpatrick, K.K., LeGrange, D., & Lock, J. (2013) Patients' characteristics and the quality of the therapeutic alliance in family-based treatment and individual therapy for adolescents with anorexia nervosa. *Journal of Family Therapy* 35 (1), 29–52.

Mairs, R. & Nicholls, D. (2016) Assessment and treatment of eating disorders in children and adolescents. *Archive of Diseases of Childhood* 101, 1168–75.

Mammel, K.A. & Ornstein, R.M. (2017) Avoidant/restrictive food intake disorder: a new eating disorder diagnosis in the diagnostic and statistical manual 5. *Current Opinion in Paediatrics* 29 (4), 407–13.

Pakes, K. & Roy-Chowdhury, S. (2007) Culturally sensitive therapy? Examining the practice of cross-cultural family therapy. *Journal of Family Therapy* 29, 267–83.

Pandya, K. & Herlihy, J. (2009) An exploratory study into how a sample of a British South Asian population perceive the therapeutic alliances in family therapy. *Journal of Family Therapy* 31, 384–404.

Rapee RM, Kennedy SJ, Ingram M., Edwards, S.L., & Sweeney, L. (2010) Altering the trajectory of anxiety in at-risk young children. *American Journal of Psychiatry* 167, 1518–25.

Rienecke, R.D. (2017) Family-based treatment of eating disorders in adolescents: current insights. *Adolescent Health Medicine and Therapeutics* 8, 69–79.

Russell, G., Szmukler, G., Dare, E., & Eisler, I. (1987) An evaluation of family therapy in anorexia nervosa and bulimia nervosa. *Archives of General Psychiatry* 44 (12), 1047–56.

Schaaf, R., Toth-Cohen, S., Johnson, S., Outten, G., & Benevides, T. (2011) The everyday routines of families of children with autism: examining the impact of sensory processing difficulties on the family. *Autism* 15 (3), 373–89.

Sharp, W., Jaquess, D.L., Morton, J., & Herzinger, C. (2010) Pediatric feeding disorders: a quantitative synthesis of treatment outcomes. *Clinical Child and Family Psychology Review* 13, 348–65.

Sundet, R., Kim, H.S., Ness, O., Borg, M., Karlsson, B., & Biong, S. (2016) Collaboration: suggested understandings. *Australian and New Zealand Journal of Family Therapy* 37, 93–104.

Thomas, J.J., Wons, O.B., & Eddy, K.T. (2018) Cognitive–behavioral treatment of avoidant/ restrictive food intake disorder. *Current Opinion in Psychiatry* 31 (6), 425–30.

Turns, B., Eddy, B.P., & Smock-Jordan, S. (2016) Working with siblings of children with autism: a solution-focused approach. *Australian and New Zealand Journal of Family Therapy* 37 (4), 558–71.

Young, S. (2013) The forgotten siblings. *Australian and New Zealand Journal of Family Therapy* 28 (1), 21–27.

Zobel-Lachiusa J., Andrianopoulos M., Mailloux Z., & Cermak S. (2015) Sensory differences and mealtime behavior in children with autism. *American Journal of Occupational Therapy* 69 (5), 1–8.

Chapter 16

Group interventions

Catherine Frogley and Karen Taylor

Introduction

Group interventions are increasingly recognised as a potentially valuable arm of treatment for a variety of mental health conditions. Mental health services routinely incorporate group work into their service provision with good clinical results. The aim of this chapter is to offer a theoretical and practical overview of group interventions for the treatment of avoidant and restrictive food intake disorder (ARFID) in children and adolescents. It begins by outlining the role and potential value of group interventions for this population as well as possible drawbacks. It proceeds with an overview of available evidence relevant to group interventions for ARFID and other feeding and eating difficulties and disorders, alongside empirical findings from the related fields of childhood behavioural difficulties and anxiety. The subsequent section describes a number of possible group interventions for parents, families and children affected by ARFID, offering guidance and practical advice about how and when these might be implemented. The chapter concludes with considerations and recommendations for future work in this area.

Advantages and disadvantages of group interventions

Group interventions have been shown to be effective, as discussed below, and to have several potential benefits. They provide participants with an opportunity to meet others experiencing similar difficulties. This in itself can reduce feelings of shame and isolation and promote a sense of acceptance and understanding. Individuals may feel more comfortable sharing thoughts, feelings and experiences, a process that can help them to make sense of the problem. Participants can access information about how others are managing difficulties, either successfully or unsuccessfully, and this can aid reflection about their own methods of coping. The group environment can also facilitate a wider pool of ideas and strategies. Not only can this enrich discussion but it can also improve people's confidence when providing support and advice to others. The group format also allows for experiential activities and opportunities to observe strategies in vivo, which may enhance learning and translation into everyday life. Importantly, amidst competing resources, group interventions are cost effective as multiple individuals can access treatment at one time.

Whilst there are many advantages to group work, it is not suitable for everyone or indeed every service. Setting up a group for the first time can be resource-intensive and may involve several professionals. This is particularly true for ARFID as the condition straddles both physical and mental health. For example, a parent group may require input from a psychologist, an occupational therapist, and a dietician to be able to offer an effective and holistic approach. Furthermore, individuals may not gain access to tailored, individualised treatment within a group environment, which may lead to frustration or information that is insufficiently targeted to specific needs. Group interventions are not a preferred option for all; some participants may feel uncomfortable sharing ideas within a group context, others may find it demoralising to compare themselves to others who they perceive to be coping better. Thoughtful leadership of the group is essential to manage group dynamics effectively and facilitators need to feel confident in their ability to do this.

Research findings

Relatively few studies have evaluated group interventions for children with feeding and eating difficulties, with only one including individuals with a confirmed diagnosis of ARFID. Existing evidence, summarised below, includes evaluations of groups for parents, multiple families, and children.

Parent groups

Two studies have evaluated the use of a behavioural parenting group for children with a diagnosis of autism and "selective eating". The first group used an applied behaviour analysis (ABA) approach and included seven sessions per day (an intensity characteristic of ABA) over several weeks (Seiverling et al., 2012). Following this intervention, children were reported to show improvements across various measures of bite acceptance, mealtime behaviour and diet variety. The second group intervention, the Autism MEAL plan, was based on behavioural therapy and ran over eight weeks for parents of children aged 3–8 years old. The authors found that parents reported high levels of efficacy and reduced stress following attendance in the group (Sharp et al., 2016). However, no significant improvements in diet variety or behaviour at mealtimes were identified. It is worth noting that despite clinical services beginning to offer regular parent workshops for those affected by ARFID, most such groups await formal evaluation to determine their efficacy.

Multi-family groups

A multi-family group intervention has been developed for children aged 8–12 years with a diagnosis of autism and "selective eating" (Kuschner et al., 2017).

The BUFFET programme (Building Up Food Flexibility and Exposure Treatment) is a 14-week group using cognitive behavioural therapy (CBT) strategies to help children develop skills to cope with anxiety and to think and act flexibly with unfamiliar foods. The sessions include a combination of family, child, and parent sessions. Preliminary results of this intervention show promise in terms of acceptability measured through attendance, child and parent feedback, and clinician satisfaction. The authors plan to evaluate the programme within a larger sample and consider its appropriateness for other populations (e.g. for those without autism).

In another study, conducted in a non-clinical population of children with "problem eating", a multi-family group intervention also demonstrated positive results (Adamson, Morawska & Sanders, 2015). The group, named Hassle Free Mealtimes, aimed at children aged 1–6 years and using a behavioural approach to target feeding, was evaluated in a randomised controlled trial. The results showed significant improvements in mealtime behaviour in addition to parental confidence, cognitions and interactions around mealtimes. These findings also remained stable at six month follow-up.

Groups for children and young people

For younger children, sensory-based exposure or "messy play" is often recommended when there are concerns around feeding and eating. Allowing children to be "messy" and play with their food forms part of the UK National Institute for Clinical Excellence (NICE) guidelines for children with faltering growth (NICE, 2017 recommendation 1.2.19). Messy food play provides an opportunity for children to explore different sensory properties of food (e.g. texture, smell) in a fun and safe way with no expectation to eat the food (see Chapter 10). This is often delivered within a group context.

The Sequential Oral Motor Sensory (SOS) approach to feeding is an assessment and treatment programme that considers sensory issues alongside oral-motor, behavioural, medical, nutritional and environmental aspects of feeding and eating difficulties (Toomey, 2010). Toomey recommends group treatment for children between 18 months and 7 years due to this age group being reported to respond best to peer role models with similar issues. This is based on evidence from social learning theory (Bandura, 1986) which suggests that children struggle to learn from role models who are too far advanced in their skills (e.g. an adult or peer with no feeding problem).

Although the SOS approach has been enthusiastically adopted by some clinical services, there remains limited published research evidence to support its use. In a doctoral dissertation, a 12-week SOS therapy group for children aged 18–61 months was evaluated by analysing the three-day food records of children attending the group over a two-year period (Boyd, 2007). It was reported that the children increased their food repertoire by 41% following the intervention. In a second study, Owen and colleagues evaluated a group based on SOS for parents and children. This included an initial parent education session, three 90-minute treatment sessions with the child and a follow-up session. The results demonstrated significant reductions on a feeding assessment scale and positive feedback from parents (Owen et al., 2012).

Further support for sensory management within a group setting comes from a five-week intervention focusing on sensory education and exploration within a non-clinical population of children aged 3–6 years (Hoppu et al., 2015). This study found improvements in children's willingness to eat selected vegetables and berries compared to a control group not receiving the intervention. It seems that, for both clinical and non-clinical populations of children, interventions that include a combination of behavioural and sensory management may be most effective.

Currently, only one study has included older children in its evaluation. The BUFFET programme included sessions for children aged 8–12 years that utilised CBT principles adapted for autism (Kuschner et al., 2017). Although there were no measures of effectiveness, both children and parents gave favourable feedback about the group. Given that individual CBT has recently demonstrated positive results for young people with ARFID (Dumont et al., 2019; see also Chapter 14), group-based CBT may represent a useful therapeutic tool to explore for older children.

For adolescents with a diagnosis of another feeding and eating disorder, namely, anorexia nervosa and bulimia nervosa, one scoping review highlighted the relative lack of research investigating group interventions for this population, despite their widespread implementation and assumed effectiveness (Downey, 2014). The review evaluated available evidence for 10–19-year-olds and suggested that multi-family group interventions showed potential in the treatment of anorexia nervosa, whilst group-based CBT showed promise for the treatment of bulimia nervosa. This is in line with the wider literature, which supports family-based treatment for anorexia nervosa and CBT for bulimia nervosa (Alckmin-Carvalho et al., 2018). Alternative group interventions have also been proposed for specific eating disorders, including art and drama therapy (Diamond-Raab & Orrell Valente, 2002), although no formal investigations have been conducted. The most recent NICE guidelines for eating disorders found no evidence for group interventions for anorexia nervosa and bulimia nervosa in children and young people (NICE Guidance on Faltering Growth, 2017). However, some evidence for group-based CBT in adults with a diagnosis of binge eating disorder was identified (NICE, 2017 recommendation 1.4.5).

What can we learn from other fields of mental health?

Although the evidence base for group interventions in children with a diagnosis of ARFID and feeding and eating difficulties more widely is still emerging, the literature regarding group interventions in other fields of mental health may offer useful insights. The following section briefly considers evidence from studies evaluating groups for behavioural difficulties and anxiety.

Behavioural difficulties

There is good evidence to support the use of group-based parenting interventions for a variety of childhood difficulties, in particular for those with behavioural difficulties. Parent training programmes utilising behavioural therapy techniques have been shown to be effective for children with difficulties such as oppositional defiant disorder and attention-deficit hyperactivity disorder, with good outcomes demonstrated in terms of efficacy and acceptability (e.g. Fabiano et al., 2015; Zwi et al., 2011).

Anxiety

Group-based parenting interventions for children with anxiety disorders have also demonstrated positive results. One ten-session intervention for parents of anxious children under nine years old resulted in over 50% of the children no longer meeting criteria for an anxiety disorder compared to 15% in the wait-list control group (Cartwright-Hatton et al., 2011). A similar group for parents was also found to be effective up to eight months post-treatment with over 70% of children being considered sufficiently improved to be discharged from the service (Evans et al., 2018). Positive results have also been found following a one-day parent workshop, as children whose parents did not attend the workshop were 16% more likely to have an anxiety disorder 12 months later (Cartwright-Hatton et al., 2018).

Groups for children have also been researched within the field of anxiety. For example, the Coping Cat programme was developed for children aged 7–13 years old using CBT principles (Kendall, 1994). An adolescent version for 14–17-year-olds also exists. The programme has been evaluated in several randomised clinical trials conducted in the United States, Norway and Australia, with one-year follow-up data reported; all have reported positive results (Barrett, Dadds & Rapee, 1996; Kendall et al., 1997; Villabø et al., 2018). Coping Cat has also been shown to be effective for children with autism (Chalfant & Rapee, 2007). Additionally, several adapted versions of the programme, for example, "Cool Kids" and "FRIENDS" (McLoone & Rapee, 2012; Shortt, Barrett & Fox, 2002) have been created for use within schools. Such interventions can be helpful in the treatment and prevention of anxiety.

Suggestions for group interventions

Having discussed the currently limited evidence base for group interventions for ARFID, the following section sets out a number of suggestions for group work which include ways of working that are anecdotally effective but await formal evaluation.

Parent and family group interventions

Involving and supporting the parents or carers of children and adolescents with a diagnosis of ARFID is an essential part of the treatment (see further Chapter 15). Nourishing and feeding a child is a crucial aspect of being a parent; when feeding is troublesome, it will almost always have some kind of impact on the caregiver – whether that be anxiety about their child's health, frustration about seeing their child in distress, or feelings of disempowerment, guilt or blame. In response to this, parents may engage in maladaptive strategies such as coercion, rewards, punishment or force, which often maintain anxiety for the child, disrupt the child–parent relationship and lead to poor feeding and eating outcomes (Chatoor et al., 2000).

A key component of improving feeding is a calm and relaxing mealtime environment (Chatoor et al., 2004). This usually involves setting limits, modelling appropriate feeding habits, and responding sensitively to the child. Alongside this, behavioural therapy techniques and sensory management have demonstrated positive results for feeding and eating difficulties both on an individual basis (see Chapter 10) and within groups. A potentially helpful aim for parent groups is therefore to improve the quality of mealtimes and provide information about behavioural and sensory strategies. As with any intervention, maintaining factors and readiness for change (for both child and parent) should be used to set clear goals for treatment (see further Chapter 11).

Psycho-education workshop

Aims:

- to educate participants on important topics related to ARFID
- to meet other parents affected by ARFID (peer support).

Frequency: This group can be run over one day or half a day. It can be offered as part of a regular, rolling intervention or as a first step.

Participants: There is scope to include more participants in this workshop than an on-going group where discussion is a significant part of the content.

Format: The workshop can include a variety of topics pertinent to ARFID, such as:

- understanding ARFID
- ensuring a "good-enough" diet
- identifying and managing sensory issues
- behavioural strategies for anxiety.

When structuring a psycho-education workshop, it is often useful to allow time for parents to talk to one another. Providing refreshments may encourage parents

Figure 16.1 Experiential activity (exposure hierarchy to unusual foods)

to remain together during breaks, whilst experiential activities can facilitate discussion and connection amongst participants. This could include a graded exposure activity using foods that often evoke a strong reaction (e.g. olives, anchovies) (see Figure 16.1) or a sensory-based activity (e.g. painting with food).

Parent skills group

Aims:

*   to teach behavioural strategies to improve feeding
*   to facilitate peer support.

Frequency: This group can be run over several weeks (for example, between six and 14 weeks) weekly or bi-weekly. The suggested length is 60 to 120 minutes.

Participants: The individual needs of each family and of the group as a whole will need to be considered to ensure cohesiveness. Effort should be made to help parents feel able to contribute and listen to others within the group. It is also advised that, where possible, families are similar in terms of their child's developmental level and feeding difficulty. The group size might be between three and ten families to allow time to hear from everyone and create a comfortable atmosphere.

Format: This type of group usefully involves participants being taught strategies each week which can then be practiced at home. It is helpful to include time to reflect on home practice and to problem-solve difficulties alongside skills teaching. Including information about creating a relaxed mealtime environment, behavioural, and (where appropriate) sensory strategies is recommended.

Multi-family group

Aims:

- to reduce stress at mealtimes and improve family interactions around food
- to enable peer support.

Frequency: This type of group can be conducted on a one-off basis, as part of day-patient treatment or intensive out-patient treatment, or as regular group spanning several weeks.

Participants: The decision to focus on the family as a whole, rather than parents only, may be useful when family members differ in their management of the feeding or eating difficulty, or when significant anxiety exists during mealtimes. Placing several families together can be helpful when similarities have been identified between families. Multi-family groups can include anywhere between two and ten families depending on space and the nature of the difficulties. Once again, careful consideration needs to be given to each family member and the dynamics within each family. For example, if one parent is particularly disapproving of the skills being suggested, this can have an impact on other family members attempting to implement the skills. It is recommended that, as far as possible, families are similar in terms of the current feeding or eating presentation, family dynamics, motivation for change and level of anxiety.

Format: Multi-family groups can be organised as an on-going group programme or as a bespoke treatment plan for several families who may require similar support at the same time. Multi-family interventions will typically include a combination of family, parent and child sessions using behavioural and (where appropriate) sensory strategies. Elements of family therapy may also be incorporated to improve family functioning and mealtime interactions (see further Chapter 15). Multi-family groups may include a combination of:

- psychoeducation
- skills teaching

- mealtime observation, video-feedback and/or therapist-facilitated mealtimes
- child sessions focusing on play, food and/or sensory-based exposure
- anxiety management strategies (for older children).

To support the therapeutic intervention and its translation into the family home, the use of therapeutic documents can be useful. This may include a child-friendly scrapbook or folder containing information, pictures, videos, and pieces of art created during the intervention (see Figures 16.2a to 16.2d).

Children and adolescents

Just as it may be beneficial for parents to come together within a group, children may also find it helpful to meet others who are struggling with food. They may have started to notice that they are different to peers or that they are causing their parents stress around food, and they may feel ashamed, blamed and/or low in confidence. Group interventions may provide a way for children to feel understood and supported by like-minded peers. They can also provide an opportunity for children to develop new ways of managing their fears around food in a comfortable, non-threatening and playful way.

Figure 16.2a Therapeutic document of worrying thoughts

Figure 16.2b Therapeutic document "Guide to success"

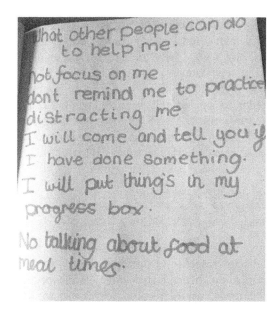

Figure 16.2c Therapeutic document "What others can do to help"

Figure 16.2d Therapeutic document "Eat up book"

Applying behavioural theory to ARFID proposes that these children have learnt to associate food with fear; usually as a result of adverse early experiences such as sensory sensitivities, physical symptoms (e.g. excessive vomiting, reflux), medical procedures, or stressful mealtimes. Therefore, some children might benefit from the opportunity to "unlearn" their fear through systematic desensitisation and exposure hierarchies. Research has also highlighted the importance of play when attempting to engage and promote a child's learning (Zosh et al., 2017) and for maintaining strong child-parent bonds (Ginsburg, 2007). It has also been highlighted as an important component of treatment for young children with ARFID (Zucker et al., 2019).

For group interventions addressing anxiety, pairing the anxiety-provoking stimulus – in this case food – with the relaxed and enjoyable association of play, is a key part of the treatment. This may be achieved in a slow, structured and gradual way to enable the child to build up their confidence at a pace that suits them. In order to support this learning, parents can be taught to use praise, play, or rewards effectively to reinforce this behaviour and support the child to feel safe. For older children who are motivated to engage in an intervention, anxiety management techniques and CBT can also be included.

Sensory- and food-based exposure groups

Aims:

- the aim of a *sensory-based* exposure group is often to reduce the child's anxiety and disgust response to different sensory stimuli through gradual exposure, habituation to the feared stimulus and positive reinforcement. This might be recommended for children whose anxiety around food is either partly or solely maintained by sensory sensitivities

- the aim of a *food-based* exposure group is to reduce the child's anxiety to food, for children whose food aversion is primarily maintained by anxiety
- the secondary aim is to support parents to respond sensitively and effectively to their child's fears and to increase the level of trust in their relationship.

Frequency: Both groups can be run over several weeks (four to eight weeks) with each session lasting somewhere between 30 to 90 minutes.

Participants: These groups may be most helpful for younger children (up to seven years old) who are not yet be able to identify their thoughts in relation to their anxiety. Both parent and child can be included within the sessions to ensure that the skills are translated into the home environment.

Format: Both groups are based on behavioural theory and rely heavily on play techniques to increase exposure to new foods in a fun, enjoyable way. This can be achieved through modelling and coaching parents alongside observation of others. Prior to the group, facilitators will need to be aware of each child's developmental level, sensory preferences and aversions, and individual interests to be able to plan activities that suit their needs. The activities can be organised by graded exposure; beginning with textures or foods that the child tolerates well before gradually incorporating new textures or foods into the activities. This might include:

- non-food sensory play (e.g. shaving foam)
- food play (e.g. running cars through cereal) (see Figure 16.3)
- food-based art (e.g. painting with yoghurt)
- preparing food (e.g. pizza making, biscuit decorating).

It is important that facilitators are responsive to participating children's cues and contributions and flexible within the sessions. They may be required to model to parents how to respond to the child's cues, taking a step back when necessary or changing the activity if it becomes too difficult.

Older children

Aims:

- to learn anxiety management techniques
- to increase exposure to feared food or textures.

Frequency: This can be conducted on a one-off basis or as part of an ongoing programme lasting between 4 and 14 weeks. Sessions are suggested to last between 60 to 120 minutes.

Participants: This type of group may be suitable for older children (aged eight years and above) who are cognitively able to understand the principles of behavioural theory and are motivated to reduce their anxiety. Some children may be able to identify thinking patterns and utilise cognitive restructuring techniques. The group

Figure 16.3 Graded exposure to textures with food play

can be conducted with individuals who are experiencing a variety of fears around food or for those with a specific anxiety disorder (e.g. emetophobia). As with other groups, the needs of each child will need to be considered and monitored throughout the group process to ensure that they feel comfortable. Group interventions are most successful when participants share some similarities e.g. age, gender, clinical presentation and severity.

Format: This group can include a mixture of didactic teaching, and opportunities for experiential learning. It may be helpful to incorporate the participants' interests and hobbies when developing activities for the group and to use playful, fun approaches when teaching new skills. Such groups typically include:

- psycho-education
- anxiety management techniques
- exposure to avoided foods (e.g. behavioural experiments)
- cognitive restructuring
- relapse prevention
- parent sessions (to compliment the work).

Future considerations

Group interventions show promise as an effective treatment for parents, families, and children affected by ARFID. They are unique in their ability to facilitate peer support and bring together individuals who may be feeling alone with their difficulties. They also allow for richer discussion and experimental learning alongside opportunities for modelling and observing healthy interactions around food, which may be both effective and less costly for services. For the most part, group interventions for ARFID have been informed by existing evidence-based group approaches, particularly from the fields of autism and anxiety. Most of the research thus far has focused on "selective eating" and therefore it is unclear whether these findings translate to children with clinically significant difficulties meeting criteria for ARFID. It is hoped that further evaluation within clearly defined populations of children with ARFID can take place to enable professionals to make confident recommendations. Psychological treatments focusing specifically on ARFID are under development, such as modifications of CBT and family-based approaches (Chapters 14 and 15). These tend to focus on individualised treatment at present but once established, may offer opportunities to develop the knowledge base for group work. Clinicians and researchers are also encouraged to continue evaluating approaches that are well-established in other areas of mental health to add to this growing field.

Summary points

- There is currently a limited evidence base in relation to group interventions specifically for children with ARFID
- Group work is generally informed by existing evidence-based approaches; namely anxiety-based interventions (behavioural and cognitive behavioural)
- Group treatment requires careful consideration of participant suitability in addition to contributing and maintaining factors
- Group interventions can be implemented for parents, families, children or for a combination of all three

References

Adamson, M., Morawska, A., & Sanders, A. (2015) Childhood feeding difficulties: a randomized controlled trial of a group-based parenting intervention. *Journal of Developmental and Behavioral Pediatrics* 36 (2), 126.

Alckmin-Carvalho, F., Vega, J.B., Cobelo, A.W., Fabbri, A.D., Pinzon, V.D., Melo, M., & da Silva, H. (2018) Evidence-based psychotherapy for treatment of anorexia nervosa in children and adolescents: systematic review. *Archives of Clinical Psychiatry (São Paulo)* 45 (2), 41–48.

Bandura, A. (1986) *Social functions of thought and action: a social cognitive theory.* New-Jersey: NJ: Prentice-Hall.

Barrett, P.M., Dadds, M.R., & Rapee, R.M. (1996) Family treatment of childhood anxiety: a controlled trial. *Journal of Consulting and Clinical Psychology* 64 (2), 333–42.

Boyd, K. (2007) The effectiveness of the sequential oral sensory approach group feeding program (Doctoral dissertation). Retrieved 27 June 2019, from ProQuest Dissertations & Theses (PQDT) database. *Dissertation Abstract International, B* 69/01, p. 665 https://search.proquest.com/docview/304762667

Cartwright-Hatton, S., Ewing, D., Dash, S., Hughes, Z., Thompson, E., Hazell, C., Field, A., & Startup, H. (2018) Preventing family transmission of anxiety: feasibility RCT of a brief intervention for parents. *British Journal of Clinical Psychology* 57 (3), 351–66.

Cartwright-Hatton, S., McNally, D., Field, A.P., Rust, S., Laskey, B., Dixon, C., Gallagher, B., Harrington, R., Miller, C., Pemberton, K., Symes, W., White, C., & Woodham, A. (2011) A new parenting-based group intervention for young anxious children: results of a randomized controlled trial. *Journal of the American Academy of Child and Adolescent Psychiatry* 50 (3), 242–51.

Chalfant, A. & Rapee, R.M. (2007) Treating anxiety disorders in children with high functioning autism spectrum disorders: a controlled trial. *Journal of Autism and Developmental Disorders* 37, 1842–57.

Chatoor, I., Ganiban, J., Hirsch, R., Borman-Spurrell, E.,, & Mrazek, D.A. (2000) Maternal characteristics and toddler temperament in infantile anorexia. *Journal of the American Academy of Child and Adolescent Psychiatry* 39 (6), 743–51.

Chatoor, I., Surles, J., Ganiban, J., Beker, L., Paez, L. & Kerzner, B. (2004) Failure to thrive and cognitive development in toddlers with infantile anorexia. *Pediatrics* 113 (5), 440–47.

Diamond-Raab, L. & Orrell Valente, J.K. (2002) Art therapy, psychodrama, and verbal therapy. An integrative model of group therapy in the treatment of adolescents with anorexia nervosa and bulimia nervosa. *Child and Adolescent Psychiatric Clinics of North America* 11 (2), 343–64.

Downey, J. (2014) Group therapy for adolescents living with an eating disorder: a scoping review. *SAGE Open* 4 (3), 10.1177/2158244014550618 accessed 14 July 2014.

Dumont, E., Jansen, A., Kroes, D., de Haan, E., & Mulkens, S. (2019) A new cognitive behavior therapy for adolescents with avoidant/restrictive food intake disorder in a day treatment setting: a clinical case series. *International Journal for Eating Disorders* 52 (4), 447–58.

Evans, R., Hill, C., O'Brien, D., & Creswell, C. (2018) Evaluation of a group format of clinician-guided, parent-delivered cognitive behavioural therapy for child anxiety in routine clinical practice: a pilot-implementation study. *Child and Adolescent Mental Health* 24 (1), 36–43.

Fabiano, G.A., Schatz, N.K., Aloe, A.M., Chacko, A., & Chronis-Tuscano, A. (2015) A systematic review of meta-analyses of psychosocial treatment for attention-deficit/ hyperactivity disorder. *Clinical Child and Family Psychology Review* 18 (1), 77–97.

Ginsburg, K.R. (2007) The importance of play in promoting healthy child development and maintaining strong parent–child bonds. *Pediatrics* 119 (1), 182–91.

Hoppu, U., Prinz, M., Ojansivu, P., Laaksonen, O., & Sandell, M.A. (2015) Impact of sensory-based food education in kindergarten on willingness to eat vegetables and berries. *Food & Nutrition Research* 59 287–95.

Kendall, P.C. (1994) Treating anxiety disorders in children: results of a randomized clinical trial. *Journal of Consulting and Clinical Psychology* 62 (1), 100–10.

Kendall, P.C., Flannery-Schroeder, E., Panichelli-Mindel, S.M., Southam-Gerow, M.A., Henin, A., & Warman, M. (1997) Therapy for youths with anxiety disorders: a second randomized clinical trial. *Journal of Consulting and Clinical Psychology* 65 (3), 366–80.

Kuschner, E., Morton, H., Maddox, B., de Marchena, A., Anthony, L., & Reaven, J. (2017) The BUFFET program: development of a cognitive behavioral treatment for selective eating in youth with autism spectrum disorder. *Clinical Child and Family Psychology Review* 20 (4), 403–21.

McLoone, J.K. & Rapee, R.M. (2012) Comparison of an anxiety management program for children implemented at home and school: lessons learned. *School Mental Health* 4 (4), 231–42.

NICE Guidance on Eating Disorders (2017) Group CBT for binge eating disorder, recommendation 1.4.5 www.nice.org.uk/guidance/ng69/chapter/Recommendations#general-principles-of-care accessed 14 July 2019.

NICE Guidance on Faltering Growth, (2017), recommendation 1. 2.19 www.nice.org.uk/guidance/ng75/chapter/Recommendations#organisation-of-care accessed 14 July 2019.

Owen, C., Ziebell, L., Lessard, C., Churcher, E., Bourget, V., & Villenueve, H. (2012) Inter-professional group intervention for parents of children age 3 and younger with feeding difficulties: pilot program evaluation. *Nutrition in Clinical Practice* 27 (1), 129–35.

Seiverling, L., Williams, K., Sturmey, P., & Hart, S. (2012) Effects of behavioral skills training on parental treatment of children's food selectivity. *Journal of Applied Behavior Analysis* 45 (1), 197–203.

Sharp, W.G., Stubbs K.H., Adams H., Wells B.M., Lesack, R.S., Criado, K.K., Simon, E.L., McCracken, C.E., West, L.L., & Scahill, L.D. (2016) Intensive, manual-based intervention for pediatric feeding disorders: results from a randomized pilot trial. *Journal of Pediatric Gastroenterology And Nutrition* 62 (4), 658–63.

Shortt, A., Barrett, P.L., & Fox, T. (2002) Evaluating the FRIENDS program: a cognitive-behavioral group treatment for anxious children and their parents. *Journal of Clinical Child Psychology* 30, 525–35.

Toomey, K. (2010) Introduction to the SOS approach to feeding program [PDF file]. Retrieved from http://sosapproach-conferences.com/wp-content/uploads/SOS-APPROACH-explanation.pdf accessed 14 July 2019.

Villabø, M., Narayanan, M., Compton, S., Kendall, P.C., & Neumer, S. (2018) Cognitive-behavioral therapy for youth anxiety: an effectiveness evaluation in community practice. *Journal of Consulting and Clinical Psychology* 86 (9), 751–64.

Zosh, J.M., Hopkins, E.J., Jensen, H., Liu, C., Neale, D., Hirsh-Pasek, K., Solis, S.L., & Whitebread, D. (2017) *Learning through play: a review of the evidence (White Paper).* The LEGO Foundation, DK.

Zucker, N.L., LaVia, M.C., Craske, M.G., Foukal, M., Harris, A.A., Datta, N., Savereide, E., & Maslow, G.R. (2019) Feeling and body investigators (FBI): ARFID division – an acceptance-based interoceptive exposure treatment for children with ARFID. *International Journal of Eating Disorders*, 52(4), 466–72.

Zwi, M., Jones, H., Thorgaard, C., York, A. & Dennis, J.A. (2011) Parent training interventions for Attention Deficit Hyperactivity Disorder (ADHD) in children aged 5 to 18 years. *Cochrane Database of Systematic Reviews* 7 (12), 10.1002/14651858 accessed 14 July 2019.

Chapter 17

Working with schools, nurseries and other agencies

Amy Siddall

Introduction

Treatment of avoidant restrictive food intake disorder (ARFID) might involve working directly with the individual (Chapter 14), with their parent/carers (Chapter 15) or involve group work (Chapter 16). However, there are times when it is also important to work with the wider system, both during assessment and treatment of ARFID. For some children, especially younger children and those with special educational needs, short, frequent treatment sessions, in familiar environments, are more likely to be effective at evoking change in oral intake. Any child's stage of cognitive development will need to be taken into account in deciding optimal pacing and environment for the work required. Children may find it anxiety provoking attending a clinic setting and working with a clinician they have only met on a few occasions. In addition, some children with ARFID demonstrate context specific eating and may not generalise progress made in a clinic to other environments, limiting the success of any intervention. Familiarity of surroundings and integration of treatment approaches into the child's usual routine can therefore support more lasting change.

By the time a child is diagnosed with ARFID, they are often part of multiple social networks, having formed relationships with their parents/caregivers, wider family, nursery and/or school staff and peers. They may also be involved with informal social organisations such as sports clubs, youth clubs, and other extra-curricular activities, and be known to wider mental health, physical health or social care teams. This chapter discusses when it might be necessary to involve and work with these wider networks and agencies, with a particular focus on the role of education and social care systems.

Why do we need to work with the wider system?

To help children achieve their potential

Health care workers and clinicians have a duty of care to safeguard children and ensure they reach their potential. It is important that they work with wider systems when there is concern that ARFID is impacting negatively on any aspect of the child's wellbeing, including their nutritional state, physical health, social and emotional development, and their educational achievement.

To provide treatment to children outside the clinic setting

Humans are social beings who are typically able to adapt their behaviour to different situations or contexts. Children may behave (and therefore eat) differently in different environments as they respond to the different social cues and demands placed upon them. Alternatively, some children, particularly young children, those with autism, intellectual and developmental disabilities, do not respond to social demands but may still demonstrate context specific eating. As Southall describes:

> From the day we are born we are engaged with the social environment in which we live. Everything we do is part of an interactive process. As children we develop through this process of interaction, with new knowledge being continually assimilated. The result is a process of constant transformation within and between individuals and relationships.
>
> (Southall, 2011, p. 133)

For these reasons it is often helpful to liaise with schools and other agencies to build a bigger picture about the child's eating difficulties and their impact, and to establish if there is a preferential environment in which to conduct treatment. For example, school attendance is associated with children learning to respect boundaries, adhere to rules, follow routines and respond to expectations; the school setting may therefore represent a promising potential environment in which to deliver treatment.

When to work with other agencies

There are a number of instances when liaison with other agencies is a helpful part of the assessment and treatment process. These are summarised below with some clinically informed case examples included to provide context.

As part of the assessment process

When conducting an assessment of a child with ARFID, it can be helpful to find out what support has already been put in place for the child and family. For example, if there are concerns about the child's physical health it can be helpful to know if there is a physical health care plan in place already, or when there are concerns about the parent–child interaction, whether social care systems are involved. Following an assessment there may be insufficient information to establish with any certainty what the main contributory and maintaining factors for the child's difficulties appear to be. It can be helpful to gather further information about the child's eating and general behaviour from other agencies, building up a detailed picture of the current situation from multiple informants and information sources. This can ensure that a comprehensive formulation is reached and an appropriate treatment intervention applied.

Prior to starting individual treatment interventions

Following assessment it may be decided that an individual treatment intervention is appropriate (see Chapter 14). Liaison with wider systems may be helpful prior to starting treatment. Information gathered from an education setting can help the clinician to tailor the work to the child's individual needs and abilities. Information about their cognitive ability, what age or stage they are functioning at, whether they prefer worksheets or verbal discussion, and if they have any identified learning difficulties can be helpful at the planning stages of treatment to maximise the change of successful intervention.

> When working with James, an 11-year-old with high functioning autism, concerns quickly arose about his cognitive ability. James appeared to be struggling to recall the content of conversations he had had a few minutes previously. It was unclear whether this was due to his cognitive ability or to anxiety. His mother reported that James was not doing well in terms of academic attainment. Liaison with his teacher revealed that James was approximately two years behind his peers in expected levels across most subjects. This information was taken into account and informed the way individual treatment was adapted and delivered.

In the event of problems with the child's food intake at school or nursery

Primary caregivers may report concern that their child is not eating and drinking enough during the school or nursery day, or that the school's lunch policy dictates that they are unable to access their preferred foods. It can sometimes be helpful to liaise with school staff to obtain more information and to see if a solution can be identified. For example, during assessment the child may be reported to have sensory difficulties and to be struggling to eat their preferred foods in the school lunch hall with peers. Whilst recommendations of an occupational therapy sensory assessment might be helpful for some children, this is not always easily available. Liaison with the school to see if any adjustment to the child's eating environment is possible, may also be helpful.

Alternatively, if the child's preferred foods are not permitted in school, liaison with school staff can be helpful. Most people understand the importance of facilitating adequate energy and fluid intake during the school day to enable children to reach their educational potential. Some problem solving might be required to determine how to balance a particular child's needs with the rules and routines of the school, which are invariably implemented for the benefit of the majority. Discussion acknowledging both perspectives may result in new solutions being generated.

Finally, it may be considered that the child might benefit from a behavioural, reward-based approach being applied in the school or nursery setting rather than in clinic. Such a recommendation may be made, for example, for children needing support to increase their oral intake during breaks or at lunchtimes, when there is a need to reduce the time taken to consume their food, or when an important goal is to establish the child being able to regularly eat a packed lunch of preferred foods ready for transition from pre-school or primary education.

> Following an assessment with Stacey, an 11-year-old with a diagnosis of autism attending a mainstream school, there was concern that she was not taking in sufficient energy overall. She ate a limited range of foods and in particular was not eating her packed lunch. Liaison with school staff made it possible to facilitate Stacey eating outside the lunch hall with a few peers. A reward system was also implemented at school to help her improve her intake during the day. Overall, the quantity of food she consumed at lunchtime increased, and eventually Stacey was also happy to use her reward (time with a learning mentor doing an activity of her choice at the end of the day) as an opportunity to consume an additional snack. She started being able to eat a cereal bar or bowl of cereal at this time, increasing her daily intake further.

When parent-led approaches implemented in the home environment are unsuccessful

In some situations a child may not respond quickly or well to interventions in the family home. This can be for a number of reasons, including parental vulnerability, parental anxiety, stressors in the family home, or difficulties in the parent-child relationship. Whilst family interventions might be recommended (see Chapter 15), it can be helpful to liaise with school or other informal agencies to see if it is possible for them to facilitate additional support needed to effect change. Treatment in the child's wider environment may range from facilitating messy food play activities, to desensitise the sensory-sensitive child (see Chapter 10), to involving "tasting times" (see below for a fuller explanation) to try and increase the child or young person's exposure to new tastes and textures. Finally, agreement and support may be required from the child's school to facilitate the administration of a nutritional supplement or other medication as required. Some schools run breakfast sessions and after-school clubs, which can be helpful contexts for some children to increase their overall oral intake in a structured environment.

If re-formulation of the child's difficulties is required

In some cases, treatment approaches may work with limited effect or not at all; at this point liaison with others regularly involved with the child, may be needed to be able to re-formulate the problem and try to understand the factors maintaining the difficulties. For example, if there are concerns that a child has some cognitive rigidity or social communication difficulties, liaison with school may reveal that these concerns are mirrored by staff, suggesting an assessment for autism might be indicated. Alternatively, information may have emerged that there are difficulties in the family that could be hindering progress; under such circumstances there may be a need to liaise and work with social care teams to support change.

> Daniel, 13 years old, had a diagnosis of high functioning autism but was motivated to change his eating. He made some significant achievements through individual treatment, becoming able to challenge his fear of choking and starting to reintroduce foods he had previously dropped. However, homework tasks set as part of the treatment were never fully completed. Daniel's parents were not facilitating the therapeutic work to continue at home. Daniel disclosed that his mother had significant physical and mental health difficulties and that the parental relationship had broken down, to the extent that there was no communication between his father and mother. Liaison between the family, the clinical team and social care colleagues resulted in the family receiving additional support from social care services. Together with staff at Daniel's school, Daniel was supported to sustain progress in making changes to his diet at school and also in the home environment.

When a child demonstrates context specific eating patterns

Some children may display different eating patterns in different environments. Typically, context specific eating is an eating pattern associated with autism. A high incidence of feeding and eating problems in children with autism, intellectual, and developmental disabilities has been reported in the literature (Schreck, Williams, & Smith, 2004; Sharp et al., 2013). Williams and colleagues report that 69% of children with autism in their study were unwilling to try new foods, with 46% of those included engaging in rituals surrounding their eating habits (Williams, Dalrymple, & Neal, 2000). Such ritualised or habitual eating behaviours have been attributed to the need to feel safe (for example, from fear and anxiety) with this, in turn, causing individuals to become fixed on certain aspects of food and the routines associated with mealtimes (Southall, 2011). Examples of this type of rigid or routine-bound behaviour include children who will only eat foods of a certain colour, children who will only eat from certain plates or with certain utensils, or those who will only eat in a specific place with specific people.

A multi-agency approach to treatment for children with autism has been advocated (see Cermak, Curtin, & Bandini, 2010; Laud et al., 2009; Subramanyam et al., 2019). Laud and colleagues also note that children with autism benefit from a rule governed approach to treatment, with structure and consistent application of behavioural principles. Such an approach can be difficult to apply in an outpatient clinic or at home and seeking support from schools to apply treatment approaches on a regular, consistent basis can have greater potential for success.

"Tasting times" – a locally implemented treatment intervention

"Tasting times" are a reward-based intervention method that can be used in treatment for ARFID. Typically, they incorporate principles such as those set out in the Sequential Oral Steps (SOS) approach to eating, which focuses on the need for the child to tolerate, interact, and smell a food before touching, tasting and swallowing it (Toomey & Ross, 2011). The approach can be applied by parents and local professionals for children who may not require or respond to treatment in a clinic setting or as an additional step to interventions provided in clinic. This method can be particularly helpful for those with autism or intellectual impairment (who may not be considered appropriate for an individual cognitive based intervention).

"Tasting time" principles

There are a number of principles that local professionals or parents might find helpful to follow when supporting a child to introduce new foods into their diet. Regular guidance and reference to these can be helpful when supporting the wider network to implement treatment.

- "Tasting time" should in most cases be presented as something that is fun. Effort should be made to make it as enjoyable and non-threatening as possible. The more fun it is, generally the more enjoyable the child or young person will find the experience. This can help to break the negative cycle of associating food with negative feelings and emotions.
- It can be very helpful to use visual communication tools to illustrate steps to eating that the child or young person is being encouraged to take. Such methods can be helpfully incorporated into the "tasting time" with the child encouraged to look at, smell and touch the food, but not pushed to try it initially. Helping them feel relaxed and comfortable in the presence of food is very important. Once they are more relaxed and comfortable, they are generally more likely to lick, bite, chew or swallow new foods.

- "Tasting time" should ideally happen away from mealtimes. This is because mealtimes are often too associated with stress, pressure, frustration, worry, or anger for children who have eating difficulties. This, in turn, can make a child more stressed and less able to respond to an intervention at the same time.
- "Tasting time" should usually only last for between 10 and 15 minutes. For some children even this might be too long and 5 minutes may be sufficient to start. A visual timer, for example, a sand-timer or a stopwatch on a smart phone, might be helpful to communicate the length of time for the task to the child or young person.
- "Tasting time" is never about failing to achieve. It can be helpful to give a sticker or other reinforcement for even the smallest achievement. In some cases touching the food item might be a huge achievement; immediate praise and instant reward usually work better than rather than delayed reactions or rewards. The child might not get to the step of putting food in the mouth and swallowing it for some time. It is important to tolerate the length of time required to achieve this rather than put unattainable expectations onto the child.
- Plan "tasting time" sessions. Two or three times per week is usually enough.
- Be consistent with the approach in each session. Only move on to the next step when the first step has been firmly established.
- Sessions should be stopped if they are causing the child significant upset or distress.
- Once the child or young person is regularly swallowing a new food during the "tasting time" it can be transitioned to a meal or snack time. Presenting the food in a packed lunch box from the start can be one helpful method. Alternatively, the staff member supporting the child to carry out the tasting tasks might be able to support the transition to another room at school, or a hand-over to lunchtime staff. Visual timetables can be useful to prepare the child for this change.
- Patience is important. The time taken for change using a "tasting time" approach can be very slow, sometimes taking up to three months for a new food to be fully incorporated to the child's diet.

Liaison required to inform a "tasting time" approach

When considering the implementation of "tasting times" in the school setting it is important to obtain information across a number of key areas to individualise the treatment appropriately and to support the safe delivery of the intervention. This might mean that liaison is required with a range of professionals involved with the child, depending on their abilities and the type of school setting.

Liaison with the child's teacher or special educational needs coordinator can be helpful to establish if the necessary resources to deliver treatment are available in the school setting. The teacher is also able to inform the reward-based approach, knowing what will motivate the child in school, for example, if there is a preferred activity or a particular toy they like to play with. Likewise, parents may require support to establish appropriate reward systems at home.

Information about the child's method of communication and level of understanding is required in order to know how to best communicate the expectations being placed upon the child. It is also important to ascertain whether the child is thought to be capable understanding the concept of now-and-next or having the ability to build such an association (i.e. can they understand that if they do A, they get B?). Some children might have been seen by a speech and language therapist or an educational psychologist, who might be able to provide results from formal assessments in this respect. Some speech and language therapists have also been involved with a child in relation to assessment of their ability to swallow. They may have also implemented some guidance regarding eating and this will be important to know prior to recommendations intended to address the eating difficulties.

It can be helpful to find out if the child has had a sensory occupational therapy assessment and if any sensory modification strategies have been recommended (see Chapter 10 for further information). An occupational therapist is also able to analyse the child's preferred foods from a food diary to provide guidance about the sensory properties of new foods to introduce, with the highest likelihood of being accepted. For example, if the child has a preference for strong rather than bland flavours, crunchy rather than soft foods, or particular colours of foods, some foods will be experienced as more challenging than others in line with these preferences. An occupational therapist may also be able to offer advice on how to optimise the school or home environment and limit potential interference from sensory issues during mealtimes.

It is important to liaise with the child's dietitian to find out which foods to prioritise with the "tasting times" based on nutritional risk. In some cases, the risk may be high and the child's eating so limited, that the intervention needs to initially be focused on accepting a nutritional supplement. If there is no nutritional risk, then foods can usually be selected based on the family's goals or to reduce the impact of the child's eating on their own and their family's stress. For example, the parent's goal may be to establish a packed lunch box which can be accessed away from the family home to facilitate going on outings or eating out.

Open communication between the clinician, school staff and parents is important, both when establishing "tasting times" and to provide ongoing advice and support.

An example of "tasting times" applied in school

Simon, an 8-year-old boy with a diagnosis of autism, was referred because he was not eating and drinking at school. At home he was completely dependent on a warmed supplement drink mixed with a smooth cereal to meet his energy and nutritional needs. He had only ever accepted this from his parents and at home. It was agreed following assessment to try and work with the school staff, and apply a "tasting time" approach to effect change. A clear visual reward system was implemented and the work was facilitated by the school speech and language therapist. Whilst Simon did not accept the supplement and cereal mix, he was able to start taking sips from a bottle of the supplement alone. As a reward for taking sips, Simon enjoyed posting tokens into a toy monster, pretending to feed him. The transition of accepting the supplement to the classroom environment, where the children usually had their snacks and meals, was harder to achieve. Simon enjoyed the one-to-one time he had during the "tasting time" and without this he was reluctant to take any supplement. "Tasting time" staff joined him in the class with his teacher before gradually withdrawing and he did eventually accept the supplement drink in the class with his peers at lunchtime. Simon also started accepting this drink away from the family home, when with his parents. Following the school holiday, he dropped this again and it was agreed to re-establish the "tasting time" for a week or two before transitioning to the classroom again. Once acceptance of the supplement in the classroom was consolidated, a new food was offered during the "tasting time". During the course of the work Simon also started trying sips of his parents' drinks at home and guidance was given to parents for other smooth foods of similar taste and texture to that of his preferred foods, which could be offered at home. Eventually this work was handed over to the local dietitian to guide the school with foods to work on going forwards.

An example of "tasting times" applied at home

Susie, an 8-year-old with ARFID, but with no other co-morbid diagnoses, had a longstanding restricted diet following an episode of tonsillitis aged 30 months. Liaison was conducted following assessment, which established that there were no concerns regarding her social development. Due to difficulties with the distance and cost of travelling to clinic the family were not able to attend on a regular basis and "tasting times" were established at home. Susie was supported to try foods at home that were similar but different to her preferred foods. For example, Susie liked chips so potato wedges and eventually baked and new potatoes were introduced through tasting times. As a reward for trying a new food Susie received a token to permit a later bedtime. Following initial tastes of new foods, Susie was supported to select a food to work on consistently trying one food daily for two to three weeks, which was then incorporated into a mealtime each week. Liaison with school staff enabled them to also support the work, facilitating the introduction of a nutritional supplement drink at break time and to help Susie try new types of bread in the morning with her peers.

Summary points

- Liaison with wider networks involved with a child and their family can be helpful in the assessment, formulation and treatment of children with ARFID
- Health care professionals have a duty of care to liaise with wider networks, agencies and individuals involved with a child, to ensure that they reach their potential; this is particularly the case when there may be safeguarding concerns
- Treatment of ARFID is not always best carried out in the clinic or home environment and schools/nurseries and informal agencies may provide potential alternative treatment settings
- "Tasting times" represent one method of intervention to broaden children's diets away from the clinic setting
- "Tasting times" require careful planning and regular reviews to enhance likelihood of success
- Progress in achieving desired changes may be slow as children proceed at varying rates
- Interventions administered outside the clinic setting should in most cases not continue if they are causing regular significant upset and distress.

References

Cermak, S.A., Curtin, C., & Bandini, L.A. (2010) Food selectivity and sensory sensitivity in children with autism spectrum disorders. *Journal of the American Dietetic Association* 110(2), 238–46.

Laud, R.B., Girolami, P.A., Boscoe, J.H., & Gulotta, C.S. (2009) Treatment outcomes for severe feeding problems in children with autism spectrum disorder. *Behaviour Modification* 33(5), 520–36.

Schreck, K.A., Williams, K., & Smith, A.F. (2004) A comparison of eating behaviors between children with and without autism. *Journal of Autism and Developmental Disorders* 34, 433–38.

Sharp, W.G., Berry, R.C., McCracken, C., & Nuhu, N. (2013) Feeding problems and nutrient intake in children with autism spectrum disorders: a meta-analysis and comprehensive review of the literature. *Journal of Autism and Developmental Disorders* 43(9), 2159–73.

Southall A. (2011) Family and wider system perspectives. In: Southall A.&. & Martin C. (eds) *Feeding problems in children: a practical guide*. (2nd ed.) Oxon: Radcliffe publishing Ltd, 133–52.

Subramanyam, A.A., Mukherjee, A., Dave M., & Chavda, K. (2019) Clinical practice guidelines for autism spectrum disorders. *Indian Journal of Psychiatry* 61(2), 254–69.

Toomey, K. & Ross, E. (2011) SOS approach to feeding. *Perspectives on Swallowing and Swallowing Disorders (Dysphagia)* 20(3), 82–87.

Williams, P.G., Dalrymple, N., & Neal, J. (2000) Eating habits of children with autism. *Pediatric Nursing* 26(3), 259–64.

Part V

Progress and future directions

Chapter 18

Prognosis and outcome

Elaine Chung

Introduction

By definition, avoidant restrictive food intake disorder (ARFID) causes significant medical and/or psychosocial difficulties. Parents frequently worry about the impact of ARFID on their children's future health, growth and social impact at school and elsewhere. This chapter describes the existing research evidence on recovery, improvement in malnutrition, weight restoration, the impact of and potential development of other psychiatric disorders including anorexia nervosa, functioning in adulthood, and potential prognostic factors. However, the research evidence on outcome and prognosis is currently limited.

Current state of research evidence

ARFID is a relatively new diagnosis hence few studies elucidating its course, outcome, and prognosis have as yet been undertaken. Existing evidence comprises mainly case studies and retrospectively diagnosed cases, and the also relatively limited evidence from the previous diagnostic classification of feeding disorder of infancy or early childhood, which did not include people with onset of difficulties over six years of age. The majority of studies compare ARFID with other restrictive eating disorders, such as anorexia nervosa. These are predominantly limited to people presenting to eating disorder services, often underweight and requiring admission. Many studies therefore likely exclude a significant number of children with ARFID in the context of longer standing medical and neurodevelopmental conditions presenting to paediatrics, whose prognosis may differ, and those within normal or overweight parameters.

ARFID comprises a heterogeneity of presentations, with the three most commonly identified underlying features being lack of interest in eating or food; avoidance based on the sensory characteristics of food; or concerns about aversive consequences of eating. As further research is carried out, it may be helpful to explore how patients with different ARFID profiles respond to various treatments. However, there is often overlap in presenting features; for example, Reilly and colleagues found that over 50% of their sample endorsed symptoms consistent with more than one phenotype (Reilly et al., 2019).

There is also a need to operationalise optimal definitions of remission and recovery to assist in evaluating treatment response and longitudinal outcomes, towards which the Radcliffe ARFID workgroup has made recommendations (Eddy et al., 2019.) Beyond no longer meeting full criteria, it is unclear what degree of weight restoration, dietary variety, and nutritional repletion constitutes recovery. Clinically it is important to treat patients individually, and a pragmatic stepwise approach is usually taken. The aim is to ensure physical safety, weight restoration, and nutritional completeness in the first instance, and to work towards the best possible outcome for an individual, taking into account their potential developmental feeding capacity and growth, which may differ from the general population (Peebles et al., 2017). These individualised outcomes, particularly for children with medical and neurodevelopmental conditions, may be harder to capture in more generalised research study outcome criteria, and in clinical practice goal based outcome measures can be useful (Law & Jacob, 2015).

Recovery from ARFID

A small number of studies provide data on recovery or remission. In one clinical case series of 11 children and adolescents with ARFID treated for four weeks with exposure-based cognitive behavioural therapy, ten were in remission at three month follow-up (Dumont et al., 2019). In a case review of 41 adolescents retrospectively diagnosed with ARFID and 203 adolescents and young adults with anorexia nervosa admitted for acute medical stabilisation, at one year follow-up 62% of those with ARFID and 46% of those with anorexia nervosa were in remission; these differences were not statistically significant (Strandjord et al., 2015). After a mean of seven years, Nakai and colleagues followed up 27 women retrospectively diagnosed with ARFID, comparing outcomes with 101 people who had had anorexia nervosa, all treated for restrictive eating in an eating disorders service having presented aged between 15 to 40. Eighteen of those with ARFID had been 15 to 19 years old at presentation. Those with ARFID had had restrictive eating in the context of emotional or gastrointestinal symptoms, but not sensory aversion or functional dysphagia, and the authors noted that their results suggested that this group was somewhat different to those described in studies of children. Treatment comprised outpatient care with individual supportive psychotherapy and/or nutritional management, and for some, inpatient admission. Significantly more of those with ARFID had fully recovered at follow-up (51.9%, n = 15); 27% (n = 10) had partially recovered, and 11.1% (n = 3) had active ARFID after seven years. 35.5% of those with anorexia nervosa had recovered. The ARFID group also showed significantly greater improvements in their eating than those with anorexia nervosa. 15% of the people with anorexia nervosa, but none with ARFID had died (Nakai et al., 2017).

Lange and colleagues undertook a long-term follow-up study of children with restrictive eating disorders treated in a regional eating disorders service when they were less than 13 years old, at a mean follow-up time of 15.9 years (range 7.2–29.3). Nineteen were retrospectively diagnosed with ARFID, one of whom also had autism; 37 had had anorexia nervosa. Fifty-three of the 56 participants were women. Mean age at treatment was 11 years (range 6.8–12.9). 26.3% (n=5) of the ARFID group continued to have ARFID at follow-up, hence almost three quarters recovered. This was similar to the rate of people with anorexia nervosa, 21.6% of whom had an eating disorder at follow-up, although there was some diagnostic crossover to other eating disorders in those who had had anorexia nervosa in childhood. There were no statistically significant differences between children who had had ARFID and those with anorexia nervosa in their other outcome measures, indicating similar prognoses, further described in sections below (Lange et al., 2019).

Food acceptance and swallowing

Sharp and colleagues undertook a systematic review of 48 single case studies comprising 98 children with feeding difficulties. They included children with neurodevelopmental difficulties (65.6%) and medical conditions (67.7%), 61.5% of whom had multiple medical conditions. The overall percentage of non-overlapping data outcomes for behavioural interventions was 87.95% within the effective range of treatment, and effect sizes were large (d=2.46). Measures of food acceptance (87.87%), frequency (88.8%) and percentages swallowing (81.75%) were within the effective range. Frequency of swallowing (98.85%) and volume of food (95.8%) were in the highly effective range. 78.1% had improvements in dietary variety, with 40% accepting foods from all food groups (Sharp et al., 2010).

Sharp and colleagues also undertook the first randomised control trial of a five-day intensive manual-based behavioural feeding intervention for ten children with ARFID aged 13 to 72 months, in the context of medical, neurodevelopmental, and sensory integration disorders, compared with ten waiting list controls, dependent on oral or enteral supplementary feeds. Statistically significant improvements were shown for bite acceptance, amount of food and mealtime disruptions (Sharp et al., 2016).

Malnutrition and weight restoration

Drawing from the literature prior to ARFID, Ammaniti and colleagues followed up a group of 72 children with "infantile anorexia" – children presenting with a lack of interest in food and eating, and growth deficiency, not due to illness or traumatic events, developing between six months to three years of age. They presented at a mean age of two years, and were followed up at five and eight years of age, but had not had treatment. These children showed a steady decline in malnutrition, with a 69% decrease in levels of malnutrition aged five years and 97% decrease aged eight. At five years, 44% had chronic malnutrition, and at eight years, about 10% continued to be moderately malnourished. These children's eating behaviour continued to be characterised by dysfunctional satiety responsiveness, lack of enjoyment of food, and increased food fussiness (Ammaniti et al., 2012).

Lucarelli and colleagues followed up a group of 113 children, about half girls, half boys, diagnosed with infantile anorexia at two years, and followed up at five, seven and 11 years, but not treated. They retrospectively clarified that this group would have met criteria for ARFID, characterised by low interest in eating. These children also showed improvement in their severity of malnutrition over time, but at 11 years of age, 73% had ongoing evidence of malnutrition, with 63% being moderate to severe, 10% mild, and 27% were not malnourished (Lucarelli et al., 2018).

In a retrospective case note review of children presenting to an eating disorders service, all 34 children with ARFID were successfully renourished (Norris et al., 2014). In a further retrospective review, at one year follow-up, 87 adolescents with ARFID presenting to adolescent medicine eating disorder services were less likely to achieve healthy weights than those with anorexia nervosa, who had two times higher odds of weight recovery, and atypical anorexia nervosa whose odds of weight recovery were four times higher. Only percentage median body mass index at presentation was found to be a significant predictor of weight recovery (Forman et al., 2014). However, in other retrospective studies, children and adolescents with ARFID attained similar percentage median body mass indices to patients treated for anorexia nervosa during treatment (Ornstein et al., 2017) and at follow-up after two and a half years (Bryson et al., 2018).

In Lange and colleagues' study, after a mean of 15.9 years following childhood treatment for ARFID, the majority were weight restored with a mean body mass index of 21.9kg/m^2 (range 16.5–29.9). At presentation all the children had been underweight with a mean percentage median body mass index of 78.2% (range 68.8–89.9%). Only two of the five people with ongoing ARFID were at low weight (Lange et al., 2019).

Bone density and other medical sequelae

ARFID can be associated with significant medical sequelae secondary to insufficient nutritional intake, including faltering growth and nutritional derangement. Case reports have documented rare cases of the impact of vitamin deficiencies, including rickets and spinal cord degeneration, and nutritional excesses such as elevated mercury levels (Thomas et al., 2017). Low weight can be associated with bradycardia, amenorrhoea and impact on bone density. Low bone mineral density has been found in 77% of 34 young people with ARFID, 25% of whom were in the osteoporotic range. Their overall bone mineral density scores were significantly lower than the comparison group of adolescents with anorexia nervosa (Norris et al., 2014). Follow-up studies are needed to explore the longer term impact of ARFID and its successful treatment on height, pubertal development and bone density.

Hospital admission

A third of 34 adolescents retrospectively diagnosed with ARFID and treated in an eating disorders service required admission for medical stabilisation in light of low weight or unstable vital signs, compared to 80% of those with anorexia nervosa (Norris et al., 2014). In a retrospective study of adolescents admitted for medical stabilisation, those with ARFID had slightly longer admissions than those with anorexia nervosa, albeit only eight compared to five days, in the context of more having required enteral feeding. 21% of adolescents with ARFID and 24% of those with anorexia nervosa required readmission (Strandjord et al., 2015).

Children and adolescents treated for ARFID with acute onset in a partial hospitalisation programme (day-patient care) required significantly shorter duration of treatment than those with anorexia nervosa, seven compared to 12 weeks, but nonetheless attained similar gains in percentage median body mass index (Ornstein et al., 2017). In a retrospective study of 27 people aged 11–26 admitted to hospital with ARFID, compared to 248 with anorexia nervosa, their rate of weight gain was slightly lower, but still good, at 1.36kg per week, compared to 1.92kg, and their body mass indices on discharge were similar. A smaller proportion transitioned to the Partial Hospitalisation Programme, for fewer days, but were equally likely to be discharged for clinical improvement (Makhzoumi et al., 2019).

Tube weaning

A systematic review and meta-analysis of nine retrospective chart reviews and two randomised controlled trials of intensive, multidisciplinary intervention for children with ARFID dependent on tube feeding, including those with medical co-morbidities, showed 80% were successfully tube weaned at follow-up (Sharp et al., 2017).

Development of other psychiatric disorders

Psychiatric comorbidity is common, with other psychiatric disorders predating, co-existing and subsequently developing in children with ARFID. It is therefore important to screen for these at assessment and follow-up, and to consider their potential relevance in terms of prognostic factors, and as potential outcomes.

In children who had had infantile anorexia, poor internal regulation of eating was associated in middle childhood with both internalising and externalising difficulties, particularly anxiety, moodiness, somatic complaints, oppositionality and social difficulties (Ammaniti et al., 2012; Lucarelli et al., 2018). In another study, the severity of comorbid psychopathological symptoms, such as anxiety, depression and attention deficit hyperactivity disorder (ADHD), have been found to worsen as selective eating became more severe (Zucker et al., 2015). Scores on measures of psychopathology in terms of eating attitudes, behaviours and anxiety, have been shown to reduce during treatment for ARFID (Ornstein et al., 2017).

In Lange and colleagues' study, after a mean of 15.9 years, 5% (five people) had another psychiatric diagnosis, two of whom had depression, four dysthymia, five anxiety disorder and one obsessive compulsive disorder. Three of those with another psychiatric diagnosis had ongoing ARFID – two of those with dysthymia and the person with obsessive compulsive disorder. The study did not describe whether these individuals had had another psychiatric diagnosis in childhood (Lange et al., 2019).

Global outcomes

Lange and colleagues used the Morgan and Russell Outcome Assessment Schedule in their long-term outcome study (Morgan & Hayward, 1988). This structured interview, developed for use in anorexia nervosa, examines outcomes in five scales: eating difficulties, menstrual state, mental state, socio-economic status and psychosexual state. The latter was not examined. The average outcome score is a composite rating on a 12-point scale in which high scores indicate a good prognosis. After a mean of 15.9 years, people treated for ARFID in childhood had a mean total outcome score of 10.1 (range 4.9–12), where 12 is the best functioning. The mean score for social functioning was 8.98 (range 1–12). Of those with ongoing ARFID, the mean total score was 8.74 (4.9–12) and social functioning 8.2 (1–12). For those without a psychiatric disorder at follow-up, the mean total score was 11.36 (10.2–12) and mean social functioning score was 10.44 (7–12), hence were doing well. 84% of the 19 children who had had a restrictive ARFID followed up after a mean of 15.9 years were in age-appropriate occupation – employment, education or paid parental leave. 100% of people without any psychiatric disorder, including ARFID, at follow-up were in occupation. Of those with ongoing ARFID, 87% were in occupation, and 60% of those with a psychiatric disorder but without ARFID (Lange et al., 2019). Those who had recovered from their ARFID in childhood were therefore doing well socially and occupationally in adulthood.

Diagnostic crossover to other eating disorders

Some parents worry whether their children will go on to develop an eating disorder such as anorexia nervosa. Some prospective epidemiological studies suggest that childhood "picky eating" is a risk factor for anorexia nervosa in adolescence and young adulthood (Marchi & Cohen, 1990). Nicholls and Viner found that infant feeding problems before six months and a history of undereating at age ten, without lower BMI, gave an odds ratio of 2.6 for the subsequent development of anorexia nervosa by age 30 (Nicholls & Viner, 2009). However, in another prospective study, there were no differences in eating between sisters who did and did not go on to develop anorexia nervosa (Micali et al., 2007). Kotler and colleagues found risk factors for developing anorexia nervosa included eating conflicts, struggles with food and unpleasant meals in early childhood, but not picky eating or eating too slowly (Kotler et al., 2001). A retrospective study of college students found that parental pressure to eat, but not childhood picky eating, predicted disordered eating symptoms (Ellis et al., 2016).

The majority of studies of children, adolescents and adults retrospectively diagnosed with ARFID to date, with longest mean follow-up of up to 15.9 years, have not found that any developed anorexia nervosa (Bryson et al., 2018; Lange et al., 2019; Nakai et al., 2017). In one study, four (12%) of the 36 adolescents with ARFID were subsequently reclassified as having anorexia nervosa; however, the authors acknowledge the complexities of eliciting eating disordered cognitions in younger children (Norris et al., 2014). In non-ARFID populations, difficult mealtimes and parental concerns about childhood overweight have been identified as risk factors for developing anorexia nervosa (Allen et al., 2009; Stein et al., 2006) and it may be helpful to further explore the former given how difficult mealtimes can be for families with children with ARFID.

Quality of life

ARFID can impact on children's lives in terms of eating at school and social events, stressful mealtimes, and hospital visits. Children with ARFID often also have co-occurring medical and psychiatric comorbidities. Health-related quality of life has been found to be low in children with ARFID, and on some factors lower than in controls with chronic illnesses (Krom et al., 2019). In two population-based surveys of people with ARFID aged 15 and older, they had poorer mental health related quality of life than those without an eating disorder, and also than those with anorexia and bulimia nervosa (Hay et al., 2017). It would be helpful if quality of life outcome measures are included clinically and in future studies.

Prognostic factors

Elucidation of prognostic factors in ARFID is still needed. Picky eating is common in early childhood, with a prevalence of up to 46% in population-based cohorts, and, whilst understandably worrying to parents, is regarded as developmentally normal, often remitting before the age of six. Around 4% of children with picky eating have been found to have persistent difficulties. Persistence of picky eating has been associated with lower birth weight, male gender, lower socioeconomic background, pervasive developmental disorders, and in some studies generalised psychopathology, anxiety, behavioural difficulties, and in some, but not others, parent–child interactions (Cardona Cano et al., 2016). Further studies elucidating which children with picky eating go on to develop ARFID, and factors impacting on this which could be targets for intervention would be helpful.

In the longitudinal follow-ups of untreated children with infantile anorexia, significant correlations have been found between children's satiety responsiveness, eating problems, severity of malnutrition, emotional and behavioural difficulties, and maternal increased emotional distress, psychopathology, and disturbed eating attitudes. It is therefore important to also assess parental well-being. Some authors have described that where parents have found it difficult to follow treatment recommendations, this is associated with poorer outcome in terms of increased fussiness, struggles with eating, early satiety, and emotional and behavioural difficulties (Lucarelli et al., 2018).

Whilst tube-feeding is sometimes medically necessary in patients with ARFID, and can be helpful in reducing difficult mealtime interactions, there are also some concerns about potential adverse effects, such as exacerbating conditioned oral aversion and missing feeding milestones (Katzman, Norris, & Zucker, 2019).

Given the commonality of comorbid psychiatric and medical difficulties in children with ARFID, it is likely that these may impact on the prognosis in terms of overall functioning and quality of life. Clinically it is important to consider a child's feeding potential in line with their developmental capacity. Treatment of some comorbid conditions, such as anxiety, is often helpful as treatment of ARFID can be further anxiety provoking. From their small case series, Dumont and colleagues suggested that comorbid generalised anxiety disorder may be a potential risk factor for relapse in ARFID (Dumont et al., 2019). Stimulant medication for ADHD has been reported as both a potential precipitating and potential exacerbating factor in ARFID (Pennell et al., 2016), and given their appetite suppressing effect is something to consider clinically in terms of impact on patients with ARFID and comorbid ADHD. However, clinically, improved concentration and hyperactivity can often facilitate better eating, and in many cases ARFID is associated with factors other than poor appetite. Where appetite is negatively affected by stimulants, alternative medications can be considered.

Finally Zimmerman and Fisher have suggested that children with ARFID of shorter duration may recover more quickly than those with more chronic difficulties (Zimmerman & Fisher, 2017).

Future directions

There is a wealth of clinical experience from feeding disorder, dietetic, paediatric, occupational and speech and language therapy, and eating disorders services, but further research evidence regarding prognostic factors and the effect of treatment on outcome is needed in relation to ARFID. Thomas and colleagues are conducting a study on neurobiological and behavioural risk mechanisms of avoidant restrictive eating trajectories, exploring the course of illness in ARFID, with a view to potentially better targeting treatment (Thomas et al., 2017). The Radcliffe working group's recommendations regarding the operationalisation of research diagnostic criteria appear helpful in guiding further research (Eddy et al., 2019.).

Summary points

- Retrospective follow-up studies suggest that up to almost 75% of children with ARFID recover in the longer term
- Case reports on new treatments specifically for ARFID are promising in terms of effectiveness
- Further research is needed into prognostic factors, particularly those that can be targets for intervention
- Assessment for and treatment of comorbid psychiatric and medical difficulties in children with ARFID is important as these may impact on prognosis
- ARFID can also impact on parental wellbeing and family dynamics, which may in turn affect prognosis, and assessment of this is needed.

References

Allen, K.L., Byrne, S.M., Forbes, D., & Oddy, W.H. (2009) Risk factors for full- and partial-syndrome early adolescent eating disorders: a population-based pregnancy cohort study. *Journal of the American Academy of Child and Adolescent Psychiatry* 48(8), 800–09.

Ammaniti, M., Lucarelli, L., Cimino, S., D'Olimpio, F., & Chatoor, I. (2012) Feeding disorders of infancy: a longitudinal study to middle childhood. *International Journal of Eating Disorders* 45, 272–80.

Bryson, A.E., Scipioni, A.M., Essayli, J.H., Mahoney, J.R., & Ornstein, R.M. (2018) Outcomes of low-weight patients with avoidant/restrictive food intake disorder and anorexia nervosa at long-term follow-up after treatment in a partial hospitalization program for eating disorders. *International Journal of Eating Disorders* 51(5), 470–74.

Cardona Cano, S., Hoek, H.W., Van Hoeken, D., de Barse, L.M., Jaddoe, V.W.V., Verhulst, F.C., & Tiemeier, H. (2016) Behavioural outcomes of picky eating in childhood: a prospective study in the general population. *Journal of Child Psychology and Psychiatry* 57(11), 1239–46.

Dumont, E., Jansen, A., Kroes, D., de Haan, E., & Mulkens, S. (2019) A new cognitive behaviour therapy for adolescents with avoidant/restrictive food intake disorder in a day treatment setting: a clinical case series. *International Journal of Eating Disorders* 52(4), 447–58.

Eddy, K.T., Harshman, S.G., Becker, K.R., Bern, E., Bryant-Waugh, R., Hilbert, A., Katzman, D.K., Lawson, E.A., Manzo, L.D., Menzel, J., Micali, N., Ornstein, R., Sally, S., Serinsky, S.P., Sharp, W., Stubbs, K., Walsh, B.T., Zickgraf, H., Zucker, N., & Thomas, J.J. (2019) Radcliffe ARFID Workgroup: toward operationalization of research diagnostic criteria and directions for the field. *International Journal of Eating Disorders* 52(4), 361–66.

Ellis, J.M., Galloway, A.T., Webb, R.M., Martz, D.M., & Farrow, C.V. (2016) Recollections of pressure to eat during childhood, but not picky eating, predict young adult eating behaviour. *Appetite* 1(97), 58–63.

Forman, S.F., McKenzie, N., Hehn, R., Monge, M.C., Kapphahn, C.J., Mammel, K.A., Callahan, S.T., Sigel, E.J., Bravender, T., Romano, M., Rome, E.S., Robinson, K.A., Fisher, M., Malizio, J.B., Rosen, D.S., Hergenroeder, A.C., Buckelew, S.M., Jay, M.S., Lindenbaum, J., Rickert, V., Garber, A., Golden, N.H., & Woods, E.R. (2014) Predictors of outcome at 1 year in adolescents with DSM-5 restrictive eating disorders: report of the national eating disorders quality improvement collaborative. *Journal of Adolescent Health* 55(6), 750–56.

Hay, P., Mitchison, D., Callado, A.E.L., González-Chica, D.A., Stocks, N., & Touyz, S. (2017) Burden and health-related qualify of life of eating disorders, including avoidant/restrictive food intake disorder (ARFID) in the Australian population. *International Journal of Eating Disorders* 5, 21.

Katzman, D.K., Norris, M.L., & Zucker, N. (2019) Avoidant restrictive food intake disorder: first do no harm. *International Journal of Eating Disorders* 52(4), 459–61.

Kotler, L.A., Cohen, P., Davies, M., Pine, D.S., & Walsh, B.T. (2001) Longitudinal relationships between childhood, adolescent, and adult eating disorders. *Journal of the American Academy of Child and Adolescent Psychiatry* 40(12), 1434–40.

Krom, H., van der Sluijs Veer, L., van Zundert, S., Otten, M.A., Benninga, M., Haverman, L., & Kindermann, A. (2019) Health related quality of life of infants and children with avoidant restrictive food intake disorder. *International Journal of Eating Disorders* 52(4), 410–18.

Lange, C.R.A., Ekedahl Fjertorp, H., Holmer, R., Wijk, E., & Wallin U. (2019) Long-term follow-up study of low-weight avoidant restrictive food intake disorder compared with childhood-onset anorexia nervosa: psychiatric and occupational outcome in 56 patients. *International Journal of Eating Disorders* 52(4), 435–38.

Law, D. & Jacob, J. (2015) *Goals and goal based outcomes (GBOs): some useful information* 3rd(3rd ed.). London; UK: CAMHS Press.

Lucarelli, L., Sechi, C., Cimino, S., & Chatoor, I. (2018) Avoidant/restrictive food intake disorder: a longitudinal study of malnutrition and psychopathological risk factors from 2 to 11 years of age. *Frontiers in Psychology* 9, 1608.

Makhzoumi, S.H., Schreyer, C.C. Hansen, J.L., Laddaran, L.A., Redgrave, G.W., & Guarda, A.S. (2019) Hospital course of underweight youth with ARFID treated with a meal-based behavioral protocol in an inpatient-partial hospitalization program for eating disorders. *International Journal of Eating Disorders* 52(4), 428–34.

Marchi, M. & Cohen, P. (1990) Early childhood eating behaviors and adolescent eating disorders. *Journal of the American Academy of Child and Adolescent Psychiatry* 29(1), 112–17.

Micali, N., Holliday, J., Karwautz, A., Haidvogl, M., Wagner, G., Fernandez-Aranda, F., Badia, A., Gimenez, L., Solano, R., Brecelj-Anderluh, M., Mohan, R., Collier, D., & Treasure, J.L. (2007) Childhood eating and weight in eating disorders: a multi-centre European study of affected women and their unaffected sisters. *Psychotherapy and Psychosomatics* 76, 234–41.

Morgan, H.G. & Hayward, A.E. (1988) Clinical assessment of anorexia nervosa. The Morgan-Russell outcome assessment schedule. *British Journal of Psychiatry* 152, 367–71.

Nakai, Y., Nin, K., Noma, S., Hamagaki, S., Takagi, R., Teramukai, S., & Wonderlich, S.A. (2017) Clinical presentation and outcome of avoidant/restrictive food intake disorder in a Japanese sample. *Eating Behaviors* 24, 49–53.

Nicholls, D.E. & Viner, R.M. (2009) Childhood risk factors for lifetime anorexia nervosa by age 30 years in a national birth cohort. *Journal of the American Academy of Child and Adolescent Psychiatry* 48(8), 791–99.

Norris, M.L., Robinson, A. Obeid, N., Harrison, M., Spettigue, W., & Henderson, K. (2014) Exploring avoidant/restrictive food intake disorder in eating disordered patients: a descriptive study. *International Journal of Eating Disorders* 47(5), 495–99.

Ornstein, R.M., Essayli, J.H., Nicely, T.A., Masciulli, E., & Lane-Loney, S. (2017) Treatment of avoidant/restrictive food intake disorder in a cohort of young patients in a partial hospitalization program for eating disorders. *International Journal of Eating Disorders* 50(9), 1067–74.

Peebles, R., Lesser, A., Park, C.C., Heckert, K., Timko, C.A., Lantzouni, E., Liebman, R., & Weaver, L. (2017) Outcomes of an inpatient medical nutritional rehabilitation protocol in children and adolescents with eating disorders. *Journal of Eating Disorders* 5, 7.

Pennell, A., Couturier, J., Grant, C., & Johnson, N. (2016) Severe avoidant/restrictive food intake disorder and coexisting stimulant treated attention deficit hyperactivity disorder. *International Journal of Eating Disorders* 49(11), 1036–39.

Reilly, E.E., Brown, T.A., Gray, E.K., Kaye, W.H., & Menzel, J.E. (2019) Exploring the cooccurrence of behavioural phenotypes for avoidant/restrictive food intake disorder in a partial hospitalisation sample. *European Eating Disorders Review* 27(4), 429–35.

Sharp, W.G., Jaquess, D.L., Morton, J.F. & Herzinger, C.V. (2010) Pediatric feeding disorders: a quantitative synthesis of treatment outcomes. *Clinical Child and Family Psychology Review* 13, 348–65.

Sharp, W.G., Stubbs, K.H., Adams, H., Wells, B.M., Lesack, R.S., Criado. K.K., Simon, E.L., McCracken, C.E., West, L.L., & Scahill, L.D. (2016) Intensive, manual-based intervention for pediatric feeding disorders: results from a randomized pilot trial. *Journal of Pediatric Gastroenterology and Nutrition* 62, 658–63.

Sharp, W.G., Volkert, V.M., Scahill, L., McCracken, C.E., & McElhanon, B. (2017) A systematic review and meta-analysis of intensive multidisciplinary intervention for pediatric feeding disorders: how standard is the standard of care?. *Journal of Paediatrics* 181, 116–24.

Stein, A., Woolley, H., Cooper, S., Winterbottom, J., Fairburn, C.G., & Cortina-Borja, M. (2006) Eating habits and attitudes among 10-year-old children of mothers with eating disorders: longitudinal study. *British Journal of Psychiatry* 189, 324–29.

Strandjord, S.E., Sieke, E.H., Richmond, M., & Rome, E.S. (2015) Avoidant/restrictive food intake disorder: illness and hospital course in patients hospitalized for nutritional insufficiency. *Journal of Adolescent Health* 57(6), 673–78.

Thomas, J.J., Lawson, E.A., Micali, N., Misra, M., Deckersbach, T., & Eddy, K.T. (2017) Avoidant/restrictive food intake disorder: a three-dimensional model of neurobiology with implications for etiology and treatment. *Current Psychiatry Reports* 19(8), 54.

Zimmerman, J. & Fisher, M. (2017) Avoidant/restrictive food intake disorder (ARFID). *Current Problems in Pediatric Adolescent Health Care* 47, 95–103.

Zucker, N., Copeland, W., Franz, L., Carpenter, K., Keeling, L. Angold. A., & Egger, H. (2015) Psychological and psychosocial impairment in pre-schoolers with selective eating. *Pediatrics* 136(3), 582–90.

Chapter 19

Future research directions

Rachel Bryant-Waugh

Introduction

The introduction of a "new" diagnostic category is not something that happens on a whim or in response to demand. It is the result of a thorough process of considering and analysing available evidence from a range of sources, followed by careful scrutiny and testing of proposed definitions and diagnostic criteria. Ultimately, it is intended, above all else, to be clinically useful. The introduction of ARFID as a diagnosis followed such a process and shares a similar aim. In general, its introduction has been well received by clinicians and researchers working in the field of feeding and eating disorders. ARFID has also been welcomed as a diagnosis by many of those affected by eating difficulties characterised by avoidance and restriction of food intake that are distinct from the restriction seen in anorexia nervosa or bulimia nervosa. Many such people recognise their own eating struggles in definitions and descriptions of ARFID, and express relief that their difficulties might now be recognised and, better still, effectively treated. However, a largely positive reception, although important, is insufficient. Research, involving the systematic gathering and unbiased analysis of data, is crucial to test the performance of any diagnostic category in the real world. In relation to ARFID, there is plenty of scope for investigators to focus their attention on the subject matter of every single chapter in this book. In this way, ARFID represents an exciting area for further exploration and evaluation. Studies carried out thus far have certainly helped to substantiate its recognition and provide justification for its introduction as a distinct disorder within the feeding and eating disorders (Norris & Katzman, 2015).

A good system of classification facilitates recognition and correct identification of its constituent parts. Yet this is only a starting point, and when the classification system is one relating to diagnoses of mental and behavioural disorders, the main focus must surely be on what happens thereafter; in other words, the main point of a diagnosis is ultimately to improve care and reduce burden and distress. Diagnostic categories are dynamic entities; our understanding of ARFID, its definition and diagnostic criteria, are likely to evolve over time as more data are gathered. Preceding chapters have included some suggestions for future work, highlighting gaps in our existing knowledge, and hopefully acting as encouragement to others interested in this field. Other authors have also promoted the importance of addressing the currently limited body of research into ARFID, including through the publication of a collection of papers focussing on children and adolescents with ARFID – an "understudied group" – with the hoped for outcome that it will catalyse clinical research in this area (Eddy & Thomas, 2019).

This final chapter proposes a number of potentially useful areas for further investigation, mentioning some studies currently underway. It is set out in line with the overall structure of this book, and as in other chapters, espouses the three-part model of evidence-based practice which proposes that alongside research trial data, clinical expertise, and patient views and values, are equally important forms of evidence to inform clinical decision-making (Sackett et al., 1996, 2002). Whether the diagnosis of ARFID proves to be clinically useful depends on evidence derived from all three.

Expert by experience perspectives

This book opens with three chapters discussing the perspectives of children and young people with ARFID, those of their parents and carers, and the importance of qualitative research. To date, there has been a striking lack of focus on "expert by experience" perspectives in the ARFID literature. There are a few related studies, for example, an interview-based exploration of the experience of being a "picky eater" (Fox et al., 2018), a survey on "picky eating" (Wildes, Zucker & Marcus, 2012), and a qualitative study designed to derive a theoretical understanding of identity related to eating (Bisogni et al., 2002). All have been carried out with adults only. It seems self-evident that future research must include well-designed qualitative studies, specifically focussing on the experiences and perspectives of children with ARFID and their families. Without this, we are missing an essential component of dialogue on the subject necessary to drive the field forwards. Future research should also focus on the design and use of patient- or person-centred outcome measures that will allow the views and values of all those directly affected by ARFID to be systematically heard and included in the shared endeavour of improving care (see further Chapter 3).

Diagnosis and presentation

The second part of this book covers diagnosis and presentation, also including discussion on aetiology, epidemiology, and the measurement and documentation of features related to ARFID. Calls have been made for clear operationalisation of diagnostic criteria for research purposes (Eddy & Thomas, 2019), which might helpfully include shared research definitions for "remission" or "recovery". This is likely to be a challenging task, as diagnostic categories are developed and intended for use in clinical practice. There is invariably an element of clinical judgement in their application, which can be at odds with the need to tightly define groups of research participants. This is an age-old dilemma; whether research should include groups of participants that more closely resemble patients seen in clinical practice, i.e. with "looser" use of diagnostic criteria, or whether they should be a highly specified group allowing greater precision in interpretation of research findings. In addition, very little work has been carried out this far across a range of different cultural contexts, which will be important to address in terms of furthering ability to correctly recognise and diagnose the disorder and any cultural variants. Remission and recovery are also both extremely difficult to define in a manner that suits all circumstances and everyone involved. Recovery might look and feel very different for different families and across different cultures, again suggesting that a combined approach integrating patient views and values, clinical expertise, and research data, might be the most productive way to proceed.

Taking a further step back, it would seem fruitful to explore similarities and differences across related difficulties, in particular across neurodevelopmental presentations such as autism and ADHD, variants of anxiety, and paediatric feeding difficulties associated with medical conditions. Much of the research interest in ARFID has, perhaps unsurprisingly, come from the eating disorders field, resulting in what might turn out to be a somewhat skewed perspective. Thoughtful exploration of possible aetiological pathways, again taking similarities and differences with other conditions into account, can result in important advances in relation the successful targeting of interventions, and is certainly an area that remains understudied. Whilst clinical formulation is important in helping people to make sense of their situation, it is a long way from determining aetiological pathways and precise mechanisms in the development of the disorder.

Epidemiological data have in part been limited by the lack of robust screening instruments. Some are now in development and currently being tested (see Chapter 6), which will hopefully lead on to improved awareness of populations at risk and better knowledge about incidence and prevalence, which is vital to be able to plan for and provide appropriate services. Some promising larger-scale studies are underway (for example, a large birth cohort study of Japanese preschool children, investigating the prevalence and course of a range of childhood eating problems, including ARFID, and their association with neurodevelopmental disorders, Dinkler, 2019), and their results are awaited with interest. Also helpful, will be the inclusion of ARFID in national registers, allowing better tracking of numbers of individuals presenting to health care services. With the inclusion of ARFID in ICD-11 (see Chapter 4), this should hopefully increase.

Assessment

Similar to the dearth of good screening instruments holding back epidemiological knowledge, the slow emergence of fully validated, ARFID-specific, standardised, assessment measures, and approaches has arguably hampered optimal assessment. This too is now changing, with a number of measures being developed and tested in different centres (see Chapter 6). From a research perspective, the ability to collect baseline data in a reliable and consistent manner is vital, not only to allow improved characterisation of ARFID presentations, but also to ensure that evidence-based approaches are available to guide clinicians in the assessment of their patients. Consensus-based assessment protocols and batteries of measures, including ARFID-specific as well as more general assessment tools covering such things as quality of life, general functioning, co-occurring difficulties, and treatment engagement and course, would allow pooling of data and enhance the identification of patterns and priorities. As discussed in the chapters in the third section of this book, assessment in relation to ARFID is recommended to be multi-component and multi-disciplinary. This is central to being able to plan appropriately for an individual patient, but on a larger scale, multiple practitioners adopting shared, consistent protocols, and combining data obtained, could represent a significant and valuable contribution to furthering knowledge and understanding.

Management

It goes without saying that there is a great need for the development of evidence-based treatment interventions for people with ARFID. Some have suggested that there is utility in adapting existing treatments for restrictive eating disorders to apply to ARFID (for example, Eddy & Thomas, 2019), which may well be the case, but there is likely to be an equal or greater argument to explore many other areas of clinical practice. In particular, it would seem that evidence-based approaches to the management of anxiety presentations, core behavioural approaches addressing expectations and learning, and perhaps some of the management strategies that have proven effective in achieving behavioural change in individuals with neurodevelopment disorders (such as Applied Behavioural Analysis and related approaches), are worthy of further consideration. A number of centres are currently trialling a range of "adapted" treatments, including the use of a cognitive behavioural therapy based manual (Thomas & Eddy, 2018) and an ARFID-specific adaptation of family based treatment for eating disorders (Lock, Sadeh-Sharvit & L'Insalata, 2019). Novel approaches are also being developed and evaluated, for example the work of Zucker and colleagues in relation to assisting children to engage more adaptively with their bodily sensations, with the aim of decreasing aversion, increasing self-awareness, and increasing approach behaviours, here in relation to food and eating (Zucker et al., 2019). Going forward, developments in management approaches will need to be guided by the views and values of those receiving the treatment as well as by findings related to aetiology, populations at risk, and characterisation, trajectory, and outcome of the eating difficulties. There may be an important role for the use of medication, but whether this will be as an adjunct to psychological interventions, or as a first line treatment, will depend on other lines of inquiry and evidence.

Course and outcome

Precise knowledge about who responds best to which intervention and why, can seem like a distant hope, but one that is nevertheless important to work towards. There is much work still to be done in determining which aspects of the course of ARFID will prove most useful to track and which aspects of outcome will be most meaningful, as this may differ depending on differing perspectives of the family, clinicians and researchers. Well-designed longitudinal studies of both clinical and population cohorts can reveal much of interest. Here again, work is underway to attempt to elucidate patterns that might shed light on potential aetiological pathways and related preventative and treatment interventions. There are currently very limited data on prognosis and prevention in ARFID, but guidance in relation to establishing appropriate infant and child feeding practices and behaviour has been recommended as potentially helpful (Zimmerman & Fisher, 2017), and work is being conducted exploring trajectories of different types of eating behaviour across childhood and their relationship with later eating difficulties (e.g. Herle et al., 2019). Longitudinal studies are often costly and complex to carry out, and it is to be hoped that funding bodies will support this type of research in relation to ARFID in the future.

Final thoughts

Whilst there is vast scope for interested investigators in the field of ARFID, with much of potential interest, it is important to reflect that the current state of research can be experienced as disappointing and frustrating for people living with ARFID. When relatively little is known, it may not be perceived as an area of opportunity, but as an area clouded by lack of awareness and ignorance. Clinician confidence may also be relatively low, both in relation to diagnosis and how to intervene (Coglan & Otasowie, 2019). There is without doubt much still to be done to increase awareness and understanding of ARFID, and to develop effective treatments. In line with the thread running throughout this book, it is proposed that this will work best when research endeavours are combined with clinical expertise and with the views and values of those affected.

Summary points

- There is much scope for research into every aspect of ARFID, as the current evidence-base remains very limited
- The views of those affected by the disorder have been particularly overlooked to date
- As research evidence accumulates it seems likely that our conceptualisation of ARFID and its management will change
- Sound research depends of robust measures; these are currently being developed and tested and will hopefully facilitate advances in the field

•   Improved knowledge about ARFID is most likely to result from combining the findings from research studies with clinical expertise and with the views and values of those affected.

References

Bisogni, C.A., Connors, M., Devine, C.M., & Sobal, J. (2002) Who we are and how we eat: a qualitative study of identities in food choice. *Journal of Nutrition Education and Behaviour*, 34 (3), 128–39.

Coglan, L. & Otasowie, J. (2019) Avoidant/restrictive food intake disorder: what do we know so far? *British Journal of Psychiatry Advances*, 25 (2), 90–98.

Dinkler, L. (2019) https://gillbergcentre.gu.se/english/research-staff-%26-associates/dinkler–lisa accessed 15 July 2019.

Eddy, K.T. & Thomas, J.J. (2019) Introduction to a special issue on child and adolescent feeding and eating disorders and avoidant/restrictive food intake disorder. *International Journal of Eating Disorders*, 52 (4), 327–30.

Fox, G., Coulthard, H., Williamson, I., & Wallis, D. (2018) "It's always on the safe list": investigating experiential accounts of picky eating adults. *Appetite* 130, 1–10.

Herle, M., De Stavola, B., Hübel, C., Abdulkadir, M., Santos Ferreira, D., Loos, R.J.F., Bryant-Waugh, R., Bulik, C., & Micali, N. (2019) Eating behaviours in childhood and later eating disorder behaviours and diagnoses: a longitudinal study. *British Journal of Psychiatry* 1–7. doi:10.1192/bjp.2019.174

Lock, J., Sadeh-Sharvit, S., & L'Insalata, A. (2019) Feasibility of conducting a randomized clinical trial using family-based treatment for avoidant/restrictive food intake disorder. *International Journal of Eating Disorders*, 52 (6), 746–51.

Norris, M.L. & Katzman, D.K. (2015) Change is never easy, but it is possible: reflections on avoidant/restrictive food intake disorder two years after its introduction in the DSM-5. *Journal of Adolescent Health*, 57 (1), 8–9.

Sackett, D.L., Rosenberg, W.M.C., Gray, J.A.M., Haynes, R.B., & Richardson, W.S. (1996) Evidence based medicine: what it is and what it isn't. *British Medical Journal*, 3 (12), 71–72.

Sackett, D.L., Strauss, S.E., Richardson, W.S., Rosenberg, W., & Haynes, R.B. (2002) *Evidence-based medicine: how to practise and teach EBM* (2nd ed.) London: Churchill Livingstone.

Thomas J.J. & Eddy, K.T. (2018) *Cognitive behavioural therapy for avoidant/restrictive food intake disorder: children, adolescents and adults.* Cambridge: Cambridge University Press.

Wildes, J.E., Zucker, N.L., & Marcus, M.D. (2012) Picky eating in adults: results of a web-based survey. *International Journal of Eating Disorders*, 45 (4), 575–82.

Zimmerman, J. & Fisher, M. (2017) Avoidant/restrictive food intake disorder (ARFID). *Current Problems in Pediatric and Adolescent Health Care*, 47 (4), 95–103.

Zucker, N., LaVia, M., Craske, M., Foukal, M., Harris, A., Datta, N., Savereide, E. & Maslow, G. (2019) Feeling and body investigators (FBI): ARFID division – an acceptance based interoceptive exposure treatment for children with ARFID. *International Journal of Eating Disorders*, 52 (4), 466–72.

Appendix: What Matters to Me?

Parent/carer version 1.3

This questionnaire is based on the views and experiences of parents and carers of children with ARFID and related eating difficulties.

It includes statements that may or may not be relevant to your situation.

Please read each statement and circle the number that best describes how things are for you **NOW**

Your name:

Your relationship to child:

Today's date:

© Rachel Bryant-Waugh and Lucy Cooke

MY CONCERNS	Not applic-able	Com-pletely disagree			Neither agree nor disagree			Com-pletely agree
1. I am very concerned about the **amount** my child eats	0	1	2	3	4	5	6	7
2. I am very concerned about the **variety** of foods my child eats	0	1	2	3	4	5	6	7
3. I am very concerned about my child **being tube fed**	0	1	2	3	4	5	6	7
4. I am very concerned about my child's **willingness to try new foods**	0	1	2	3	4	5	6	7
5. I am very concerned about my child's ability to **manage solid foods**	0	1	2	3	4	5	6	7
6. I am very concerned about the overall **nutritional quality** of my child's diet	0	1	2	3	4	5	6	7
7. I am very concerned about my child's ability to **chew and/or swallow**	0	1	2	3	4	5	6	7
8. I am very concerned about my child's **fear of food**	0	1	2	3	4	5	6	7
9. I am very concerned about my child's **behaviour at mealtimes**	0	1	2	3	4	5	6	7
10. I am very concerned about my child's **lack of interest and/ or enjoyment of food**	0	1	2	3	4	5	6	7
11. I am very concerned about my child's **eating speed**	0	1	2	3	4	5	6	7
12. I am very concerned about my child's **food allergies/ intolerances**	0	1	2	3	4	5	6	7
13. **Other important concerns that I have** (please specify):	0	1	2	3	4	5	6	7

RESOURCES

THE IMPACT OF MY CHILD'S EATING DIFFICULTY

	Not applic-able	Com-pletely disagree			Neither agree nor disagree			Com-pletely agree
14. My child's eating difficulty has a negative effect on their **social** life	0	1	2	3	4	5	6	7
15. My child's eating difficulty has a negative effect on their **growth**	0	1	2	3	4	5	6	7
16. My child's eating difficulty has a negative effect on their **phys-ical health**	0	1	2	3	4	5	6	7
17. My child's eating difficulty has a negative effect on their **intake of vitamins and minerals**	0	1	2	3	4	5	6	7
18. My child's eating difficulty has a negative effect on their **mood**	0	1	2	3	4	5	6	7
19. My child's eating difficulty has a negative effect on their **exist-ing illness**	0	1	2	3	4	5	6	7
20. My child's eating difficulty has a negative effect on **family mealtimes**	0	1	2	3	4	5	6	7
21. My child's eating difficulty has a negative effect on their **energy or stamina**	0	1	2	3	4	5	6	7
22. My child's eating difficulty has a negative effect on **family life**	0	1	2	3	4	5	6	7
23. My child's eating difficulty has a negative effect on their **learn-ing at school/nursery**	0	1	2	3	4	5	6	7
24. My child's eating difficulty causes significant **anxiety to me**	0	1	2	3	4	5	6	7
25. My child's eating difficulty causes significant **anxiety to my partner/my child's other parent**	0	1	2	3	4	5	6	7
26. My child's eating difficulty has a negative effect on **my mood**	0	1	2	3	4	5	6	7
27. My child's eating difficulty has a negative effect on **my part-ner's/my child's other parent's mood**	0	1	2	3	4	5	6	7
28. **Other impact that my child's eating difficulty has** (please specify):	0	1	2	3	4	5	6	7

MY HOPES FOR TREATMENT/MY GOALS

	Not applic-able	Com-pletely dis-agree			Neither agree nor disagree			Com-pletely agree
29. I would like my child to eat a **greater quantity** of food	0	1	2	3	4	5	6	7
30. I would like my child to **enjoy** food	0	1	2	3	4	5	6	7
31. I would like my child to eat a **wider variety** of foods	0	1	2	3	4	5	6	7
32. I would like my child to be **less anxious** around food	0	1	2	3	4	5	6	7
33. I would like my child to be more **willing to try new foods**	0	1	2	3	4	5	6	7
34. I would like my child to **stop needing to be tube-fed**	0	1	2	3	4	5	6	7
35. I would like my child not to need to take **nutritional supplements**	0	1	2	3	4	5	6	7
36. I would like my child to be able to eat **different textures** of foods	0	1	2	3	4	5	6	7
37. I would like us to be able **to eat out as a family**	0	1	2	3	4	5	6	7
38. I would like us to have **normal family mealtimes**	0	1	2	3	4	5	6	7
39. I would like my child to be able to **feed themself**	0	1	2	3	4	5	6	7
40. I would like my child to **eat more quickly**	0	1	2	3	4	5	6	7
41. **Other important goals that I have** (please specify):	0	1	2	3	4	5	6	7

Now that you have been through all the statements and rated these, please could you look back over your answers and identify the *three items* that best reflect the things about your child's current eating difficulty that you would most like to change:

Please place one item number in each of the boxes below and add any comments you would like to make/say how close you are to achieving each of them

How close are you to achieving this? (Please circle one number)

NOT AT ALL 0 1 2 3 4 5 6 7 8 9 10 GOAL REACHED

How close are you to achieving this? (Please circle one number)

NOT AT ALL 0 1 2 3 4 5 6 7 8 9 10 GOAL REACHED

How close are you to achieving this (Please circle one number)

NOT AT ALL 0 1 2 3 4 5 6 7 8 9 10 GOAL REACHED

Thank you!

Glossary

Amenorrhoea   absence of menstruation

Anorexia nervosa   one of the formal feeding and eating disorders in DSM-5 and ICD-11; characterised by dietary restriction and persistent behaviours leading to low weight for the individual, associated with disturbance in perception of weight and appearance

Anthropometric   pertaining to measurement of proportions of the human body, e.g. weight, height, body mass index, waist circumference, skinfold thickness

Anti-tissue transglutaminase antibody (Anti-TTG)   an auto-antibody with high sensitivity and specificity for coeliac disease

Applied behaviour analysis   a form of behavioural therapy that seeks to develop socially acceptable alternatives for aberrant behaviour

Aspiration   when material enters the airway below the level of the vocal cords

Attention deficit hyperactivity disorder   a neurodevelopmental disorder characterised by inattention, hyperactivity, and impulsivity

Behavioural therapy   therapy based on psychological theory proposing that human behaviours are learned through experience

Binge eating disorder   one of the formal feeding and eating disorders in DSM-5 and ICD-11; characterised by regular binge eating in the absence of regular compensatory behaviours

Biofeedback   electronic monitoring of automatic bodily function, often used to train someone to acquire voluntary control of that function

Bisphosphonate   a class of medications used to increase bone density, especially in osteoporosis

Blenderised, or blended, diets   a diet that may range from purees mixed with manufactured formula feeds to blended whole table foods

Body mass index (BMI)   a means of representing weight standardised for height and sex, calculated as weight in kilogrammes divided by height in metres squared

Bolus   a ball or round mass of food or liquid ready to be swallowed

Bone mineral density   the amount, specifically as density, of mineralised bone in bone tissue

Bradycardia   a slow heart rate

Bulimia nervosa   one of the formal feeding and eating disorders in DSM-5 and ICD-11; characterised by regular binge eating accompanied by compensatory behaviours, such as self-induced vomiting or laxative misuse and/or other behaviours to prevent weight gain

Carotenaemia   the yellow-orange tinge staining of visible body surfaces due to raised beta-carotene levels in blood resulting from excess consumption of beta-carotene-containing foods

Classical conditioning   a learning process that occurs when two stimuli are repeatedly paired

Cognitive behavioural therapy   a psychological intervention based on the proposal that thoughts, feelings and behaviour are inter-connected and focussing on strategies to change these

Cognitive rigidity   a lack of mental flexibility

Co-morbid conditions   conditions that co-occur with another diagnosis; if diagnostic criteria are met for each condition, an individual may be assigned two or more diagnoses concurrently

Concurrent validity   when results of a new measure are similar to results from an established measure of a similar construct

Conditioned food aversion   the process by which consuming an innocuous food followed by an aversive stimulus causes the food to become displeasing

Constitutional growth delay   temporary delay in vertical growth in the absence of other medical causes of growth delay

Contingency   a tangible reward given directly after a desired behaviour in order to increase the frequency of the behaviour

Convergent validity   tests two measures that are supposed to be similar and shows that they are related

Crico-pharyngeal sphincter   a ring of muscle at the top of the oesophagus, also called the upper oesophageal sphincter

Decisional balance worksheet   allows advantages and disadvantages that might follow a decision to be weighed up, allowing consideration of whether the decision is "good" or "bad" under specific circumstances

Defensiveness   sometimes used to describe a sensory system that an individual is over-sensitive to and avoids e.g. tactile or oral defensiveness

Desensitisation   process in which an emotional response or arousal is reduced with repeated exposure

Developmental disability   an impairment in physical, learning, language or behaviour areas

Differential diagnosis   another medical or psychiatric condition that may present with similar signs or symptoms to those of the diagnosis under consideration

Divergent validity   tests that constructs that should have no relationship do, in fact, not have any relationship

Dysthymia   chronic low mood

Emetophobia   a phobia characterised by significant fear of vomiting, in some cases, leading to restricted eating

Endocrine   relating to hormones in human physiology

Enteral feeding   tube feeding where nutrition is administered directly into the stomach or small intestine – e.g. via a nasogastric tube, percutaneous endoscopic gastrostomy tube (PEG) or gastrostomy button

Enteral nutrition   refers to the delivery of a nutritionally complete feed directly into the stomach, duodenum or jejunum

Expectancy violation   when individual perception of an interaction/experience goes against what is expected/predicted

Experiential   learning based on experience or observation

Exposure hierarchy   a technique often used in anxiety treatment to assist with systematic desensitisation; the hierarchy is a list of feared objects or situations, starting with the one the person considers least challenging and ending with those considered most difficult

Exposure-based therapy   a treatment approach in anxiety whereby an individual is exposed to an anxiety source or its context to help them overcome their anxiety or distress

Externalising difficulties   problem behaviours directed toward the external environment e.g. disruptive behaviour disorders – attention deficit hyperactivity disorder, oppositional defiant disorder, conduct disorder

Faltering growth   a slower rate of gain in weight and height in childhood than expected for age and sex

Feeding disorder of infancy and/or early childhood   a diagnostic category in DSM IV and ICD-10 characterised by inadequate food intake, low weight, and age of onset below six years; now replaced and extended by ARFID

Fight or flight response   a term used to describe a physiological when reaction humans or other animals perceive threat or experience stress; arousal of the sympathetic nervous system releases hormones that prepare the individual to fight or to flee

Follicle stimulating hormone (FSH)   an endocrine hormone produced in the pituitary gland involved in the regulation of the reproductive system in males and females

Food avoidance emotional disorder   a descriptive term, not a formal diagnosis, used to describe a presentation in which *restricted intake is linked to emotion regulation difficulties, usually* resulting in weight loss

Food chaining   a behavioural technique based on a gradual broadening out of foods using an individual's taste, texture, and temperature preferences; demonstrated to be effective in widening dietary intake as the magnitude of difference in "new" foods is minimised

Food fortification   the process of adding calories or nutrients to food

Food neophobia   the reluctance to eat, or the avoidance of, new foods

Food responsiveness   the tendency to eat when food is present irrespective of degree of hunger

Food supplement drink   a preparation intended to supplement the diet and provide nutrients that may be missing from the diet or not consumed in sufficient quantity

Formulation   a stage in the process of psychological evaluation, consisting of an attempt to draw together all strands of information gathered in the assessment, representing an attempt to understand why difficulties have arisen and what may be contributing to their maintenance

Fortified foods   foods that have had energy or micro-nutrients added to increase their nutritional value

Functional dysphagia   the sensation of solid and/or liquid foods sticking, lodging, or passing abnormally through the oesophagus without an organic cause

Fundoscopy   the clinical examination of the back of the eye using an opthalmoscope

Gastro-oesophageal reflux   when food and drink travels down the digestive tract normally but some food, drink, and acid travels back up, instead of passing through to the large and small intestines, often irritating the lining of the digestive tract

Goal based outcome measures   personalised outcome measures where goals are set by the individual and progress measured against these

Graded exposure   gradual exposure to a feared or anxiety-provoking situation to enable control of the physiological response at one step before exposure to the next, slightly more anxiety-provoking step

Habituation   the reduced physiological response to a stimulus over time as it becomes familiar

Hypernatraemia   a high blood sodium concentration

Hypopharynx   part of the throat between the epiglottis and the larynx

Hypotension   a low blood pressure (either diastolic or systolic)

Infantile anorexia   characterised by a lack of interest in food and eating with associated growth impairment, usually developing between six months to three years of age

Internal consistency   the extent to which all items in a questionnaire are measuring the same construct

Internalising difficulties   negative, problematic thoughts and behaviours directed towards the self, e.g. depression and anxiety

Interoception   the sense from receptors inside the body, such as thirst, nausea, body temperature, emotions

Inter-rater reliability   the extent to which two raters will give the same rating

Karyotype   the microscopic appearance of the number and form of the chromosomes

Luteinising hormone (LH)   an endocrine hormone produced in the pituitary gland involved in the regulation of the reproductive system in males and females, LH acts in collaboration with follicle stimulating hormone

Macro-nutrient   main groups of foodstuffs in the diet, e.g. protein, fat, and carbohydrate

Micro-nutrients part of the diet which are needed in small, or trace quantities such as vitamins and minerals

Nasogastric feeding a medical process involving the insertion of a plastic tube (nasogastric tube) through the nose, past the throat, and down into the stomach

Neurodevelopmental conditions impairments of the growth and development of the brain or central nervous system affecting emotion, learning, self-control and memory, including autism spectrum conditions, attention deficit hyperactivity and learning disorders

Neurological thresholds the number of stimuli needed for a neuron/neuron system to respond; a lower threshold requires less stimulus for a response (over-sensitivity); a higher threshold requires more sensory input for a response (under-sensitivity), lower registration, and a delayed response

Neutropenia a low level of neutrophils in the blood, a class of white cell involved in immunity; often low in malnutrition

Nutritional supplement any dietary supplement (in liquid, powder, capsule or tablet form) intended to provide nutrients that may otherwise not be consumed

Obsessive compulsive disorder characterised by repetitive, intrusive thoughts or images, and or repetitive, unwanted compulsive actions

Operant conditioning a learning process in which behaviour is modified by reinforcement or punishment

Oral nutritional supplement a supplement taken orally that will add micro- and macro-nutrients, not necessarily nutritionally complete

Orexigenic hormone a hormone that has the effect of increasing appetite

Oro-pharynx part of the mouth incorporating the back of the oral cavity to above the epiglottis

Oro-pharyngeal dysphagia difficulty in swallowing

Orthorexia nervosa a descriptive term, not a formal diagnosis, characterised by exclusive eating of foods deemed to be "healthy", often resulting in significantly inadequate nutritional intake

Other specified feeding or eating disorder (OSFED) a formal diagnosis in DSM-5, including a number of recognised clinical presentations and atypical variants of the main diagnostic categories

Over-sensitivity low threshold to sensory stimuli (also known as hyper sensitive, sensory sensitivity, overresponsive, over reactive or low threshold); with failure of the normal inhibitory mechanism and over activity of the sympathetic nervous system

Partial hospitalisation programme day patient treatment

Percentage median body mass index the percentage that an individual's BMI is of the 50th centile, or median, BMI for biological sex and age; frequently used to standardise degree of underweight, alongside z-scores and centiles

Percentage of non-overlapping data   a non-regression metric statistic determining the percentage of treatment data not overlapping with baseline data; possible scores range from 0 to 100%, with higher scores reflecting more effective treatments

Percutaneous endoscopic gastrostomy (PEG)   a surgical procedure for placing a tube for feeding without having to perform an open operation on the abdomen

Peristaltic wave   when muscles in the body automatically contract and relax sequentially in a wave

Phenotype   the observable characteristics of an individual

Pica   one of the formal feeding and eating disorders in DSM-5 and ICD-11; characterised by eating non-food, non-nutritive items (e.g. chalk or soil)

Prokinetic medications   medications used to speed up transit time of food in the gastro-intestinal tract

Proprioception   the sense from muscles and joints that tells us where our body is in space

Psychometric   measurement or assessment of individual differences in abilities, aptitudes, attitudes, behaviour, intelligence, and other attributes

QTc   the corrected time between the Q wave and a T wave on an ECG; the most common equation used to correct the QT (the time between Q and T-wave) is Bazett's formula whereby the QT is divided by the time between R waves, squared

Refeeding syndrome   a complication that can result following re-introduction of nutrition in the starved state, due to the sudden increase of glucose and insulin concentrations and leading to a transcellular shift in electrolytes that can cause clinical complications and an electrolyte imbalance, including hypophosphataemia

Remission   usually when someone no longer fulfils diagnostic criteria; variously defined by different authors

Rickets   skeletal disorder caused by a lack of vitamin D, calcium, or phosphate affecting bone development in children with deficient mineralisation at the growth plate of long bones

Rumination disorder   one of the formal feeding and eating disorders in DSM-5 and ICD-11; characterised by the regular regurgitation of food, which is then re-chewed, re-swallowed or spat out

Russell-Silver/Silver-Russell Syndrome   a rare genetic condition typified by slow growth, short stature and characteristic facial features

Satiety responsiveness   the ability to recognise that one is full and to stop eating even when there is still food available

Self-regulation strategies (in the context of sensory modulation) behaviours that are used to maintain an appropriate level of arousal or alertness needed for the situation, e.g. seeking sensory input or avoiding it

Semi-structured interview   the interviewer does not strictly follow a formalised list of questions, but asks more open-ended questions, allowing for discussion

Sensory interventions   sensory-based activities aimed at supporting regulation through use of sensory activities sometimes known as a "sensory diet"; might include activities such as bouncing on a gym ball, use of sensory equipment (e.g. ear defenders), or altering the environment to meet the individual's sensory needs

Sensory modulation   the process by which the brain regulates and organises the sensory input that is constantly being received, and produces an appropriate behavioural response

Sensory processing   the process of receiving, perceiving, integrating, and response to all the sensory input that is continuously received by the brain

Sensory seeking   drive for enhanced sensory experiences

Sensory thresholds – see neurological thresholds

Social learning theory   a psychological theory that suggests people learn from one another via observation, imitation, and modelling

Somatic complaints   significant focus on physical symptoms causing distress or disturbance in functioning, without or disproportional to organic causes

Special educational needs   a child with special education needs has a learning difficulty or disability that requires a special education provision to be made for them

Spinal cord degeneration   degeneration of the posterior and lateral columns of the spinal cord as a result of vitamin B_{12}, vitamin E, and copper deficiency

Stunting   impaired growth, most commonly a consequence of inadequate nutrition; commonly used to denote permanently impaired growth with a reduced final height as an adult.

Supplemental feeding   any method of giving food or fluid, including breast or formula products, orally, intravenously, or via a tube, to supplement the usual diet, often as a powder, formula, or tablet.

Systematic desensitisation   a technique often used in the treatment of anxiety, frequently with an exposure hierarchy, where the individual is gradually exposed to increasingly challenging situations alongside encouragement to utilise skills and strategies to manage to any accompanying increase in anxiety

Tanner staging   a conventional method for staging level of pubertal development in males and females

Tasting time   a structured and graded process to trying a new food based on principles of desensitisation; usually coupled with a tangible reward immediately after trying a new food.

Test-re-test reliability   the extent to which scores on a test taken by an individual will be the same or similar if the same individual takes the same test at a later date

Under-sensitive   high threshold to sensory input (also known as hypo-sensitive, under-reactive) that leads to poor registration and/or a delayed response.

Unspecified feeding or eating disorder   category in the feeding and eating disorders section of DSM-5; used when an individual presents with a clinically significant eating disturbance that does not fit any of the other available diagnostic categories

Valleculae   space behind the root of the tongue above the epiglottis

Vestibular   the sense from the inner ear telling us which way up we are and how we are moving

Visual timetable   a visual picture of what is happening to aid understanding of what will happen over a period of time

Vitamin D   a fat soluble steroid, a micro-nutrient, which plays an important role in calcium and phosphate metabolism in the body

Subject index

Made in the USA
Middletown, DE
01 March 2020

85351984R00152